Rick Steves'

PRAGUE
& THE CZECH REPUBLIC

2006

Rick Steves & Jan (Honza) Vihan

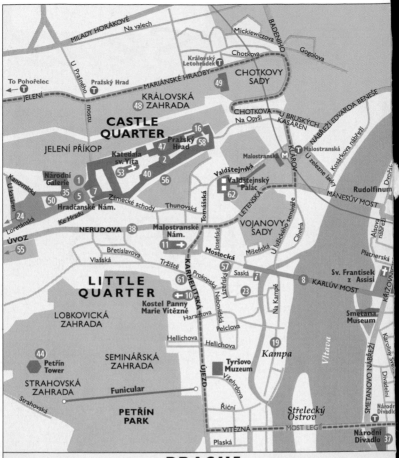

PRAGUE

1. Archbishop's Palace
2. Basilica of St. George and Convent
3. Bethlehem Chapel
4. Black Light Theater (2)
5. Castle Square
6. Ceremonial Hall
7. Changing of the Guard
8. Charles Bridge
9. Charles University
10. Church of St. Mary the Victorious
11. Church of St. Nicholas (in Little Quarter)
12. Church of St. Nicholas (in Old Town)
13. Convent of St. Agnes of Bohemia
14. To Dancing House
15. Estates Theatre
16. Golden Lane
17. Havelská Market
18. Jewish Quarter
19. Kampa Island
20. Karlova Street
21. Klaus Synagogue
22. Klementinum
23. Lennon Wall
24. To Loreta Church
25. Lucerna Gallery
26. Maisel Synagogue
27. Mucha Museum
28. Municipal House
29. Mus. of Applied Arts
30. Mus. of Communism
31. Museum of Czech Cubism (in Black Madonna House)
32. To Museum of Modern Art
33. Na Příkopě Street
34. Náprstek's Museum of Asian, African & American Cultures
35. National Gallery in Sternberg Palace
36. National Museum
37. National Theatre
38. Nerudova Street
39. Old Jewish Cemetery
40. Old Royal Palace
41. Old Town Hall, Astronomical Clock, Tower & Chapel
42. Old Town Square & Jan Hus Memorial
43. Old-New Synagogue
44. Petřín Tower & Mus. of Jára Cimrman
45. Pinkas Synagogue
46. Powder Tower
47. Prague Castle
48. Royal Gardens
49. Royal Summer Palace
50. Schwarzenberg Palace
51. Spanish Synagogue
52. St. Martin in the Wall
53. St. Vitus Cathedral
54. St. Wenceslas Statue
55. To Strahov Monastery & Library
56. Terraced Gardens
57. Torture Museum
58. Toy and Barbie Museum
59. Týn Church
60. Ungelt Courtyard
61. Vrtba Garden
62. Wallenstein Palace & Garden
63. Wenceslas Square

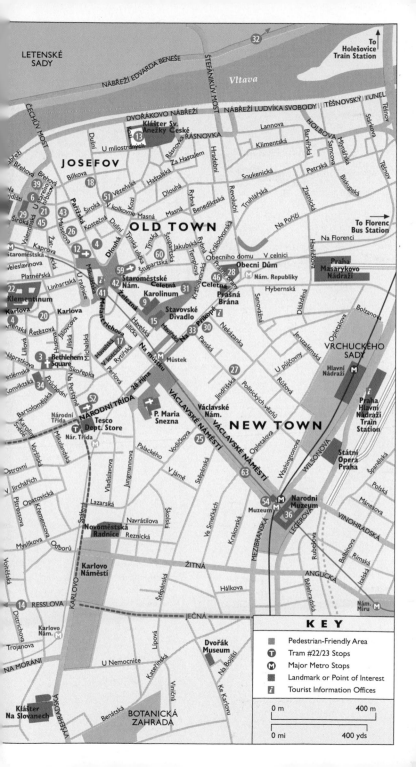

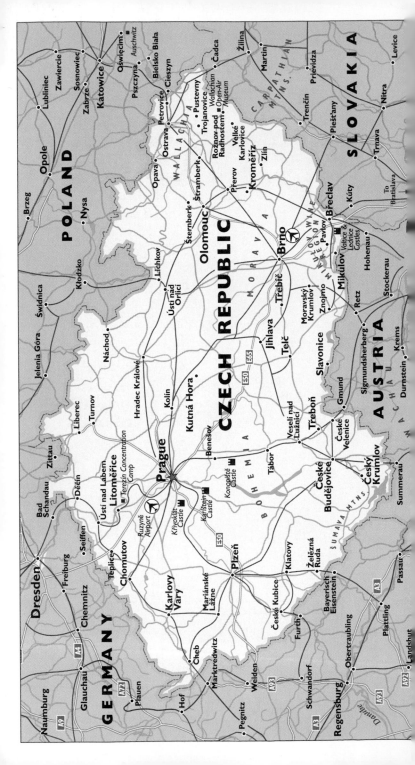

Rick Steves'

PRAGUE

& THE CZECH REPUBLIC

2006

VLTAVA

Prague Castle

Strahov Monastery

Little Quarter

St. Nicholas

Petřín Hill

Pivo!

Jewish Quarter

Charles Bridge

National Theatre

Dancing House

Hus Memorial

Old Town Square

Wenceslas Square

National Museum

Municipal House

Mucha Museum

DCH

AVALON
TRAVEL

CONTENTS

Top Destinations in the Czech Republic

DAY TRIPS:
KUTNÁ HORA,
TEREZÍN &
CASTLES

PRAGUE

WALLACHIA

OLOMOUC

TŘEBOŇ, TELČ
& TŘEBÍČ

MORAVSKÝ
KRUMLOV

ČESKÝ
KRUMLOV

SLAVONICE

MIKULOV
WINE REGION

DCH

INTRODUCTION

Wedged between Germany and Austria, the Czech Republic is one of the most comfortable and easy-to-explore countries of the former Warsaw Pact. Since the fall of communism in 1989, the Czech capital, Prague, has quickly become one of Europe's most popular destinations. Come see what all the fuss is about...but don't overlook the rest of the country. Even in a quick visit, you can enjoy a fine introduction to the entire Czech Republic.

This book focuses on Prague, but also includes the best small-town and back-to-nature destinations in the countryside. It gives you all the information and opinions necessary to wring the maximum value out of your limited time and money. If you want to experience the best two weeks the Czech Republic has to offer, this book is all you need.

Experiencing Europe's culture, people, and natural wonders economically and hassle-free has been my goal for three decades of traveling, tour guiding, and writing. With this book, I pass on to you the lessons I've learned, updated for 2006.

This book is selective, including only the top destinations and sights. For example, the Czech Republic has dozens of charming medieval towns, but I take you to only the most pleasant: Třeboň and Slavonice.

The best is, of course, only my opinion. But after spending half my adult life researching Europe, I've developed a sixth sense for what travelers enjoy.

This Information Is Accurate and Up-to-Date

This book is updated every year. Most guidebook publishers can only afford an update once every two or three years (and even then, it's often by e-mail or fax). Since this book is selective, covering only the places that make the best two weeks or so in the Czech

Republic, it's easy for me to get it updated in person each summer. The telephone numbers and hours of sights listed in this book are accurate as of mid-2005. Even with annual updates, things change. Still, if you're traveling with the current edition of this book, I guarantee you're using the most up-to-date information available in print (for the latest, see www.ricksteves.com/update). Also at our Web site, you'll find a valuable list of reports and experiences—good and bad—from fellow travelers who have used this book (www.ricksteves.com/feedback).

Use this year's edition. People who try to save a few bucks by traveling with an old book are not smart. They learn the seriousness of their mistake...in Prague. Your trip costs about $10 per waking hour. Your time is valuable. This guidebook saves lots of time.

About This Book

Rick Steves' Prague & the Czech Republic is a personal tour guide in your pocket. Better yet, it's actually two tour guides in your pocket: My co-writer/researcher for this guidebook is Honza Vihan, a Prague native who leads Eastern Europe tours for my travel company, Rick Steves' Europe Through the Back Door. Together, Honza and I will keep this book up-to-date and accurate. For simplicity, from this point, "we" will shed our respective egos and become "I"—but, at times, you'll know from the intimacy of some of the comments that Honza is sharing his perspective as a Czech citizen.

The first half of this book focuses on Prague, following this format:

Orientation helps you get the lay of the land, with tourist information; tips on getting around and avoiding scams; and details on tours and local guides to enhance your appreciation of the city. The "Planning Your Time" section offers a suggested schedule, with thoughts on how best to use your time.

The **Town** and **Quarter** chapters provide a succinct overview of Prague's most important sights, arranged by neighborhood, with ratings: ▲▲▲—Don't miss; ▲▲—Try hard to see; ▲—Worthwhile if you can make it; No rating—Worth knowing about.

Sleeping is a guide to my favorite good-value hotels.

Eating offers a wide assortment of restaurants, ranging from fun, inexpensive eateries to classy splurges.

Shopping gives you tips on where to shop and how to get VAT refunds.

Entertainment is your guide to fun, including a wide array of concerts and nightclubs—as well as other Czech entertainment options, from the unique Black Light Theater to hockey and soccer matches.

Transportation Connections covers connections by train and bus to destinations throughout the Czech Republic and beyond.

The second half of the book, **Beyond Prague,** is devoted to the rest of the Czech Republic. It includes day trips from Prague as well as various destinations. Each one is covered as a mini-vacation of its own, containing information formatted in a style similar to the one described above.

At the end of the book, you'll find a couple more handy tools:

Czech History explains the complicated, tumultuous, and ultimately uplifting background of this country.

The **appendix** is a traveler's tool kit, with a telephone calling chart, a list of national holidays, and a climate chart.

Browse through this book, choose your favorite destinations, and link them together. Then have a great trip! You'll travel like a temporary local, getting the absolute most out of every mile, minute, and dollar. As you travel the route I know and love, I'm happy you'll be meeting some of my favorite Czech people.

PLANNING

Trip Costs

Traveling in the Czech Republic is generally cheap. Things that natives buy—such as food, transportation, and museum tickets—are affordable (in line with the local economy). Hotels, on the other hand, are expensive, often surpassing even Western prices for comparable quality. Still, if you avoid restaurants with inflated prices on the main tourist drag, and if you use my listings to stay only at the best-value hotels, a trip to the Czech Republic can be substantially less expensive than a trip to Western European destinations.

Five components make up your trip cost: airfare, surface transportation, room and board, sightseeing/entertainment, and shopping/miscellany. While Prague is relatively expensive (by Czech standards), things tend to be much cheaper elsewhere in the country.

Airfare: Don't try to sort through the mess. Find and use a good travel agent. A basic, round-trip flight from the U.S. to Prague should cost $600 to $1,200 (even cheaper in winter), depending on where you fly from and when.

Surface Transportation: Point-to-point train and bus tickets within the Czech Republic are inexpensive—a second-class train ticket from Prague to the farthest reaches of the country won't run you more than about $25. Renting a car is convenient for exploring the Czech countryside, but is much more expensive than public transportation (figure around $500 per week, including gas and insurance). And those with more money than time could consider hiring a car with a private driver (a full-day round-trip excursion from Prague to Český Krumlov runs about $140; see page 154).

Room and Board: Plan on spending an average of $80 a day per person for room and board in Prague. An $80-a-day budget per person allows $10 for lunch, $20 for dinner, and $50 for lodging (based on 2 people splitting the cost of a $100 double room that includes breakfast). That's doable. Outside of Prague and Český Krumlov, hotel rates plummet to $50 or less for a decent double, and food prices also drop—making $50 per person per day a reasonable budget in the Czech countryside. Even in Prague, students and tightwads can get by on $30 a day ($15 per bed, $15 for meals and snacks)

Sightseeing and Entertainment: Sightseeing is inexpensive here. Most sights generally cost around $2 to $4; a few biggies cost much more (such as Prague Castle—up to $14, or the Jewish Quarter—$20), but that's rare. Figure $20 for concerts and other splurge experiences. You can hire a private guide for as little as $65 for four hours. An overall average of $20 a day works for most travelers. Don't skimp here. After all, this category is the driving force behind your trip—you came to sightsee, enjoy, and experience the Czech Republic.

Shopping and Miscellany: Figure $1 per postcard, coffee, beer, and ice-cream cone. Shopping can vary in cost from nearly nothing to a small fortune. Good budget travelers find that this category has little to do with assembling a trip full of lifelong and wonderful memories.

When to Go

The "tourist season" runs roughly from Easter (April 16 in 2006) through late September. July and August have their advantages, with the best weather, very long days (light until after 21:00), fewer tourists in Prague than in the peak months of May and September, and busy festivals held in small towns around the country.

In spring and fall (May, June, Sept, and early Oct), the weather is milder, and the colors and scents are powerful.

Winter travelers find the concert season in full swing, with remarkably fewer tourists, but some accommodations and sights are either closed or run on a limited schedule. Seeing Charles Bridge blanketed by fresh snow easily makes the hours spent out in the cold worthwhile. But the weather can be too cold and dreary, and night will draw the shades on your sightseeing before dinnertime. Use the climate chart in the appendix as a guide.

Sightseeing Priorities

Depending on the length of your trip, here are my recommended priorities. Presuming you're traveling by public transportation,

I've taken geographical proximity into account.

3 days:	Prague
5 days, add:	Your choice of one or two nearby day trips (Kutná Hora, Terezín Concentration Camp, and the 3 castles: Konopiště, Karlštejn, or Křivoklát)
7 days, add:	Český Krumlov
9 days, add:	Olomouc and Moravský Krumlov
10 days, add:	Třeboň
Morc:	Your choice among Wallachia, Telč, Slavonice, Třebíč, Mikulov Wine Region, and Lednice/Valtice.

This list assumes you're primarily interested in the Czech Republic. But note that Prague also splices neatly into a wider-ranging trip including such nearby destinations as Vienna, Budapest, Kraków, Munich, and Berlin.

Travel Smart

Your trip is like a complex play—easier to follow and really appreciate on a second viewing. While no one does the same trip twice to gain that advantage, reading this book in its entirety before your trip accomplishes much the same thing. As a practical matter (to avoid redundancy), many cultural or historic details are explained for one sight and not repeated for another—even if they would pump up your understanding and appreciation of that second sight.

Design an itinerary that enables you to hit museums and festivals on the right days. As you read this book, note that Monday is a problem day outside of Prague, when many museums are closed. Sundays have the same pros and cons as they do for travelers in the U.S. Sightseeing attractions are generally open, shops and banks are closed, and public-transportation options are fewer. City traffic is light. Rowdy evenings are rare on Sundays. Saturday morning feels like any bustling weekday, but at lunchtime, many shops close down until Monday morning.

Plan ahead for banking, laundry, post-office chores, and picnics. Maximize rootedness by minimizing one-night stands. Mix intense and relaxed periods. Every trip (and every traveler) needs at least a few slack days. Pace yourself. Assume you will return.

Reread this book as you travel and visit local tourist information offices. Upon arrival in a new town, lay the groundwork for a smooth departure; write down the schedule for the train or bus you'll take when you depart. Buy a phone card (or mobile phone) and use it for reservations and reconfirmations. Outsmart Prague's notorious taxis to get around cheaply and efficiently.

Connect with the culture. Set up your own quest to find the most Czech pub you can. (Anything with an English menu doesn't

The Czech Republic's Best Two-Week Trip by Car

Day	Plan	Sleep in
1	Arrive in Prague	Prague
2	Prague	Prague
3	Prague	Prague
4	Day-trip to Kutná Hora or Terezín Concentration Camp	Prague
5	To Český Krumlov via one of the castles near Prague (Konopiště, Karlštejn, or Křivoklát)	Český Krumlov
6	Český Krumlov	Český Krumlov
7	To Třeboň	Třeboň
8	To Slavonice via Telč	Slavonice
9	To Pavlov via Třebíč and Moravský Krumlov	Pavlov
10	Mikulov Wine Region	Pavlov
11	To Olomouc via Kroměříž	Olomouc
12	Olomouc	Olomouc
13	To Wallachia	Trojanovice
14	Return to Prague (via Kutná Hora, if you haven't day-tripped there yet)	Prague

count.) Once inside, get recommendations from the locals on the best type of beer, and make it your goal to get the most interesting story you possibly can out of them.

Enjoy the friendliness of the Czech people. Ask questions. Most locals are eager to point you in their idea of the right direction. Keep a notepad in your pocket for organizing your thoughts. Those who expect to travel smart, do.

The Czech Republic's
Best 12-Day Trip by Bus and Train

Day	Plan	Sleep in
1	Arrive in Prague	Prague
2	Prague	Prague
3	Prague	Prague
4	Day-trip to Kutná Hora, Terezín Concentration Camp, or one of the castles near Prague (Konopiště, Karlštejn, or Křivoklát)	Prague
5	More day trips near Prague (same choices as Day 4)	Prague
6	To Český Krumlov	Český Krumlov
7	Český Krumlov	Český Krumlov
8	To Třeboň	Třeboň
9	To Telč	Telč
10	To Olomouc via Moravský Krumlov (bus to Brno, train to Moravský Krumlov, then train back to Brno and on to Olomouc)	Olomouc
11	Olomouc	Olomouc
12	Return to Prague	Prague

With more time in the Czech Republic, consider a pair of other destinations that are a little more difficult—but still possible—to reach by public transportation: Hikers enjoy **Wallachia,** which fits easily into the above schedule after Olomouc (home-base in Trojanovice). Wine-lovers head for the **Mikulov Wine Region,** easiest to visit between Telč and Olomouc (home-base in Pavlov).

Beyond the Czech borders, consider adding **Budapest,** Hungary, and **Kraków,** Poland—each an easy, direct night-train away from Prague (or even quicker connection from Olomouc). For more on these destinations beyond the Czech Republic, see the current edition of *Rick Steves' Best of Eastern Europe.*

RESOURCES

Tourist Information Offices

In the U.S.

The Czech national tourist office is a wealth of information. Before your trip, get the free general information packet and request any specifics you may want (such as regional and city maps and festival schedules) from the **Czech Tourist Authority:** 1109 Madison Ave., New York, NY 10028, tel. 212/288-0830, fax 212/288-0971, www.czechtourism.com/usa, info-usa@czechtourism.com. Basic information and a map are free; additional materials are $4 (prepaid by check).

In the Czech Republic

The tourist information office is your best first stop in any new town. Try to arrive, or at least telephone, before it closes. In this book, I'll refer to a tourist information office as a **TI.**

In virtually every town covered in this book, you'll find a TI on the main square. Most of these TIs offer English-speaking staff; a free map of the town; a selection of hiking and biking maps; listings of events, activities, and accommodations (but usually not a room-booking service); bus and train schedules; Internet access; and an opportunity to buy concert tickets or hire a local guide. Virtually all local tourist offices in the Czech Republic are run by the town governments, which means their information isn't colored by a drive for profit.

Rick Steves' Guidebooks, Public Television Show, and Radio Show

Rick Steves' Europe Through the Back Door gives you budget-travel skills, such as minimizing jet lag, packing light, planning your itinerary, traveling by car or train, finding rooms, changing money, avoiding rip-offs, buying a mobile phone, hurdling the language barrier, staying healthy, taking great photographs, using a bidet, and much more. The book also includes chapters on 38 of my favorite "Back Doors," including one on Prague.

Country Guides: These annually updated books offer you the latest on the top sights and destinations, with tips on how to make your trip efficient and fun. Here are the titles:

Rick Steves' Best of Europe	*Rick Steves' Great Britain*
Rick Steves' Best of *Eastern Europe*	*Rick Steves' Ireland*
	Rick Steves' Italy
Rick Steves' England (new in 2006)	*Rick Steves' Portugal*
	Rick Steves' Scandinavia
Rick Steves' France	*Rick Steves' Spain*
Rick Steves' Germany *& Austria*	*Rick Steves' Switzerland*

City and Regional Guides: Updated every year, these focus on Europe's most compelling destinations. Along with specifics on sights, restaurants, hotels, and nightlife, you'll get self-guided, illustrated tours of the outstanding museums and most characteristic neighborhoods.

Rick Steves' Amsterdam,
  Bruges & Brussels
Rick Steves' Florence
  & Tuscany
Rick Steves' London
Rick Steves' Paris

Rick Steves' Prague
  & the Czech Republic
Rick Steves' Provence
  & the French Riviera
Rick Steves' Rome
Rick Steves' Venice

Rick Steves' Phrase Books: In Europe, a phrase book is as fun as it is necessary. This practical and budget-oriented series covers Spanish, Portuguese, Italian, French, German, and French/Italian/German. You'll be able to make hotel reservations over the phone, chat with your cabbie, and bargain at street markets.

And More Books: *Rick Steves' Europe 101: History and Art for the Traveler* (with Gene Openshaw) gives you the story of Europe's people, history, and art. Written for smart people who were sleeping in their history and art classes before they knew they were going to Europe, *101* helps Europe's sights come alive. This book is more focused on Western Europe than the Czech Republic, however.

Rick Steves' Easy Access Europe, geared for travelers with limited mobility, covers London, Paris, Bruges, Amsterdam, and the Rhine River.

Rick Steves' Postcards from Europe, my autobiographical book, packs 25 years of travel anecdotes and insights into the ultimate 2,000-mile European adventure.

My latest book, *Rick Steves' European Christmas,* covers the joys, history, and quirky traditions of the holiday season in seven European countries.

Public Television Show: My series, *Rick Steves' Europe,* keeps churning out shows (more than 60 at last count), including one on Prague.

Radio Show: My new weekly radio show, which combines call-in questions (à la *Car Talk*) and interviews with travel experts, airs on public radio stations. For a schedule of upcoming topics, an archive of past programs, and details on how to call in, see www.ricksteves.com/radio.

Other Guidebooks

Especially if you'll be traveling beyond my recommended destinations, you may want some supplemental information. When you consider the improvements they'll make in your $3,000 vacation, $30 for extra maps and books is money well spent. Particularly for several people traveling by car, the extra weight and expense of a small trip library are negligible. One budget tip can save the price of an extra guidebook.

Lonely Planet's guides to the Czech and Slovak Republics and Prague are thorough, well-researched, and packed with good maps

---

Begin Your Trip at www.ricksteves.com

At www.ricksteves.com you'll find a wealth of **free information** on destinations covered in this book, including fresh European travel and tour news every month and helpful "Graffiti Wall" tips from thousands of fellow travelers.

While you're there, the **online Travel Store** is a great place to save money on travel bags and accessories designed by Rick Steves to help you travel smarter and lighter, plus a wide selection of guidebooks, planning maps, and DVDs.

Traveling through Europe by rail is a breeze, but choosing the right railpass for your trip—amidst hundreds of options— can drive you nutty. At www.ricksteves.com, you'll find **Rick Steves' Annual Guide to European Railpasses**—your best way to convert chaos into pure travel energy. Buy your railpass from Rick, and you'll get a bunch of free extras to boot.

Travel agents will tell you about mainstream tours of Europe, but they won't tell you about **Rick Steves' tours.** Rick Steves' Europe Through the Back Door travel company offers more than two dozen itineraries and 300 departures reaching the best destinations in this book...and beyond. You'll enjoy the services of a great guide, a fun bunch of travel partners (with group sizes in the 20s), and plenty of room to spread out in a big, comfy bus. You'll find trips to fit every vacation size, from week-long city getaways to longer cross-country adventures. For details, visit www.ricksteves.com or call 425/771-8303 ext 217.

---

and hotel recommendations. The similar Rough Guides to these destinations are hip and insightful, written by British researchers. Neither of these is updated annually—use them only with a one- or two-year-old copyright. Students and vagabonds will like the highly opinionated Let's Go series, researched every year by Harvard students. If you're a low-budget train traveler interested in hosteling and the youth and nightlife scene (which I have basically ignored), get *Let's Go: Eastern Europe* or *Let's Go: Austria & Switzerland* (includes coverage of Prague). Older travelers enjoy *Frommer's Prague and the Best of the Czech Republic* even though it, like the Fodor's guide, ignores alternatives that enable travelers to save money by dirtying their fingers in the local culture.

The popular, skinny *Michelin Green Guide to Prague* is excellent, known for its city and sightseeing maps, dry but concise and helpful information on all major sights, and good cultural and historical background. The encyclopedic Blue Guides to Prague and the Czech and Slovak Republics are dry but just right for scholarly types.

The Eyewitness series has editions covering Prague and the Czech and Slovak Republics. They're popular for great, easy-to-grasp graphics and photos, 3-D cutaways of buildings, aerial-view maps of historic neighborhoods, and cultural background. But written content in Eyewitness is relatively skimpy, and the books weigh a ton. I simply borrow them for a minute from other travelers at certain sights to make sure I'm aware of that place's highlights. The Time Out travel guide to Prague provides good, detailed coverage, particularly on arts and entertainment.

Maps

The black-and-white maps in this book, designed and drawn by Dave Hoerlein, are concise and simple. Dave, who is well-traveled in the Czech Republic, has created the maps to help you locate recommended places and get to the tourist offices, where you can pick up a more in-depth map of the city or region (usually free).

Many of Prague's bookstores have road, hiking, and cycling maps covering all of the country. One of the best is the Kiwi Map Store near Wenceslas Square (see page 143).

For drivers, I'd recommend a 1:100,000 atlas of the Czech Republic. If you have hiking plans (near Křivoklát, around Český Krumlov, in the Šumava and Beskydy Mountains, around Třeboň, or near Slavonice), get the excellent 1:50,000 *Edice Klub Českých Turistů* maps (based on military reconnaissance maps), or the much less detailed but sufficient 1:100,000 *Kartografie Praha* maps. Train travelers usually manage fine with the maps they get from the local tourist offices.

PRACTICALITIES

Red Tape: Currently, Americans and Canadians need only a passport, but no visa or shots, to travel in the Czech Republic.

Time: In Europe—and throughout this book—you'll be using the 24-hour clock. After 12:00 noon, keep going—13:00, 14:00, and so on. For anything over 12, subtract 12 and add p.m. (14:00 is 2:00 p.m.)

The Czech Republic is six/nine hours ahead of the East/West Coasts of the U.S.

Discounts: While discounts for sightseeing and transportation are not listed in this book, youths (under 18) and students (only with International Student Identity Cards) often get discounts—but only by asking.

Metric: Get used to metric. A liter is about a quart, four to a gallon. A kilometer is six-tenths of a mile. I figure kilometers to miles by cutting them in half and adding back 10 percent of the original (120 km: 60 + 12 = 72 miles, 300 km: 150 + 30 = 180 miles).

Czech Literature and Film

Children, adults, and grandparents delight in telling stories. In Czech fairy tales, there are no dwarfs and monsters. To experience the full absurdity and hilarity of Czech culture, you need a child's imagination and the understanding that the best fun comes from being able to laugh at yourself. Czech writers invented the robot, the pistol, and Black Light Theater (an absurd show of illusion, puppetry, mime, and modern dance). Literature and film are the most transparent window into the Czech soul.

The most famous Czech literary figure is the title character of **Jaroslav Hašek's** *Good Soldier Švejk,* who frustrates the WWI Austro-Hungarian army he serves by cleverly playing dumb.

Bohumil Hrabal, writing in a stream-of-consciousness style, mixes tales he had heard in pubs from sailors, self-made philosophers, and kind-hearted prostitutes into enchanting fictions that express the Czech spirit and sense of humor better than any other work; the best are *I Served the King of England, The Town Where Time Stood Still*, and *Too Loud a Solitude*. (Jiří Menzel turned some of Hrabal's writings into films, the most famous of which is the Oscar-winning *Closely Watched Trains*—for more on Czech cinema, see below.)

Other well-known Czech writers include **Václav Havel** (playwright who went on to become Czechoslovakia's first post-communist president; he authored many essays and plays, including *The Garden Party*); **Milan Kundera** (author of *The Unbearable Lightness of Being,* set during the "Prague Spring" uprising); and **Karel Čapek** (novelist and playwright who created the robot in the play *R.U.R.*).

But the most famous Czech writer of all is the existentialist great, **Franz Kafka**—a Prague Jew who wrote in German about people turning into giant cockroaches *(The Metamorphosis)* and urbanites being pursued and persecuted for crimes they knew nothing about *(The Trial)*.

Some less-known Czech writers are also worth discovering. **Arnošt Lustig's** *Dita Saxová* covers the fate of Czech Jews

Shoppers: For information on VAT tax refunds and customs regulations, see page 143.

Watt's up? If you're bringing electrical gear, you'll need a two-prong adapter plug and a converter. Travel appliances often have convenient built-in converters; look for a voltage switch marked 120V (U.S.) and 240V (Europe).

News: Americans keep in touch in Europe with the *International Herald Tribune* (published almost daily via satellite).

during the war, while **Josef Škvorecký**'s *The Cowards (Zbabělci)* describes the world of a generation coming of age just after the war. Surprisingly, the 1990s were not a very exciting time for Czech literature. The one exception, and the definitive book of the 1989 generation, is **Jáchym Topol's** *Sister*. Topol captures "the years after the Time exploded" in a rich mixture of colloquial Czech full of German and English loanwords and neologisms. The English translation is superb.

The Nobel Prize-winning poet **Jaroslav Seifert** experienced during his long life all the diverse movements of the 20th century—dadaism, surrealism, communism, anti-communism—creating a medium of his own, in which everyone finds a poem to her own liking.

The Czech film tradition has always been strong, and the 1960s were its heyday, giving birth to **Jiří Menzel's** *Closely Watched Trains* and *Larks on the String*; **Vojtěch Jasný's** *Intimate Lighting*; and **Miloš Forman's** *Fireman's Ball* and *Loves of a Blonde* (after his 1968 escape from communist Czechoslovakia, Forman made it big in the U.S. with films such as *One Flew Over the Cuckoo's Nest* and *Amadeus*).

The 1990s saw the arrival of two excellent Czech filmmakers, **Jan Svěrák** (*The Elementary School* and the Oscar-winning *Kolya*) and **Jiří Hřebejk** (*Divided We Fall*, nominated for an Academy Award).

One of the most inspiring Czech artists is a painter, animator, director, and surrealist—**Jan Švankmajer**. His *Something from Alice*, *Lesson Faust*, and *Food* combine all of the author's artistic skills into a highly original style that is guaranteed to change the way you look at the world.

Czechs have wonderful animation that successfully competes with Walt Disney in Eastern Europe and China. *Pat a Mat*, *Krteček (The Little Mole)*, or *Maxipes Fík* are intelligent gifts to bring to your little ones at home.

Every Tuesday, the European editions of *Time* and *Newsweek* hit the stands with articles of particular interest to European travelers. Sports addicts can get their fix from *USA Today*. Good Web sites include www.prague.com and http://news.bbc.co.uk. For the local perspective, I pick up a copy of the English-language *Prague Post*.

Telephone Tips: Dial 112 for emergencies, 158 for police. If an 0800 number doesn't work, replace the 0800 with 822.

MONEY

Banking

Bring plastic (ATM, credit, or debit cards) along with several hundred dollars in hard cash as an emergency backup. Traveler's checks are a waste of time and money.

The best and easiest way to get Czech cash is to use the omnipresent cash machines (called *Bankomats*). You'll find these all over the Czech Republic—they're always open and provide quick transactions. Before you go, verify with your bank that your card will work, inquire about fees (can be up to $5 per transaction), and alert them that you'll be making withdrawals in Europe; otherwise, the bank may not approve transactions if it perceives unusual spending patterns. Bring an extra card in case one gets demagnetized or gobbled up by a machine.

Although the Czech Republic hasn't officially adopted the euro, many hotels, restaurants, and shops accept euro bills. Most businesses will not take euro coins or larger bills, and you'll usually get bad rates (and your change in the local currency). If you're just passing through the country, your euros will probably get you by—and can actually be helpful in an emergency. But if you're staying awhile, get the local currency.

Just like at home, credit or debit cards work easily at larger hotels, restaurants, and stores. Visa and MasterCard are more commonly accepted than American Express. Note that restaurants and smaller businesses far prefer payment in cash and in local currency. If you have lots of large bills, break them at a bank, especially if you like shopping or eating at mom-and-pop places; they rarely have huge amounts of change.

If you do need to exchange money, you can buy and sell easily at train stations (5 percent fee), banks, or hotels. Assume anyone trying to sell money on the streets is peddling obsolete (or

---

Exchange Rate

Though the Czech Republic joined the European Union in 2004, it'll be another few years before they officially begin using the euro. For now, the Czech Republic continues to use its traditional currency, the Czech crown (*koruna*, abbreviated Kč).

25 Czech crowns (Kč) = about $1. This is the cost of one pint of beer.

To roughly convert Czech crowns into dollars, drop the last two digits and multiply by four (e.g., 750 Kč = $28— actually $30).

Damage Control for Lost or Stolen Cards

If you lose your credit, debit, or ATM card, you can stop people from using your card by reporting the loss immediately to the respective global customer-assistance centers. Call these 24-hour U.S. numbers collect: Visa (tel. 410/581-9994), MasterCard (tel. 636/722-7111), and American Express (tel. 336/393-1111).

Have, at a minimum, the following information ready: the name of the financial institution that issued you the card, along with the type of card (classic, platinum, or whatever). Ideally, plan ahead and pack photocopies of your cards— front and back—to expedite their replacement. Providing the following information will allow for a quicker cancellation of your missing card: full card number, whether you are the primary or secondary cardholder, the cardholder's name exactly as printed on the card, billing address, home phone number, circumstances of the loss or theft, and identification verification (your birth date, your mother's maiden name, or your Social Security number—memorize this, don't carry a copy). If you are the secondary cardholder, you'll also need to provide the primary cardholder's identification verification details. You can generally receive a temporary card within two or three business days in Europe.

If you promptly report your card lost or stolen, you typically won't be responsible for any unauthorized transactions on your account, although many banks charge a liability fee of $50.

Bulgarian) currency. Change bureaus advertise no commission and offer decent but deceptive rates. (These rates are for selling dollars—their rates for buying your dollars are worse.) Hidden fees abound; ask exactly how many crowns you'll walk away with before you agree to the transaction.

You should use a money belt (a pouch with a strap that you buckle around your waist like a belt and wear under your clothes). Thieves target tourists. A money belt provides peace of mind and allows you to carry lots of cash safely.

Don't be petty about getting money. Withdraw a week's worth of cash, stuff it in your money belt, and travel!

Tips on Tipping

Tipping in the Czech Republic isn't as automatic and generous as it is in the U. S.—but for special service, tips are appreciated, if not expected. As in the U. S., the proper amount depends on your resources, tipping philosophy, and the circumstance, but some general guidelines apply.

Restaurants: Tipping is an issue only at restaurants that have waiters and waitresses. If you order your food at a counter, don't tip. At Czech restaurants that have a waitstaff, locals round up the bill after a good meal (usually 5 percent; e.g., for a 380-Kč meal, pay 400 Kč). If you warm up the waiter with a few Czech words, such as please (*prosím*; PROH-zeem) and thank you (*děkuji*; DYACK-quee), you'll get better service and won't be expected to tip more than a local. But if you greet your waiter in English, he'll want a 15 percent tip. Believe me, the slightest attempt at speaking Czech (see phrases on page 23) will turn you from a targeted tourist into a special guest, even in the most touristy restaurants.

Taxis: To tip the cabbie, round up about five percent. If the cabbie hauls your bags and zips you to the airport to help you catch your flight, you might want to toss in a little more. But if you feel like you're being driven in circles or otherwise ripped off, skip the tip. Again, if you use some Czech words, it's less likely that your cabbie will try to scam you.

Hotels: I don't tip at hotels, but if you do, give the porter about 20 Kč for carrying bags and, at the end of your stay, leave around 50 Kč for the maid if the room was kept clean.

Special Services: Tour guides at public sites sometimes hold out their hands for tips after they give their spiels. If I've already paid for the tour, I don't tip extra. In general, if someone in the service industry does a super job for you, a small tip (around 50 Kč) is appropriate...but not required.

When in Doubt, Ask. If you're not sure whether (or how much) to tip for a service, ask your hotelier or the local tourist information office; they'll fill you in on how it's done on their turf.

TRANSPORTATION

By Car or Train?

Within Prague, a car is a worthless headache. If you're staying mostly in Prague and tackling a few convenient side-trips (such as Kutná Hora and Český Krumlov), public transportation works well. If you'll be venturing farther into the countryside, trains and buses will get you where you need to go—but renting a car gives you greater flexibility. For connecting Prague to international destinations (like Budapest or Kraków), stick with the train.

Trains

Trains are fairly punctual (running about 10 min late) and cover cities well, but frustrating schedules make a few out-of-the-way destinations I recommend not worth the time and trouble for the less determined (try buses instead; see below).

Czech Public Transportation

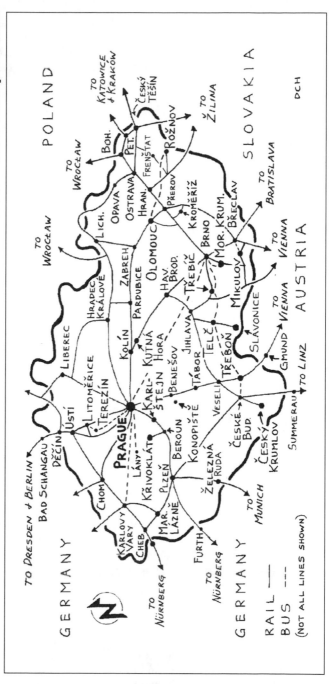

Schedules: For Czech train and bus timetables, visit www.vlak-bus.cz or Germany's excellent all-Europe timetable: http://bahn.hafas.de/bin/query.exe/en. Consider buying the *Traťové Jízdní Řády*, a comprehensive, easy-to-use schedule of all trains in the country (includes English instructions, sold at major station ticket windows for 30 Kč). Although it's easy to look up a connection on the Internet, having the schedule and a map of railway lines with you gives you freedom to easily change or make new plans as you travel.

Tickets and Tips: Tickets within the Czech Republic are valid for two days, and international tickets are good from three days to two months (the shorter-term ones are often cheaper). Tickets are valid for travel along the entire stretch from Prague to your destination, not just for one trip on a specific train—so take advantage of the freedom it gives you and hop on and hop off along the way. You'll rarely need a reservation, except for international night trains.

If you have one or more companions traveling with you by train, ask for a group ticket. This gets you a 50 percent discount for every extra ticket (i.e., only 1 person pays the full price).

If you're heading to a city near the Czech border (such as Vienna, Bratislava, Dresden, or Nürnberg), it often pays to buy two separate tickets: one to the Czech border, and another from the border to your destination. This also allows you to take advantage of particular discounts in that country, such as the group discount.

Railpasses: The Czech Republic has its own railpass, but since point-to-point tickets are so inexpensive, it's rarely worthwhile. Find our free Railpass Guide online at www.ricksteves.com/rail. The Czech Republic is not a Eurail country, so Eurailpasses and Eurail Selectpasses are not valid here. To connect Prague with international destinations, consider a Prague Excursion Pass (see page 153).

Buses

To reach many of the destinations in this book, buses are faster and cheaper than trains. Buses are also generally more punctual. No reservations are needed for buses—simply buy tickets directly from the driver (who will appreciate exact change and will have difficulty breaking big bills). You'll be required to put big bags in the luggage compartment under the bus (12–24 Kč extra, depending on the distance), so have a small day-bag ready to take on the bus with you. Buses don't have bathrooms, nor do they stop for bathroom breaks.

Always let the bus driver know where you want to get off. Some stops are by request only (for example, the Small Fortress at Terezín Concentration Camp), and most bus drivers are happy to let you know when your stop is coming up.

Car Rental

It's smart (though not essential) to set up your car rental in advance from the U.S. Especially during the summer, the best deals at Czech car-rental companies need to be arranged two to three weeks ahead. Renting from a local Czech company (see page 55) is as convenient as using Budget or Avis; most will bring the car to your hotel. There are about a hundred car-rental companies in Prague. Alimex is a good bet (see page 55). Or do a Google search from home, take your pick, and reserve by e-mail.

Czechs are once again proud of their locally built Škoda cars (since the 1920s, the Ford of Eastern Europe). Now owned by Volkswagen, Škoda is the biggest post-communist success story in the country. By renting one, you'll learn why most Eastern Europeans stay loyal to the brand, even as cheap Japanese cars inundate the market.

When renting, I usually get a Škoda Felicia or Fabia; for more luggage space and more oomph, step up to the Škoda Octavia. On average, you should be able to get a Škoda with full insurance and unlimited mileage for $40–50 per day. Škodas usually have standard transmission and come with alarms; you might want to supplement the alarm with a lock for the steering wheel or stick shift.

At about $1.25 per liter ($5 per gallon) for unleaded ("Natural 95"), gas in the Czech Republic is still considerably cheaper than in Western Europe.

For peace of mind, I spring for the Collision Damage Waiver insurance (CDW, about $15–25 per day), which limits my financial responsibility in case of an accident. Unfortunately, CDW now has a high deductible hovering around $1,200. When you pick up your car, many car-rental companies will try to sell you "super CDW" at an additional cost of $7–15 per day to lower the deductible to zero.

Some credit cards offer CDW-type coverage for no charge to their customers. Quiz your credit-card company on the worst-case scenario. You have to choose either the coverage offered by your car-rental company or by your credit-card company. This means that if you go with the credit-card coverage, you'll have to decline the CDW offered by the car-rental company. In this situation, some car-rental companies put a hold on your credit card for the amount of the full deductible (which can equal the value of the car). This is bad news if your credit limit is low—particularly if you plan on using that card for other purchases during your trip.

Another alternative is buying CDW insurance from Travel Guard for $9 a day (U.S. tel. 800/826-4919, www.travelguard .com). It's valid throughout Europe, but some car-rental companies refuse to honor it, especially in Italy and the Republic of Ireland. Oddly, residents of some states (including Washington) are not allowed to buy this coverage.

In sum, buying CDW—and the supplemental insurance to buy down the deductible, if you choose—is the easiest but priciest option. Using the coverage that comes with your credit card is cheaper, but can involve more hassle. If you're taking a short trip, an easy solution is to buy Travel Guard's very affordable CDW. For longer trips of three weeks or more, leasing (which automatically includes CDW insurance) is the best way to go.

For driving in Eastern Europe, it's wise to get an International Driving Permit ahead of time at your local AAA office ($10 plus 2 passport-type photos).

Generally speaking, if you rent a car in Eastern Europe, you can cross borders within the East. But you might get hassled if you're going between Western and Eastern Europe. No matter where you're going, state your travel plans up front to the rental company. Some won't allow any of their rental cars to enter Eastern Europe, and some restrict certain types of cars: BMWs, Mercedes, and convertibles. Ask about extra fees—some companies automatically tack on theft and collision coverage for an Eastern European excursion. To avoid hassles at the borders, ask the rental agent to mark your contract with the company's permission to cross.

Driving

During the communist era, Eastern Europe's infrastructure lagged far behind the West's. Now that the Iron Curtain is long gone, superhighways are popping up like crazy all over the Czech Republic. You'll sometimes discover that a much faster freeway option has been built between major destinations since your three-year-old map was published (a good reason to travel with the most up-to-date maps available). As soon as a long-enough section is completed, the roads are opened to the public. Only rarely are backcountry roads the only option (as with part of the trip between Prague and Kraków). These can be bumpy and slow, but they're almost always paved (or, at least, they once were).

Learn the universal road signs. Seat belts are required, and two beers under those belts are enough to land you in jail.

Driving in the Czech Republic: Distance and Time

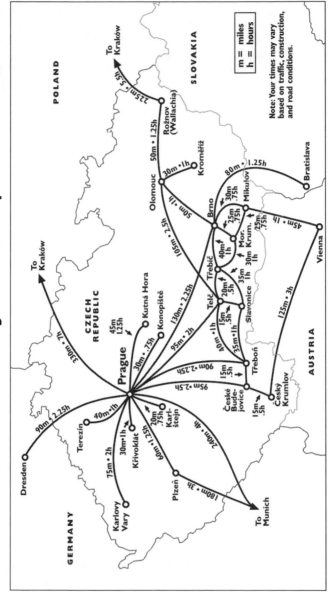

Tolls: If you're driving on highways in the Czech Republic, buy a toll sticker *(dálniční známka)* at the border, a post office, or a gas station (200 Kč/15 days, 300 Kč/2 months). Your rental car may come with the necessary sticker—ask.

Parking: You'll pay about $10–15 a day to park safely in Prague. Formerly notorious for its Russian car-theft gangs, Prague is safer now—but it's still wise to be careful. Ask at your hotel for advice. In small towns such as Český Krumlov or Slavonice, you have nothing to worry about. I keep a pile of coins in my ashtray for parking meters, public phones, launderettes, and wishing wells.

COMMUNICATING

Hurdling the Language Barrier

The language barrier in the Czech Republic is no bigger than in Western Europe. In fact, I find that it's even easier to communicate in Český Krumlov than it is in Madrid. Immediately after the Iron Curtain fell in 1989, English-speakers were rare. But today, you'll find that most people in the tourist industry—and virtually all young people—speak good English.

Of course, not everyone speaks English. You'll run into the most substantial language barriers in situations when you need to deal with a clerk or service person aged forty or above (train station and post office staff, maids, museum guards, bakers, and so on). Be reasonable in your expectations. Czech post-office clerks and museum ticket-sellers are every bit as friendly, cheery, and multilingual as they are in the U.S. Luckily, it's relatively easy to get your point across in these places. I've often bought a train ticket simply by writing out the name of my destination; the time I want to travel (using the 24-hour clock); and if necessary, the date I want to leave (day first, then month, then year). Here's an example of what I'd show a ticket-seller at a train station: "Olomouc–17:30–15.7.2006."

If you speak German, it will likely come in handy—especially in the south of the country, where the economy is almost entirely dependent on Austrian tourists from across the border.

Czech Language

Czech, a Slavic language closely related to its neighbors Polish and Slovak, bears little resemblance to Western European languages. Slavic pronunciation can be tricky. In fact, when the first Christian missionaries, Cyril and Methodius, came to Eastern Europe a millennium ago, they invented a whole new alphabet to represent these strange Slavic sounds. The Cyrillic alphabet is still used today in the eastern Slavic countries (such as Serbia and Russia).

Key Czech Phrases

English	Czech	Pronounced
Hello. (formal)	**Dobrý den.**	DOH-bree dehn
Hi. / Bye. (informal)	**Ahoj.**	AH-hoy
Do you speak English?	**Mluvíte anglicky?**	MLOO-vee-teh ANG-lits-kee
Yes. / No.	**Ano. / Ne.**	AH-no / neh
Please. / You're welcome. / Can I help you?	**Prosím.**	PROH-zeem
Thank you.	**Děkuji.**	DYACK-quee
I'm sorry. / Excuse me.	**Promiňte.**	PROH-meen-teh
Good.	**Dobře.**	DOHB-zhay
Goodbye.	**Na shledanou.**	nah SKLEH-dah-now
one / two	**jeden / dva**	YAY-dehn / dvah
three / four	**tři / čtyři**	tree / chuh-TEE-ree
five / six	**pět / šest**	pyeht / shehst
seven / eight	**sedm / osm**	SEH-dum / OH-sum
nine / ten	**devět / deset**	DEHV-yeht / DEH-seht
hundred	**sto**	stoh
thousand	**tisíc**	TYEE-seets
How much?	**Kolik?**	KOH-leek
local currency	**koruna (Kč)**	koh-ROO-nah
Where is...?	**Kde je...?**	gday yeh
...the toilet	**...vécé**	vayt-SAY
men	**muži**	MOO-zhee
women	**ženy**	ZHAY-nee
water / coffee	**voda / káva**	VOH-dah / KAH-vah
beer / wine	**pivo / víno**	PEE-voh / VEE-noh
Cheers!	**Na zdraví!**	nah zdrah-VEE
The bill, please.	**Účet, prosím.**	OO-cheht PROH-zeem

Pronouncing Czech Place Names

Here's a rough pronunciation key for destinations in this guide-book. Note that I haven't tried to duplicate the sounds represented by ř (which sounds like a cross between a rolled "r" and "zh") and ň (which sounds like an "n" followed by an extremely slight "y" sound). As these sounds are notoriously impossible for foreigners to duplicate, it's easiest just to replace them with simple "r" and "n" sounds.

For pronunciation help for specific sights and neighborhoods within Prague, see page 49.

Name	Pronounced
Beskydy (mountains)	BEH-skih-dee
Brno	BURR-noh
České Budějovice	CHESS-keh BOO-dyeh-yoh-vee-tseh
Český Krumlov	CHESS-key KROOM-loff
Karlštejn (castle)	KARL-shtayn
Konopiště (castle)	KOH-noh-peesh-tyeh
Křivoklát (castle)	KREE-vohk-laht
Kroměříž	KROH-myehr-eezh
Kutná Hora	KOOT-nah HO-rah
Lednice	LEHD-nee-tseh

Fortunately, the Czechs long ago converted to the same Roman alphabet we use, but they've added lots of different diacritics—little markings below and above letters—to represent a wide

range of sounds. An acute accent *(á, é, í, ó, ú, ý)* means you linger on that vowel. The letter *c* always sounds like "ts" (as in "cats"). The little accent *(háček)* above the *č, š,* or *ž* makes it sound like "ch," "sh", or "zh" (as in "leisure"), respectively. A *háček* above *ň* makes it sound like "ny" (as in "canyon"), and over *ě* makes it sound like "ye." Czech has one sound that occurs in no other language: *ř* (as in "Dvořák"), which sounds like a cross between a rolled "r" and "zh."

Give it your best shot. The locals will appreciate your efforts.

Litoměřice	LEE-toh-myer-zhee-tseh
Mikulov	MEE-kuh-lohv
Moravský Krumlov	MOH-rahv-skee KROOM-loff
Mucha (painter)	MOO-kah
Olomouc	OH-loh-moats
Pálava (hills)	PAH-lah-vah
Pavlov	PAHV-lohv
Pustevny	POO-stehv-nee
Rožnov	ROHZH-nohv
Slavonice	SLAH-voh-neet-seh
Šumava (mountains)	SHOO-mah-vah
Telč	telch
Terezín (concentration camp)	TEH-reh-zeen
Třebíč	TREH-beech
Třeboň	TREH-bohn
Trojanovice	TROH-yah-noh-vee-tseh
Valtice	VAHL-tee-tseh
Velké Karlovice	VEHL-keh KAR-loh-vee-tseh
Valašsko	vah-LAH-she-skoh

Telephones

Smart travelers learn the phone system and use it daily to reserve or reconfirm rooms, get tourist information, or phone home.

Types of Phones

You'll encounter various kinds of phones in your European travels.

Most Czech **pay phones** take insertable phone cards (see page 26) rather than coins. Simply take the phone off the hook, insert the prepaid card, wait for a dial tone, and dial away.

Hotel room phones are fairly cheap for local calls, but pricey for international calls, unless you use an international phone card (see page 26).

American mobile phones work in Europe if they're GSM-enabled, tri-band (or quad-band), and on a calling plan that includes international calls. With a T-Mobile phone, you can roam using your home number, and pay $1–2 per minute for making or receiving calls.

Some travelers buy a **European mobile phone** in Europe. For about $125, you can get a phone that will work in most countries once you pick up the necessary chip (about $30) per country. Or you can buy a cheaper, "locked" phone that only works in the country where you purchased it (about $100, includes $20 worth of calls). If you're interested, stop by any European shop that sells mobile phones; you'll see prominent store window displays. You aren't required to (and shouldn't) buy a monthly contract—buy prepaid calling time instead (as you use it up, buy additional minutes at newsstands or mobile-phone shops). If you're on a budget, skip mobile phones and use international phone cards instead.

Paying for Calls

You can spend a fortune making phone calls in Europe...but why would you? Here's the skinny on different ways to pay, including the best deals.

Czech phone cards come in two types: official phone cards that you insert into a pay phone, and international phone cards that can be used from virtually any phone. Either type of phone card works only in the Czech Republic.

An **insertable phone card** is used to make calls from a pay phone. These are a good deal for calling within Europe, but can make calling home to the U.S. expensive (at least 50 cents/min).

An **international phone card** is a better deal for overseas calls (calls to the U.S. generally cost 20–30 cents per minute). Unlike the official phone cards, an international phone card is *not* inserted into the phone. Instead, you dial the toll-free number listed on the card, reaching an automated operator. When prompted, you dial in a scratch-to-reveal code number, also written on the card. Then dial your number. You can use the cards to make local and domestic long-distance calls as well. Since they're not insertable, you can use them from any phone—including the one in your hotel room (if your phone is set on pulse, switch it to tone).

While you can't find these cards everywhere, their availability is growing fast, and you should be able to get them in most of the Czech Republic. Look for fliers advertising long-distance rates, or ask about the cards at newsstands, exchange bureaus, souvenir shops, and mini-marts. Request an international telephone card and tell the vendor where you'll be making most calls ("to America"), and he'll select the brand with the best deal. Because cards are occasionally duds, avoid the high denominations. I find the "Smartcall" card, sold in newsstands at places like Prague's Wenceslas Square, most reliable.

Dialing direct from your hotel room without using an international phone card is usually quite expensive for international calls, but it's convenient. I always ask first how much I'll be charged. Keep in mind that you have to pay for local and occasionally even toll-free calls.

Receiving calls in your hotel room is often the cheapest way to keep in touch with the folks back home—especially if your family has an inexpensive way to call you (either a good deal on their long-distance plan, or a prepaid calling card with good rates to Europe). Give them a list of your hotels' phone numbers before you go. As you travel, send your family an e-mail or make a quick payphone call to set up a time for them to call you, and then wait for the ring.

U.S. calling cards (such as the ones offered by AT&T, MCI, or Sprint) are the worst option. You'll nearly always save a lot of money by paying with an insertable phone card, or—better yet—an international phone card that you buy in the Czech Republic.

How to Dial

Calling from the U.S. to the Czech Republic, or vice versa, is simple—once you break the code. If you have trouble making a connection, double-check the prefix numbers you're using. The European calling chart on page 248 will walk you through it. Remember that the Czech Republic time is six/nine hours ahead of the East/West Coasts of the U.S.

Dialing within the Czech Republic: You'll save money by dialing direct, rather than going through an operator. The Czech Republic has a direct-dial phone system (no area codes). To call anywhere within the Czech Republic, just dial the number. For example, one of my recommended Prague hotels is 224-812-041. To call it from a Prague train station, just dial 224-812-041. If you call it from Český Krumlov, it's the same: 224-812-041. All phone numbers in the Czech Republic are nine digits.

Dialing International Calls: When calling internationally, dial the international access code (00 if you're calling from Europe, 011 from the U.S. or Canada), the country code of the country you're calling (420 for the Czech Republic; see appendix for list of other countries), and the local number. So, to call the Prague hotel from the U.S., dial 011 (the U.S. international access code), 420 (the Czech Republic's country code), then 224-812-041. To call my office in Edmonds, Washington, from the Czech Republic, I dial 00 (Europe's international access code), 1 (the U.S. country code), 425 (Edmonds' area code), and 771-8303.

E-mail and Mail

E-mail: You'll find Internet cafés and connection points in every city and at many hotels throughout the Czech Republic. Most hotels have e-mail addresses and Web sites (listed in this book) and prefer to receive bookings online rather than by fax or phone. Some family-run pensions can become overwhelmed by the volume of e-mail they receive, so be patient if you don't get an immediate response.

Mail: Get stamps at the neighborhood post office, at news-stands inside fancy hotels, and at some mini-marts and card shops. While you can arrange for mail delivery to your hotel (allow 10–15 days for a letter to arrive), phoning and e-mailing are so easy that I've dispensed with mail stops altogether.

SLEEPING

In this book, I've focused my listings on small hotels, and prefer options that are friendly, comfortable, professional-feeling, centrally located, English-speaking, and family-run. Obviously, a place meeting every criterion is rare, and all of my recommendations fall short of perfection—sometimes miserably. But I've listed the best values for each price category, given the above criteria. I've also thrown in a few hostels, private rooms, and other cheap options for budget travelers.

Hotel prices in Prague are at Western European levels, but once you get out of the city, you'll pay half as much for a similar room. Plan on spending $70 to $120 per hotel double in Prague, and $30 to $70 in smaller towns. While most of my listings fall within those ranges, I also include a few $10 bunks and $150-plus doubles. Breakfasts are usually included in room prices.

Three or four people can save money by requesting one big room. Traveling alone can be expensive: A single room is often only 20 percent cheaper than a double.

For environmental reasons, towels are often replaced in hotels only when you leave them on the floor. In cheaper places, they aren't replaced at all, so hang them up to dry and reuse.

Before accepting a room, confirm your understanding of the complete price. The only tip my recommended hotels would like is a friendly, easygoing guest. And, as always, I appreciate feedback on your hotel experiences.

Private Rooms

A cheap option in the Czech Republic is a room in a private home (called "pension," sometimes advertised with the German phrase *Zimmer frei*). These places are inexpensive, at least as comfortable as a cheap hotel, and a good way to get some local insight. The boss changes the sheets, so people staying several nights are most desirable—and stays of less than three nights are often charged up to 30 percent more.

Hostels

For $10 to $20 a night, you can stay at a youth hostel. Travelers of any age are welcome, as long as they don't mind dorm-style accommodations and lots of traveling friends. Cheap meals are

Sleep Code

I've divided the rooms into three categories, based on the price for a standard double room with bath:

$$$ **Higher Priced**
$$ **Moderately Priced**
$ **Lower Priced**

To save space while giving more specific information for people with special concerns, I've described my recommended hotels with a standard code. Prices listed are per room, not per person. When a range of prices is listed for a room, the price fluctuates with room size or season. You can assume a hotel takes credit cards unless you see "cash only" in the listing. The hotel staff speaks basic English unless otherwise noted.

S = Single room (or price for 1 person in a double).

D = Double or twin. Double beds are usually big enough for non-romantic couples.

T = Triple (often a double bed with a single bed moved in).

Q = Quad (an extra child's bed is usually cheaper).

b = Private bathroom with toilet and shower or tub.

s = Private shower or tub only (the toilet is down the hall).

According to this code, a couple staying at a "Db-2,700 Kč" hotel in Prague would pay a total of 2,700 Czech crowns (about $108) for a double room with a private bathroom. English is spoken and credit cards are accepted.

sometimes available, and kitchen facilities are usually provided for do-it-yourselfers. Expect crowds in the summer, snoring, and lots of youth groups giggling and making rude noises while you try to sleep. Family rooms and doubles are often available on request, unlike in Western Europe most hostels in the Czech Republic are in university dorms where two or three person rooms are the norm. Hosteling is ideal for those traveling single: Prices are per bed, not per room, and you'll have an instant circle of friends. More and more hostels are getting their business acts together, taking credit-card reservations over the phone and leaving sign-in forms on the door for each available room. If you're serious about traveling cheaply, get a card (www.hihostels.com), carry your own sheets, and cook in the members' kitchens.

Making Reservations

It's possible to travel at any time of year without reservations (especially if you arrive early in the day), but given the high stakes, the erratic accommodations values, and the quality of the places I've found for this book, I'd recommend reserving rooms ahead, either directly with the hotel or through one of Prague's room-booking services (see page 117).

You can reserve rooms long in advance from home or by calling a day or two in advance as you travel. Even if a hotel clerk says the hotel is fully booked, you can try calling between 9:00 and 10:00 on the day you plan to arrive. That's when the hotel clerk knows exactly who's checking out and which rooms will be available.

I've taken great pains to list telephone numbers with long-distance instructions (see "Telephones," page 25; also see the appendix). Use the telephone and convenient telephone cards. Most hotels listed are accustomed to English-only speakers. (If you have difficulty, ask the fluent receptionist at your current hotel to call for you.) A hotel receptionist will usually trust you and hold a room until 16:00 without a deposit, though some will ask for a credit-card number.

If you know where you want to stay each day (and you don't need or want flexibility), reserve your rooms from the U.S. in advance. To book from home, you can e-mail, phone, or fax your request. Phone and fax costs are reasonable, e-mail is a steal (and preferred by most hotels), and simple English is usually fine. To fax, use the handy form in the appendix (online at www.ricksteves .com/reservation). If you don't get an answer to your fax request, consider that a "no." (Many little places get 20 faxes a day after they're full, and they can't afford to respond.)

A two-night stay in August would be "2 nights, 16/8/06 to 18/8/06." (Europeans write the date in this order—day/month/year—and hotel jargon uses your day of departure.)

If you receive a response from the hotel stating its rates and room availability, it's not a confirmation. You must confirm that you indeed want a room at the given rate. One night's deposit is generally required. Your credit-card number will usually be accepted as the deposit. Be sure to fax your card number (rather than e-mail it) to keep it private, safer, and out of cyberspace. You can pay with your card or cash when you arrive; if you don't show up, your card will be billed for one night. To make things easier on yourself and the hotel, be sure you really intend to stay at the hotel on the dates you requested. These family-run businesses lose money if they turn away customers while holding a room for someone who doesn't show up. Understandably, some hotels bill no-shows for one night. *If you must cancel, do so well in advance.* Long distance is cheap and easy from public phone booths. Don't let these people down—I promised you'd call and cancel if for some reason you won't show up.

Reconfirm your reservations a few days in advance for safety, and let them know about what time you'll arrive. Don't needlessly confirm rooms through the tourist office or Web services; they'll take a commission of up to 20 percent. On the small chance that a hotel loses track of your reservation, bring along their faxed confirmation or a hard copy of their e-mailed confirmation.

EATING

You'll find that the local cafés, cuisine, beer, and wine are highlights of your Czech adventure. This is affordable sightseeing for your palate.

When restaurant-hunting, choose a spot filled with locals, not the place with the big neon signs boasting "We Speak English and Accept Credit Cards." Incredible deals abound in the Czech Republic, where locals routinely eat well for $5. Venturing even a block or two off the main drag leads to authentic, higher quality food for less than half the price of the tourist-oriented places. Most restaurants tack a menu onto their door for browsers and have an English menu inside. Only a rude waiter will rush you. Good service is relaxed (slow to an American). Most Czech restaurants are open Sunday through Thursday 11:00–22:00, Friday through Saturday 11:00–24:00. You can stay in a pub as long as you want—no one will bring you the *účet* (bill) until you ask for it: *"Pane vrchní, zaplatím!"* (PAH-neh VURCH-nee zah-plah-TEEM; "Mr. Waiter, now I pay!").

When you're in the mood for something halfway between a restaurant and a picnic meal, look for take-out food stands, bakeries (with sandwiches and small pizzas to go), delis with stools or a table, department-store cafeterias, salad bars, or simple little eateries for fast and easy sit-down restaurant food.

Czech Food

Czech cuisine is heavy, hearty, and tasty. Expect lots of meat, potatoes, and cabbage. Still, there's more variety than you might expect. Ethnic restaurants provide a welcome break from Slavic fare. Seek out vegetarian, Italian, or Chinese—these are especially good in bigger towns such as Prague, Olomouc, Český Krumlov, and Kutná Hora.

After a sip of beer, ask for the *jídelní lístek* (menu). *Polévka* (soup) is the most essential part of a meal. The saying goes: "The soup fills you up, the dish plugs it up." Some of the thick soups for a cold day are *zelná* or *zelňačka* (cabbage), *čočková* (lentil), *fazolová* (bean), and *dršťková* (tripe—delicious if fresh, chewy as gum if not). The lighter soups are *hovězí* or *slepičí vývar s nudlemi* (beef or chicken broth with noodles), *pórková* (leek), and *květáková* (cauliflower). *Pečivo* (bread) is either delivered with the soup or you need to ask for it; it's always charged separately depending on how many *rohlíky* (rolls) or slices of *chleba* (yeast bread) you eat.

Main dishes are divided into *hotová jídla* (quick, ready-to-serve standard dishes, in some places available only during lunch hours, 11:30–14:30) and the more specialized *jídla na objednávku* or *minutky* (plates prepared when you order). Even the supposedly quick *hotová jídla* will take longer than fast food you're used to back home.

A Czech restaurant is a social place where people come to relax. Tables are not private. You can ask to join someone and will most likely make some new friends. Instead of worrying about how much sightseeing you're missing during your two-hour lunch, appreciate the opportunity to learn more about Czech culture.

Hotová jídla (ready-to-serve dishes) come with set garnishes. The standard menu across the country includes *smažený řízek s bramborem* (fried pork fillet with potatoes), *svíčková na smetaně s knedlíkem* (beef tenderloin in cream sauce with dumplings), *vepřová s knedlíkem a se zelím* (pork with dumplings and cabbage), *pečená kachna s knedlíkem a se zelím* (roasted duck with dumplings and cabbage), *maďarský guláš s knedlíkem* (the Czech version of Hungarian goulash), and *pečené kuře s bramborem* (roasted chicken with potatoes). In this landlocked country, fish options are limited to *kapr* (carp) and *pstruh* (trout), prepared in a variety of ways and served with potatoes or fries. Vegetarians can go for the delicious *smažený sýr s bramborem* (fried cheese with potatoes) or default for *čočka s vejci* (lentils with fried egg). If you are spending the night out with friends, have a beer and feast on the huge *vepřové koleno s hořčicí a křenem* (pork knuckle with mustard and horseradish sauce) with *chleba* (yeast bread).

The range of the *jídla na objednávku* (meals prepared to order) depends on the chef. You choose your garnishes, which are charged separately.

Šopský salát, like a Greek salad, is usually the best salad option (a mix of tomatoes, cucumbers, peppers, onion, and feta cheese with vinegar and olive oil). The waiter will bring it with the main dish, unless you specify that you want it before.

For *moučník* (dessert), there are *palačinka* (crêpes served with fruit or jam), *lívance* (small pancakes with jam and curd), or *zmrzlinový pohár* (ice-cream sundae). Many restaurants will offer different sorts of *koláče* (pastries) and *štrůdl* (apple strudel), but it's much better to get these directly from a bakery.

Czech Beer

Czechs are among the world's most enthusiastic beer *(pivo)* drinkers—adults drink about 80 gallons a year. The pub is a place to have fun, complain, discuss art and politics, talk hockey, and chat with locals and visitors alike. The *pivo* that was drunk in the country before the Industrial Revolution was much thicker, providing the main source of nourishment for the peasant folk. As a result, even today it doesn't matter whether you are in a *restaurace* (restaurant), a *hostinec* (pub), or a *hospoda* (bar)—a beer will land on your table upon the slightest hint to  the waiter, and a new pint will automatically appear when the old glass is almost empty. (You must tell the waiter *not* to bring more.) Order beer from the tap (*točené* means "draft," *sudové pivo* means "keg beer"). A *pivo* is large (.5 liter, or 17 oz); a *malé pivo* is small (.3 liter, or 10 oz). Men invariably order the large size. *Pivo* for lunch has me sightseeing for the rest of the day on Czech knees.

The Czechs invented lager in nearby Plzeň ("Pilsen" in German). This is the famous Pilsner Urquell, on tap in many local pubs. But be sure to venture beyond Pilsner Urquell. There are plenty of other good Czech beers, including Krušovice,

Gambrinus, Staropramen, and Kozel. Budvar, from the town of Budějovice ("Budweis" in German), is popular with Anheuser-Busch's attorneys. (The Czech and the American breweries for years disputed the "Budweiser" brand name. The solution: The Czech Budweiser—actually owned by South Africans—is sold under its own name in Europe, China, and Africa, while in America it markets itself as Czechvar.)

The big degree symbol on bottles does not indicate the percentage of alcohol content. Twelve degrees is about 4.2 percent alcohol, 10 degrees is about 3.5 percent alcohol, and 11 and 15 degrees are dark beers.

Each establishment has only one kind of beer on tap; to try a particular brand, look for its sign outside. A typical pub serves only one brand of 10-degree beer, one brand of 12-degree beer, and one brand of dark beer. Czechs do not mix beer with anything, and do not hop from pub to pub (in one night, it is said, you must stay loyal to one woman and to one beer). *Na zdraví* means "to your health" in Czech.

No Czech meal is complete without a cup of strong *turecká káva* (Turkish coffee—finely ground coffee that only partly dissolves, leaving "mud" on the bottom, drunk without milk). Although espressos and instant coffees have made headway in the past few years, many Czechs regard them as a threat to their culture.

A good alternative to a beer is *minerálka* (mineral water). These healthy waters have a high mineral content. They're naturally carbonated because they come from the springs in the many Czech spas (Mattoni, the most common brand, is from Carlsbad). If you want plain water, ask for *voda bez bublinek* (water without bubbles).

Bohemia is beer country (see sidebar, page 33), with Europe's best and cheapest brew. Locals also like the herb liquor *becherovka*. Moravians prefer wine and *slivovice* (SLEE-voh-veet-seh)—a plum

brandy so highly valued that it's the de facto currency of the Carpathian Mountains (often used for bartering with farmers and other mountain folk). *Medovina* (literally, "honey wine") is mead.

In bars and restaurants, you can go wild with memorable liqueurs, most of which cost about a dollar a shot. Experiment. *Fernet,* a bitter drink made from many herbs, is the leading Czech apéritif. *Absinthe,* made from wormwood and herbs, is a watered-down version of the hallucinogenic drink that's illegal in the U.S. and much of Europe. It's famous as the muse of many artists (including Henri de Toulouse-Lautrec in Paris more than a century ago). *Becherovka,* made of 13 herbs and 38 percent alcohol, was used to settle upset aristocratic tummies and as an aphrodisiac. This velvety drink remains popular today. *Becherovka* and tonic mixed together is nicknamed *beton* ("concrete"). If you drink three, you'll find out why.

TRAVELING AS A TEMPORARY LOCAL

We travel all the way to Europe to enjoy differences—to become temporary locals. You'll experience frustrations. Certain truths that we find "God-given" or "self-evident," such as cold beer, ice in drinks, bottomless cups of coffee, hot showers, and bigger being better, are suddenly not so true. One of the benefits of travel is the eye-opening realization that there are logical, civil, and even better alternatives. A willingness to go local ensures that you'll enjoy a full dose of Czech hospitality.

If there is a negative aspect to the image Europeans have of Americans, it is that we are big, aggressive, impolite, rich, loud,

---

Send Me a Postcard, Drop Me a Line

If you enjoy a successful trip with the help of this book and would like to share your discoveries, please fill out the survey at www.ricksteves.com/feedback or e-mail me at rick@ricksteves.com. I personally read and value all feedback.

---

and a bit naive. Americans tend to be noisy in public places, such as restaurants and trains. Our raised voices can demolish Europe's reserved and elegant ambience. Talk softly. While Europeans look bemusedly at some of our Yankee excesses—and worriedly at others—they nearly always afford us individual travelers all the warmth we deserve.

Judging from all the happy postcards I receive from travelers who have used this book, it's safe to assume you'll enjoy a great, affordable vacation—with the finesse of an independent, experienced traveler. Thanks, and happy travels!

BACK DOOR TRAVEL PHILOSOPHY
From *Rick Steves' Europe Through the Back Door*

Travel is intensified living—maximum thrills per minute and one of the last great sources of legal adventure. Travel is freedom. It's recess, and we need it.

Experiencing the real Europe requires catching it by surprise, going casual..."Through the Back Door."

Affording travel is a matter of priorities. (Make do with the old car.) You can travel—simply, safely, and comfortably—anywhere in Europe for $100 a day plus transportation costs. In many ways, spending more money only builds a thicker wall between you and what you came to see. Europe is a cultural carnival, and, time after time, you'll find that its best acts are free and the best seats are the cheap ones.

A tight budget forces you to travel close to the ground, meeting and communicating with the people, not relying on service with a purchased smile. Never sacrifice sleep, nutrition, safety, or cleanliness in the name of budget. Simply enjoy the local-style alternatives to expensive hotels and restaurants.

Extroverts have more fun. If your trip is low on magic moments, kick yourself and make things happen. If you don't enjoy a place, maybe you don't know enough about it. Seek the truth. Recognize tourist traps. Give a culture the benefit of your open mind. See things as different but not better or worse. Any culture has much to share.

Of course, travel, like the world, is a series of hills and valleys. Be fanatically positive and militantly optimistic. If something's not to your liking, change your liking. Travel is addictive. It can make you a happier American as well as a citizen of the world. Our Earth is home to six billion equally important people. It's humbling to travel and find that people don't envy Americans. They like us, but, with all due respect, they wouldn't trade passports.

Globe-trotting destroys ethnocentricity. It helps you understand and appreciate different cultures. Regrettably, there are forces in our society that want you dumbed down for their convenience. Don't let it happen. Thoughtful travel engages you with the world—more important than ever these days. Travel changes people. It broadens perspectives and teaches new ways to measure quality of life. Many travelers toss aside their hometown blinders. Their prized souvenirs are the strands of different cultures they decide to knit into their own character. The world is a cultural yarn shop. And Back Door travelers are weaving the ultimate tapestry. Come on, join in!

CZECH REPUBLIC

(Česká Republika)

The Czech Republic is geographically small. In a quick visit, you can enjoy a fine introduction while still packing in plenty of surprises.

Despite their difficult 20th-century experience, the Czechs managed to preserve their history. In Czech towns and villages, you'll find a simple joy of life—a holdover from the days of the Renaissance. The deep spirituality of the Baroque era still shapes the national character. The magic of Prague, the beauty of Český Krumlov, and the lyrical quality of the countryside relieve the heaviness caused by the turmoil that passed through here. Get

Czech Republic Almanac

Birth of Two Nations: The nation of Czechoslovakia—formed after World War I, and dominated by the U.S.S.R. after World War II—split on January 1, 1993, into two separate nations: the Czech Republic (Česká Republika) and Slovakia.

Population: 10 million people. About 95 percent are ethnic Czechs, who speak Czech. Unlike some of their neighbors (including the very Catholic Poles and Slovaks), Czechs are inclined to be agnostic: One in four is Roman Catholic, but the majority (60 percent) list their religion as unaffiliated.

Latitude and Longitude: 50°N and 15°E (similar latitude to Vancouver, B.C.)

Area: 31,000 square miles (similar to South Carolina or Maine).

Geography: The Czech Republic is made up of three regions—Bohemia (Čechy), Moravia (Morava), and a small slice of Silesia (Slezsko). The climate is generally cool and cloudy.

Biggest Cities: Prague (the capital, 1.2 million), Brno (380,000), Ostrava (318,000), and Plzeň (165,000).

Economy: The Gross Domestic Product is $172 billion (similar to Indiana). The GDP per capita is $17,000 (less than half that of the average American). Some major money-makers for the country are machine parts, cars and trucks, and beer (including Pilsner Urquell and the original Budweiser—called "Czechvar" in the U.S.). More than a third of trade is with next-door-neighbor Germany. Privatization of formerly government-run industries goes on.

Currency: 25 Czech crowns (*koruna*, Kč) = about $1.

Government: Until 1989, Czechoslovakia was a communist state under Soviet control. Today, the Czech Republic is a vibrant democracy where no single political party dominates. The two-house parliament (of 281 directly elected legislators) selects the president, who appoints the prime minister. The current president, Václav Klaus (a conservative), and his appointed (left-of-center) prime minister, Jiří Paroubek, head a coalition government. The Czech Republic joined the European Union in 2004.

Flag: The Czech flag is red (bottom), white (top), and blue (a triangle along the hoist side).

The Average Czech: The average Czech has 1.2 kids (rising again, after the sharp decline that followed the end of communism), will live 76 years (fewer if he's a man), and has one television in the house.

beyond Prague and explore the country's medieval towns. These rugged woods and hilltop castles will make you feel like you're walking through the garden of your childhood dreams.

Of the Czech Republic's three main regions—Bohemia, Moravia, and small Silesia—the best known is Bohemia. It has nothing to do with beatnik bohemians, but with the Celtic tribe of Boheia that inhabited the land before the coming of the Slavs. A long-time home of the Czechs, Bohemia is circled by a naturally fortifying ring of mountains and cut down the middle by the Vltava River, with Prague as its capital. The wine-growing region of Moravia (to the east) is more hilly, Slavic, and colorful.

Tourists often conjure up images of Bohemia when they think of the Czech Republic. But the country consists of more than rollicking beer halls and gently rolling landscapes. It's also about dreamy wine cellars and fertile Moravian plains, with the rugged Carpathian Mountains on the horizon. Politically and geologically, Bohemia and Moravia are two distinct regions. The soils and climates in which the hops and wine grapes grow are very different...and so are the two regions' mentalities. The boisterousness of the Czech polka contrasts with the melancholy of the Moravian ballad; the politics of the Prague power-broker is at odds with the spirituality of the Moravian bard. Only a tiny bit of Silesia—around the town of Opava—is part of the Czech Republic today; the rest of the region is in Germany and Poland. (The Hapsburgs lost traditionally Czech Silesia to Prussia in the 1740s, and 200 years later, Germany in turn ceded it to Poland.) People in Silesia speak a wide variety of dialects that mix Czech, German, and Polish. Perhaps due to their diverse genome and cultural heritage, women from Silesia are famous for being intelligent and beautiful.

Since 1989, when the Czechs won their independence from Soviet control, more Czechs have been traveling. People are working harder—but the average monthly wage is still only about $600. Roads have been patched up, facades have gotten facelifts, and neighborhood grocery stores have been pushed out by supermarkets.

Most young Czechs are caught up in the new freedom. Everyone wants to travel—to the practical West to study law, or to the mystical East to learn to speak Thai. They want to work for big bucks at a multinational investment bank, or for a meager salary at a non-profit organization based in Chechnya. With so many material dreams suddenly within reach, few Czechs are having children. In the 1990s, the birth rate fell dramatically, but since 2001 it has been slowly rising again.

Yet, even faced with a bright future, some locals maintain a healthy dose of pessimism and are reluctant to dive headlong into the Western rat race. Things still go a little slower here, and people find pleasure in simple things.

Ninety percent of the tourists who visit the Czech Republic see only Prague. But if you venture outside the capital, you'll enjoy traditional towns and villages, great prices, a friendly and gentle countryside dotted by nettles and wild poppies, and almost no Western tourists. Since the time of the Hapsburgs, fruit trees have lined the country roads for everyone to share. Take your pick.

PRAGUE

Prague

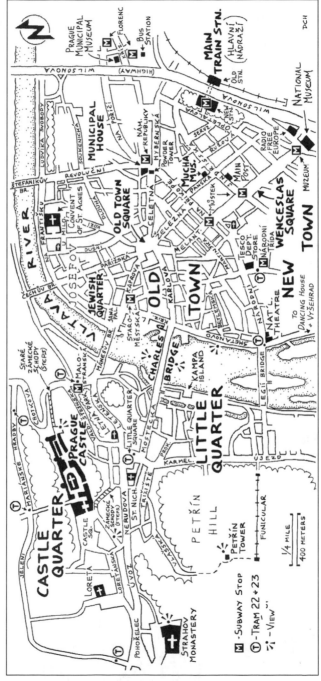

ORIENTATION

It's amazing what a decade and a half of freedom can do. Prague has always been historic. Now it's fun, too. No other place in Europe has become so popular so quickly. And for good reason: Prague—the only Central European capital to escape the bombs of the last century's wars—is one of Europe's best-preserved cities. It's filled with sumptuous Art Nouveau facades, offers tons of cheap Mozart and Vivaldi, and brews the best beer in Europe. Beyond its architecture and traditional culture, it's an explosion of pent-up entrepreneurial energy jumping for joy after 40 years of communist rule. Its low prices can cause you to jump for joy, too. Travel in Prague is like travel in Western Europe...15 years ago and for half the price.

Planning Your Time

A week in Prague is plenty of time to get a solid feel for the city and enjoy excursions to Český Krumlov and Kutná Hora. If you're in a rush, you need a minimum of two full days (with 3 nights, or 2 nights and a night train) for a good introduction to the city. From Munich, Berlin, and Vienna, Prague is about a six-hour train ride by day (you also have the option of a longer night train from Munich). From Budapest, Warsaw, or Kraków, you can take a handy overnight train.

With two days in Prague, I'd spend a morning seeing the castle and a morning in the Jewish Quarter. Use your afternoons for loitering around the Old Town, Charles Bridge, and the Little Quarter, and split your nights between beer halls and live music. Keep in mind that Jewish Quarter sights close on Saturday.

With the luxury of four or more days in Prague, focus on being in the right places at the right times: on Charles Bridge at dawn, up at the Strahov Monastery overlook at sunrise, at the door

Daily Reminder

Sunday: The St. Vitus Cathedral at Prague Castle is closed Sunday morning for Mass. Some stores have shorter hours or are closed.

Monday: The major sights—such as Prague Castle—are open, but a number of the lesser sights are closed, including the Bethlehem Chapel, Museum of Czech Cubism, Museum of Applied Arts, Convent of St. Agnes of Bohemia, Museum of Modern and Contemporary Art, Troja Castle, Prague Municipal Museum, Loreta Church, Dvořák Museum, and Náprstek's Museum of Asian, African, and American Cultures.

If you're day-tripping today, only Terezín is open. Kutná Hora's Bone Chapel and the three castles—Konopiště, Karlštejn, and Křivoklát—are closed.

In Prague's Old Town, musicians have a jam session at 17:00 at St. Martin in the Wall, and cover is free at Roxy's music club at 20:00.

Tuesday–Friday: All sights are open.

Saturday: The Jewish Quarter sights are closed.

Crowd-Beating Tips: Visit Prague Castle either first thing in the morning (be at St. Vitus Cathedral at 9:00—except Sun morning, when it's closed for Mass) or before it closes (17:00 in summer, 16:00 in winter).

Summer Movies: Outdoor movies are shown at 21:00 from mid-July through early September on Střelecký Island.

of St. Vitus Cathedral or in the Jewish Cemetery at 9:00 (at opening time, to avoid crowds), in Žižkov for a good rock concert or at Reduta for the best jazz in Eastern Europe, on the Old Town Square at midnight, or on Wenceslas Square at any time. Pace yourself, and enjoy the cheap beer and coffee. The more in-depth your experience in Prague, the better you'll know the city—and the more you'll want to come back.

OVERVIEW

Prague unnerves many travelers—it's behind the former Iron Curtain, and you've heard stories of rip-offs and sky-high hotel prices (both are real problems, but avoidable if you're smart). Despite your fears, Prague is charming, safe, and ready to show you a good time. The language barrier is tiny. It seems like every well-educated young person speaks English.

Locals call their town "Praha" (PRAH-hah). It's big, with 1.2 million people, but focus on its relatively compact old center

during a quick visit. As you wander, take advantage of brown street signs directing you to tourist landmarks.

The Vltava River divides the west side (Castle Quarter and Little Quarter) from the east side (New Town, Old Town, Jewish Quarter, Main Train Station, and most of the recommended hotels).

Prague addresses come with references to a general zone. Praha 1 is in the old center on either side of the river. Praha 2 is in the new city, southeast of Wenceslas Square. Praha 3 and higher indicate a location farther from the center. Virtually everything I list is in Praha 1 (unless noted otherwise).

Tourist Information

TIs are at four key locations: **Main Train Station** (roughly Easter–Oct Mon–Fri 9:00–19:00, Sat–Sun 9:00–16:00—but often closed Sat-Sun; Nov–Easter Mon–Fri 9:00–18:00, Sat 9:00–15:00, closed Sun), **Old Town Square** (Easter–Oct Mon–Fri 9:00–19:00, Sat–Sun 9:00–18:00; Nov–Easter Mon–Fri 9:00–18:00, Sat–Sun 9:00–17:00; tel. 224-482-018), below **Wenceslas Square** at Na Příkopě 20 (Easter–Oct Mon–Fri 9:00–19:00, Sat–Sun 9:00–17:00; Nov–Easter Mon–Fri 9:00–18:00, Sat 9:00–15:00, closed Sun; tel. 224-226-087), and the castle side of **Charles Bridge** (Easter–Oct daily 10:00–18:00, closed Nov–Easter). For general tourist information in English, dial 12444 (Mon–Fri 8:00–19:00) or check the TIs' useful Web site: www.pis.cz.

The TIs offer maps, phone cards, a useful transit guide, information on guided walks and bus tours, and bookings for private guides, concerts, hotel rooms, and rooms in private homes.

There are several monthly events guides—all of them packed with ads—including *Prague Guide* (29 Kč), *Prague This Month* (free), and *Heart of Europe* (free, summer only). The English-language weekly *Prague Post* newspaper is handy for entertainment listings and current events (sold cheap at newsstands).

Arrival in Prague

Upon arrival, be sure to buy a city map, with trams and Metro lines marked and tiny sketches of the sights for ease in navigating (30–70 Kč, many different brands; sold at kiosks, exchange windows, or tobacco stands). It's a mistake to try doing Prague without a good map—you'll refer to it constantly.

Prague at a Glance

In the Old Town

▲▲▲**Old Town Square** Colorful, magical main square of Old World Prague, with dozens of colorful facades, the dramatic Jan Hus Memorial, looming Týn Church, and fanciful Astronomical Clock. **Hours:** Always open.

▲▲▲**Jewish Quarter** The best Jewish sight in Europe, featuring various synagogues and an evocative cemetery. **Hours:** Sun–Fri 9:00–18:00, closed Sat.

▲▲▲**Charles Bridge** Atmospheric, statue-lined bridge connecting the Old Town to the Little Quarter and Prague Castle. **Hours:** Always open.

Havelská Market Colorful open-air market selling crafts and produce. **Hours:** Daily 9:00–18:00.

Convent of St. Agnes of Bohemia Medieval convent housing museum of Gothic art. **Hours:** Tue–Sun 10:00–18:00, closed Mon.

Museum of Applied Arts Arts and crafts from the Czech lands. **Hours:** Tue 10:00–20:00, Wed–Sun 10:00–18:00, closed Mon.

Museum of Czech Cubism Exhibit of early-20th-century Czech artistic school, in the Old Town's interesting Black Madonna House. **Hours:** Tue–Sun 10:00–18:00, closed Mon.

Bethlehem Chapel Reconstructed 15th-century chapel with Jan Hus' former pulpit. **Hours:** April–Oct daily 10:00–18:30; Nov–March Tue–Sun 10:00–17:30, closed Mon and during university functions.

Náprstek's Museum of Asian, African, and American Cultures Quirky exhibit with an emphasis on Native Americans (including Sitting Bull's clothes). **Hours:** Tue–Sun 10:00–17:00, closed Mon.

In the New Town

▲▲**Wenceslas Square** Lively boulevard at the heart of modern Prague. **Hours:** Always open.

▲▲**Mucha Museum** Likeable collection of Art Nouveau works by Czech artist Alfons Mucha. **Hours:** Daily 10:00–18:00.

▲**Museum of Communism** The rise and fall of the regime, from start to Velvet finish. **Hours:** Daily 9:00–21:00.

Dancing House Frank Gehry-designed building on the Vltava riverbank, depicting a pair of Czech patriots. . .or Fred and Ginger. **Hours:** Always viewable.

In the Little Quarter
Torture Museum Prague "goes medieval" in this cheesy and gruesome tourist trap. **Hours**: Daily 10:00–22:00.

Church of St. Nicholas Jesuit centerpiece of Little Quarter Square, with ultimate High Baroque decor and a climbable bell tower. **Hours:** Church—daily 9:00–17:00; tower—April–Oct daily 10:00–18:00, closed Nov–March.

Wallenstein Palace and Garden Beautiful Little Quarter mansion with delightful Renaissance garden. **Hours:** Garden—April–Oct daily 10:00–18:00, closed Nov–March.

Petřín Hill Little Quarter hill with public art, a funicular, a replica of the Eiffel Tower, and the museum of a nonexistent Czech hero. **Hours:** Funicular—daily 8:00–22:00; museum—daily 10:00–22:00.

In the Castle Quarter
▲▲▲**St. Vitus Cathedral** The Czech Republic's most important church, featuring a climbable tower and a striking stained-glass window by Art Nouveau artist Alfons Mucha. **Hours:** Daily April–Oct 9:00–17:00, Nov–March 9:00–16:00—but closed Sunday mornings year-round for Mass.

▲▲**Prague Castle** Traditional seat of Czech rulers, with St. Vitus Cathedral (see above), Old Royal Palace, Basilica of St. George, shop-lined Golden Lane, and lots of crowds. **Hours:** Castle sights—daily April–Oct 9:00–17:00, Nov–March 9:00–16:00; castle grounds—daily 5:00–23:00.

▲**Strahov Monastery and Library** Baroque center of learning, with ornate reading rooms and old-fashioned science exhibits. **Hours:** Daily 9:00–12:00 & 13:00–17:00.

Loreta Church Baroque church featuring what's supposedly the actual house of the Virgin Mary. **Hours:** Tue–Sun 9:00–12:15 & 13:00–16:30, closed Mon.

Toy and Barbie Museum Several centuries of toys, starring an army of Barbies. **Hours**: Daily 9:30–17:30.

By Train

Most travelers coming from and going to major international destinations use the Main Station (Hlavní Nádraží)—as do travelers to and from Český Krumlov, Kutná Hora, Olomouc, Třeboň, and some other Czech towns. Other trains use the secondary station (Nádraží Holešovice). Trains to and from Karlštejn and Křivoklát use the Smíchov station. (For information on getting to Prague, see Transportation Connections chapter, page 153.)

Upon arrival, get money. The stations have ATMs (best rates) and exchange bureaus (rates are generally bad, but can vary—compare by asking at 2 windows what you'll get for $100, but keep in mind that many of the windows are run by the same company). Then buy your map and confirm your departure plans. Consider arranging a room or tour through the AVE travel agency (branches in both stations—see page 117). Anyone arriving on an international train will be met at the tracks by room hustlers, trying to snare tourists for cheap rooms.

Main Station (Hlavní Nádraží): This station's low-ceilinged hall contains a fascinating mix of travelers, kiosks, gamblers, loitering teenagers, and older riffraff. The creepy station ambience is the work of communist architects, who expanded a classy building to make it just big, painting it the compulsory dreary gray with reddish trim. An ATM is near the subway entrance. The station's baggage-storage counter is reportedly safer than the lockers. The Wasteels office can help you figure out train connections, and sells cheap phone cards and train tickets for anywhere in Europe (no commission; Mon–Fri 9:00–17:00, Sat 9:00–16:00, closed Sun, tel. 224-641-954, www.wasteels.cz). The information office for Czech Railways (downstairs on the left) is less helpful, and the ticket windows downstairs don't give schedule information. The windows marked *vnitrostátní* sell tickets within the Czech Republic.

If you're killing time here (or for a wistful glimpse of a more genteel age), go upstairs into the Art Nouveau hall. Here, under an elegant dome, you can sip coffee, enjoy music from the 1920s, watch boy prostitutes looking for work, and see new arrivals spilling into the city. The station was originally named for Emperor Franz Josef. Later, it was renamed for President Woodrow Wilson, because his promotion of self-determination led to the creation of the free state of Czechoslovakia in 1918. Look for a commemorative plaque with Wilson's face at the main exit hall from the platforms. Under the communists (who weren't big fans of Wilson), it was bluntly

Prague Landmarks

English	Czech	Pronounced
Main Train Station	**Hlavní Nádraží**	hlav-NEE NAH-drah-zhee
Old Town	**Staré Město**	STAH-reh myehs-toh
Old Town Square	**Staroměstské Náměstí**	STAR-roh-myehst-skeh NAH-myehs-tee
New Town	**Nové Město**	NOH-vay myehs-toh
Little Quarter	**Malá Strana**	MAH-lah strah-nah
Jewish Quarter	**Josefov**	YOO-zehf-fohf
Castle Quarter	**Hradčany**	HRAD-chah-nee
Charles Bridge	**Karlův Most**	KAR-loov most
Wenceslas Square	**Václavske Náměstí**	VAHT-slahf-skeh NAH-myehs-tee
Vltava River	**Vltava**	VUL-tah-vah

renamed simply Hlavní Nádraží—literally, "Main Station."

Even though the Main Station is basically downtown, it can be a little tricky to get to your hotel. The biggest challenge is that the **taxi** cabbies at the train station are a gang of no-neck mafia thugs who wait around to charge an arriving tourist five times the regular rate. To get an honest cabbie, I'd walk a few blocks (or ride the Metro one stop), hail one off the street, or call AAA Taxi (tel. 233-113-311). A taxi should get you to your hotel for no more than 200 Kč (see "Getting Around Prague," below). Cheaper—and with far less danger of being ripped off—is to take the **Metro** (inside station, look for the red M with two directions: Háje or Ládví). To get to hotels in the Old Town, catch a Háje-bound train to the Muzeum stop, then transfer to the green line (direction: Dejvická) and get off at either Můstek or Staroměstská; these stops straddle the Old Town. Or, if your hotel is close enough, consider **walking** (Wenceslas Square, a downtown landmark, is about a 10-minute walk away: Turn left out of the station and follow Washingtonova street to the huge National Museum).

Holešovice Station (Nádraží Holešovice): This station, slightly farther from the center, is suburban mellow. The main hall has all the services of the Main Station in a compact area. The friendly, little-frequented café allows you to place cheap international calls through the Internet (7 Kč/min to the U.S., daily 8:00–19:30). Outside the first glass doors, the ATM is on the left, the Czech Railways information office is on the right (daily 9:00–17:00), and the Metro is straight ahead (follow signs toward *Vstup,* which means

Prague's Four Towns

Until about 1800, Prague was actually four distinct towns with four town squares, all separated by fortified walls. Each town had a unique character, which came from the personality of the people who initially settled it. Today much of Prague's charm survives in the distinct spirit of each of its towns.

Castle Quarter (Hradčany): Since the ninth century, when the first castle was built on the promontory overlooking a ford across the Vltava River, Castle Hill has been occupied by the ruling class. When Christianity arrived in the Czech lands, this hilltop—oriented along an east-west axis—proved a perfect spot for a church and, later, the cathedral (which, according to custom, must be built with the altar pointing east). Finally, the nobles built their representative palaces in proximity to the castle to compete with the Church for influence on the king. Even today, you feel like clip-clopping through this neighborhood in a fancy carriage. The Castle Quarter—which hosts the offices of the president and prime minister—has high art and grand buildings, little commerce, and few pubs.

Little Quarter (Malá Strana): This Baroque town of fine palaces and gardens rose from ashes of a merchant settlement that burned in the 1540s. The Czech and European nobility that settled here took pride in the grand design of their gardens. In the 1990s, after decades of decay, these gardens were carefully restored. While some are open only to the successors of the former nobility—including the Czech Parliament and the American, German, and Polish Embassies—many are open to visitors.

Old Town (Staré Město): Charles Bridge connects the Little Quarter with the Old Town. A boomtown since the 10th century, this has long been the busy commercial quarter—filled with merchants, guilds, and supporters of Jan Hus (folks who wanted a Czech stamp on their religion). Trace the walls of this town in the modern road plan (the Powder Tower is a remnant of a wall system that completed a fortified ring, half provided by the river). The marshy area closest to the bend—least inhabitable and therefore allotted to the Jewish community—became the ghetto (today's Josefov, or Jewish Quarter).

New Town (Nové Město): The New Town rings the Old Town—cutting a swath from riverbank to riverbank—and is fortified with Prague's outer wall. In the 14th century, the king created this town, tripling the size of what would become Prague. Wenceslas Square was once the horse market of this busy work-

Prague Overview

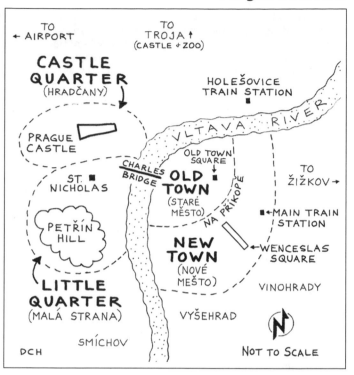

ing-class district. Even today, the New Town is separated from the Old Town by a "moat" (the literal meaning of the street called Na Příkopě). As you cross bustling Na Příkopě, you leave the glass and souvenir shops behind and enter a town of malls and fancy shops that cater to locals and visitors alike.

Cutting through the four towns—from St. Vitus Cathedral down to the Charles Bridge, and then from the bridge to the Powder Tower—is the Royal Way (Královská Cesta), the ancient path of coronation processions. Today this city spine is marred by tacky trinket shops and jammed by tour groups. Use it for orientation only—try to avoid it if you want to see the real Prague.

Rip-Offs in Prague

Prague's new freedom comes with new scams. There's no particular risk of violent crime, but green, rich tourists do get taken by con artists. Simply be on guard, particularly when: traveling on trains (thieves thrive on overnight trains), changing money (tellers with bad arithmetic and inexplicable pauses while counting back your change), dealing with taxis (see "By Taxi," page 57), paying in restaurants (see Eating chapter, page 129), and in seedy neighborhoods (see below).

Anytime you pay for something, make a careful note of how much it costs, how much you're handing over, and how much you expect back. Count your change. Someone selling you a phone card marked 190 Kč might first tell you it's 790 Kč, hoping to pocket the difference. Call the bluff and they'll pretend it never happened.

Plainclothes policemen "looking for counterfeit money" are con artists. Don't show them any cash or your wallet. If you're threatened with an inexplicable fine by a "policeman," conductor, or other official, you can walk away, scare him away by saying you'll need a receipt (which real officials are legally required to provide), or ask a passerby if the fine is legit. On the other hand, do not ignore the plainclothes inspectors on the Metro and trams who have shown you their badges.

"entrance"; take it 3 stops to Hlavní Nádraží—the Main Station, or 4 stops to the city-center Muzeum stop). Taxis and trams are outside to the right (allow 200 Kč for a cab to the center).

By Plane

Prague's modern, tidy, low-key **Ruzyně Airport**—a delightful contrast to the old, hulking Main Train Station—is 12 miles (about 30 min) west of the city center. The airport has ATMs (avoid the change desks); desks promoting their transportation service (such as city transit and shuttle buses); kiosks selling city maps and phone cards; and a tourist service with little printed material. Airport info: tel. 220-113-314, operator tel. 220-111-111.

Getting to and from the airport is easy. You have four options:

Dirt cheap: Take bus #119 to the Dejvická Metro station, or #100 to the Zličín Metro station (20 min), then take the Metro

Pickpockets can be little children, or adults dressed as professionals or even as tourists. They target Western visitors. Many thieves drape jackets over their arms to disguise busy fingers. Thieves work the crowded and touristy places in teams. They use mobile phones to coordinate their bumps and grinds. Be careful if anyone creates a commotion at the door of a Metro or tram car (especially around the Národní Třída and Vodičkova tram stops, or on the made-for-tourists trams #22 and #23)—it's a smokescreen for theft. Car theft is also a big problem in Prague (many Western European car-rental companies don't allow their rentals to cross the Czech border). Never leave anything valuable in your car—not even in broad daylight on a busy street. The sex clubs on Skořepka street, just south of Havelská Market, routinely rip off naive tourists and can be dangerous. They're filled mostly with Russian girls and German and Asian guys. Lately this district has become the rage for British "stag" parties (happy to take cheap off-season flights to get to cheap beer and cheap girls). Be warned: Even on the street, aggressive girls can be all over gawkers.

This all sounds intimidating. But Prague is safe. It has its share of petty thieves and con artists, but very little violent crime. Don't be scared—just be alert. You can join in on a local running joke on the pickpockets: A professor of Buddhism from a prestigious American university keeps an empty wallet with a picture of a man giving the finger prominently displayed in his pocket during every Prague visit. So far, he has yet to be robbed. See if you have more luck.

into the center (20 Kč, info desk in airport arrival hall).

Cheap: Take the Čedaz minibus shuttle to Náměstí Republiky, across from Kotva department store (daily 5:30-21:30, 2/hr, pay 90 Kč directly to driver, info desk in arrival hall).

Moderate: Take a Čedaz minibus directly to your hotel, with a couple of stops likely en route (360 Kč for a group of up to 4, tel. 220-114-286).

Expensive: Catch a taxi. Cabbies wait at the curb directly in front of the arrival hall. Airport taxi cabbies are honest but more expensive. Carefully confirm the complete price before getting in. It's a fixed rate of 600–700 Kč, with no meter.

Helpful Hints

Medical Help: A 24-hour pharmacy is at Palackého 5 (a block from Wenceslas Square, tel. 224-946-982). First aid and emergency medical service in the Czech Republic are free for everyone. For standard assistance, there are two state hospitals in the center: the General Hospital (open daily 24 hours, moderate wait time, U Nemocnice 2, Praha 2, use entry G, right above Karlovo Náměstí, tel. 224-962-564); and the Na Františku Hospital (go to the main entrance, Na Františku 1, on the embankment next to Hotel InterContinental; for English assistance call Mr. Hacker between 8:00–14:00, tel. 222-801-278 or tel. 222-801-371, serious problems only). The reception staff may not speak English, but doctors do.

For better-than-standard assistance in English (including dental service), consider the top-quality Hospital Na Homolce (less than 1,000 Kč for an appointment, from 8:00–16:00 call 252-922-146, after-hours emergency call 257-211-111, Roentgenova 2, Praha 5, bus #167 from Anděl Metro station). The Canadian Medical Care Center is a small, private clinic with English-speaking Czech staff at Veleslavínská 1 in Praha 6 (tel. 235-360-133, after-hours emergency call 724-300-301, halfway between the city and the airport, 3,000 Kč for an appointment, 4,500 Kč for a house call).

Internet Access: Internet cafés are interspersed through Old and New Towns. Consider Bohemia Bagel, with two locations, one in the Jewish Quarter in the Old Town, and the other in the Little Quarter (see page 140). Káva Káva Káva Coffee, on the boundary between the Old and New Towns, is in the Platýz courtyard off Národní 37.

Bookstore: For some good bookstores in Prague, see page 142 in the Shopping chapter.

Laundry: A full-service laundry near most of the recommended hotels is at Karolíny Světlé 10 (200 Kč/8-pound load, wash and dry in 2 hrs, Mon–Fri 7:30–19:00, closed Sat–Sun, 200 yards from Charles Bridge on Old Town side). Or surf the Internet while your undies tumble-dry at Korunní 14 (160 Kč/load wash and dry, Internet-2 Kč/min, daily 8:00–20:00, Praha 2, near Náměstí Míru Metro stop).

American Express: It's right on Wenceslas Square (foreign exchange daily 9:00–19:00; travel service Mon–Fri 9:00–18:00, Sat 9:00–12:00, closed Sun; Václavské Náměstí 56, tel. 222-800-237). AmEx also has offices on Celetná street in the Old Town and on the Old Town Square.

Local Help: Magic Praha is a tiny travel service run by hardworking Lída Šteflová. A charming Jill-of-all-trades who takes her clients' needs seriously, she's particularly helpful with accommodations and transfers throughout the Czech Republic, private tours, and side-trips to historic towns (Spálená 21, 1st floor, tel. & fax 224-931-674, mobile 604-207-225, www.magicpraha.cz, magicpraha@magicpraha.cz). **Athos Travel**

books rooms (see page 117), rents cars, and has guides for hire (1–5 people-700 Kč/hr—see page 59).

Car Rental: All of the biggies have offices in Prague (check each company's Web site, or ask at the TI). For a local alternative, consider **Alimex**, which features a wide variety of new vehicles (tel. 233-350-001, toll-free tel. 800-150-170, www.alimexcr .cz). The cheapest model, a Škoda Fabia, is a great value (450 Kč/day with basic insurance, plus 238 Kč/day for full theft and damage insurance; additional fees: 500-Kč tax for airport pickup, 357 Kč for delivery to your hotel; discounts if you book online, smart to reserve up to a week ahead in peak season). They have branches at the airport (daily 8:00–22:00) and near the Holešovice train station (daily 8:00–18:00).

Best Views: Enjoy the "Golden City of a Hundred Spires" during the early evening, when the light is warm and the colors are rich. Good viewpoints include the terrace at the Strahov Monastery (above the castle), the top of St. Vitus Cathedral (at the castle), the top of either tower on Charles Bridge, the Old Town Square clock tower (has an elevator), the Restaurant u Prince Terrace (see page 133), and the steps of the National Museum overlooking Wenceslas Square.

Getting Around Prague

You can walk nearly everywhere. But the Metro is slick, the trams fun, and the taxis quick and easy, once you're initiated. For details, pick up the handy transit guide at the TI. City maps show the tram, bus, and Metro lines.

By Metro and Train

Affordable and excellent public transit is perhaps the best legacy of the communist era (locals ride all month for 460 Kč). The three-line Metro system is handy and simple, but doesn't always get you right to the tourist sights (landmarks such as the Old Town Square and Prague Castle are several blocks from the nearest Metro stops). The trams take you just about anywhere.

Tickets: The trams and Metro work on the same cheap tickets:

- 20-minute basic ticket with limited transfer options—14 Kč *základní s omezenou přestupností*. With this ticket, no transfers are allowed on trams and buses, but on the Metro, you can go up to five stops with one transfer (not valid for night trams or night buses).
- 75-minute transfer ticket with unlimited transfers (*základní přestupní*)—20 Kč.
- 24-hour pass *(jízdenka na 24 hodin)*—80 Kč.
- 3-day pass *(jízdenka na 3 dny)*—220 Kč.
- 7-day pass *(jízdenka na 7 dní)*—280 Kč.

Prague Metro

Buy tickets from your hotel, at newsstand kiosks, or from automated machines (select ticket price, then insert coins). For convenience, buy all the tickets you think you'll need—but estimate conservatively. Remember, Prague is a great walking town, so unless you're commuting from a hotel far outside the center, you will likely find that individual tickets work best. Be sure to validate your ticket on the tram, bus, or Metro by sticking it in the machine (which stamps a time on it—watch locals and imitate). Inspectors routinely ambush ticketless riders (including tourists) and fine them 400 Kč on the spot.

Tips: Navigate by signs listing end stations. When you come to your stop, push the yellow button if the doors don't automatically

open. Although it seems that all Metro doors lead to the neighborhood of Výstup, that's simply the Czech word for "exit." When a tram pulls up to a stop, two different names are announced: first, the name of the stop you're currently at, followed by the name of the stop that's coming up next. Confused tourists, thinking they've heard their stop, are notorious for rushing off the tram one stop too soon. Trams run every 5–10 minutes in the daytime (a schedule is posted at each stop). The Metro closes at midnight, and the nighttime tram routes (identified with white numbers on blue backgrounds at tram stops) run all night in 30-minute intervals. There's more information and a complete route planner at www .dp-praha.cz.

Handy Trams: Trams #22 and #23 are practically made for sightseeing, using the same route to connect the New Town with the Castle Quarter (see tram route marked on color map at beginning of this book). The trams use some of the same stops as the Metro (making it easy to get to—or travel on from—the tram route). Of the many stops these trams make, the most convenient are two in the New Town (Národní Třída Metro stop, between the bottom of Wenceslas Square and the river; and Národní Divadlo, at the National Theatre), one stop in the Little Quarter (Malostranská Metro stop), and three  stops above Prague Castle (Královský Letohrádek, Pražský Hrad, and Pohořelec; for details, see "Getting to Prague Castle—By Tram" on page 102).

By Taxi

Prague's taxis—notorious for hyperactive meters—are being tamed. New legislation is in place to curb crooked cabbies, and police will always take your side in an argument. Many cabbies are crooks who consider it a good day's work to take one sucker for a ride. You'll make things difficult for a dishonest cabbie by challenging an unfair fare.

While most hotel receptionists and guidebooks advise avoiding taxis, I find Prague to be a great taxi town and use them routinely. With the local rate, they're cheap (read the rates on the door: drop charge—30 Kč; per-kilometer charge—20–30 Kč; and waiting time per minute—5 Kč). The key is to be sure the cabbie turns on the meter at the #1 tariff (look for the word *sazba*, meaning "tariff," on the meter). Avoid cabs waiting at tourist attractions and train stations. To improve your odds of getting a fair meter rate—which starts only when you take off—call for a cab (or have your hotel or restaurant call one for you). AAA Taxi (tel. 233-113-311) and City Taxi (tel. 257-257-257) are the most likely to have English-speaking staff—and honest cabbies. I also find that hailing a passing taxi usually gets me a decent price.

If a cabbie surprises you at the end with an astronomical fare, simply pay 200 Kč, which should cover you for a long ride anywhere in the center. Then go into your hotel. On the miniscule chance he follows you, the receptionist will back you up.

TOURS

Walking Tours—Prague Walks offers walking tours of the Old Town, the castle, the Jewish Quarter, and more (250–1,000 Kč, 1.5–6 hrs, tel. 222-322-309, fax 261-214-603, mobile 603-271-911, www.praguewalks.com, pwalks@comp.cz). Consider their clever Good Morning Walk, which starts at 8:00 (April–Aug only), before the crowds hit. Several other companies offer good guided walks. For the latest, pick up the walking tour fliers at the TI.

Private Guides—Hiring your own personal guide can be an exceptional value in Prague, especially if you're traveling in a group. Guides meet you wherever you like and tailor the tour to your interests. **Šárka Pelantová** gets beyond the dates and famous buildings to provide insight into her culture, and is eager to build a walk around your interests (€13/hr, mobile 777-225-205, www .prague-guide.info, saraguide@volny.cz). **Katka Svobodová**—a hardworking guide who knows her stuff and speaks excellent English—enjoys showing individuals and small groups around. She studies anthropology and wrote her thesis on Jewish burial customs (400 Kč or €13 per hour, minimum 3 hrs, tel. 224-818-267, mobile 603-181-300, www.praguewalker.com, katerina@praguewalker .com). **Jana Hronková** knows Hebrew and has a natural style—a welcome change from the more strict professionalism of some of the busier guides (mobile 732-185-180, janahronkova@hotmail .com). My readers have also recommended **Renata Blažková** (tel.

222-716-870, mobile 602-353-186, blazer@volny.cz) and **Martin Bělohradský** (martinb@uochb.cas.cz).

Athos Travel's licensed guides can lead you on a general sight-seeing tour or fit the walk to your interests: music, Art Nouveau, Jewish life, architecture, Franz Kafka, and more (1–5 people-700 Kč/hr, more than 5 people-800 Kč/hr, arrange tour at least 24 hours in advance, tel. 241-440-571, www.athos.cz, info@athos.cz).

To get beyond Prague, call **Thomas Zahn,** who runs Pathways Guided Travel. Thomas, an American who married into the Czech Republic, specializes in helping Americans of Czech descent find their roots. He also organizes and leads creative, affordable (mostly 1-day and 2-day) excursions from Prague. Hiking, biking, horseback riding, or canoeing, you'll explore the unknown charms of the region with a small group and a committed guide. Explore Thomas' Web site for ways to connect with the rural Czech countryside and experience more than Prague on your visit (tel. 257-940-113, mobile 603-758-983, www.pathfinders.cz).

The **TI** also has plenty of private guides (rates for a 3-hour tour: 1,200 Kč/1 person, 1,400 Kč/2 people, 1,600 Kč/3 people, 2,000 Kč/4 people; desk at Old Town Square TI, arrange and pay in person at least 2 hours in advance, tel. 224-482-562, guides@pis.cz). For a listing of more private guides, see www.guide-prague.cz.

Tram Joyride—Trams #22 and #23 (following the same route) both make a fine joyride through town. Consider it a scenic lead-up to touring the castle. Catch it at the Náměstí Míru Metro station; roll through a bit of the New Town, the Old Town, and across the river, and hop out just above the castle (at Hotel Savoy, stop: Pohořelec); then hike down the hill into the Castle Quarter.

Bus Tours—Cheap big-bus orientation tours provide an efficient, once-over-lightly look at Prague and a convenient way to see the castle. But in a city as walkable as Prague, bus tours should be used only in case of rain, laziness, or both. Several companies have kiosks on Na Příkopě. Premiant City Tours offers 20 different tours, including several overview tours of the city (250 Kč/1 hr, 380 Kč/2 hrs, 750 Kč/3.5 hrs), the Jewish Quarter (700 Kč, 2 hrs), Prague by night, Bohemian glass, Terezín Concentration Camp, Karlštejn Castle, Český Krumlov (1,750 Kč, 10 hrs), and a river cruise. The tours feature live guides and depart from near the bottom of Wenceslas Square at Na Příkopě 23. Get tickets at an AVE travel agency, hotel, on the bus, or at Na Příkopě 23 (tel. 224-946-922, mobile 606-600-123, www.premiant.cz). Tour salespeople are notorious for telling you anything to sell a ticket. Some tours, especially those heading into the countryside, can be in as many as four different languages. Hiring a private guide can be a much better value (see above).

Cruises—Prague isn't great for a boat tour. Still, the hour-long Vltava River cruises, which leave from near the castle end of Charles Bridge about hourly, are scenic and relaxing, though not informative (100 Kč). You can rent a small rowboat or paddleboat on the island by the  National Theatre, and float among the swans at your own pace (about 80 Kč/hr, bring photo ID for deposit).

THE OLD TOWN

(Staré Město)

From Prague's dramatic centerpiece, the Old Town Square, sight-seeing options fan out in all directions. Get oriented on the square before venturing onward. You can find out about Jewish heritage in the Jewish Quarter (Josefov), a few blocks from the Old Town Square. Closer to the square are the quaint and historic Ungelt courtyard and Celetná street, which leads to the Museum of Czech Cubism and the landmark Estates Theatre. If you're intrigued by Jan Hus, the preacher and martyr, look for his pulpit in the chapel on Bethlehem Square. Nearby, Karlova street leads to the famous Charles Bridge.

Old Town Square (Staroměstské Náměstí)

The focal point for most visits, Prague's Old Town Square is well worth ▲▲▲. This has been a market square since the 11th century.

It became the nucleus of the Old Town (Staré Město) in the 13th century, when its Town Hall was built. Today, the old-time market stalls have been replaced by cafés, touristy horse buggies, and souvenir hawkers. But under this shallow surface the square hides a magic power to evoke the history that has passed through here.

• *Gawk your way to the square's centerpiece, the...*

Jan Hus Memorial: This monument, erected in 1915 (500 years after the Czech reformer's martyrdom by fire), symbolizes the long struggle for Czech freedom (see sidebar on page 63). Walk around the memorial. Jan Hus stands tall between two groups of people: victorious Hussite patriots and Protestants defeated by

Prague's Old Town

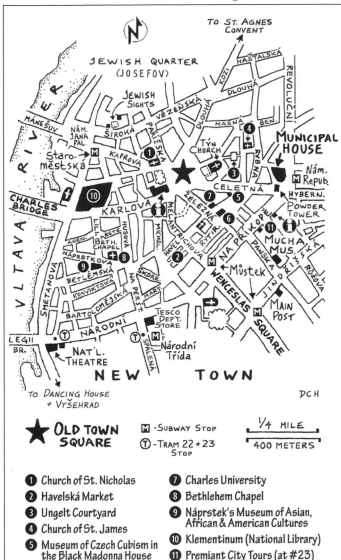

★ **OLD TOWN SQUARE**

Ⓜ – SUBWAY STOP

Ⓣ – TRAM 22 + 23 STOP

¼ MILE / 400 METERS

❶ Church of St. Nicholas
❷ Havelská Market
❸ Ungelt Courtyard
❹ Church of St. James
❺ Museum of Czech Cubism in the Black Madonna House
❻ Estates Theatre
❼ Charles University
❽ Bethlehem Chapel
❾ Náprstek's Museum of Asian, African & American Cultures
❿ Klementinum (National Library)
⓫ Premiant City Tours (at #23)

Hus and Luther

The word *catholic* means "universal." The Roman Catholic Church—in many ways the administrative ghost of the Roman Empire—is the only organization to survive from ancient times. For more than a thousand years, it enforced its notion that the Vatican was the sole interpreter of God's word on earth, and the only legitimate way to be a Christian was as a Roman Catholic. Jan Hus (c. 1369–1415) lived and preached a century before Martin Luther. Both were college professors, as well as priests. Both drew huge public crowds as they preached in their university chapels. Both promoted a local religious autonomy. Both helped establish their national languages. (Hus gave the Czechs their unique accent marks to enable the letters to fit the sounds.) And both got in big trouble. While Hus was burned, Luther survived. Living after Gutenberg, Luther was able to spread his message more cheaply and effectively, thanks to the new printing press. Since Luther was high-profile and German, killing him would have caused major political complications. While Hus may have loosened Rome's grip on Christianity, Luther orchestrated the Reformation that finally broke it. Today, both are honored as national heroes as well as religious reformers.

the Hapsburgs. One of the patriots holds a cup—in the medieval Church, only priests could drink the wine at Communion. Since the Hussites fought for their right to take both the wine and the bread, the cup is their symbol. Behind Jan Hus, a mother with her children represents the ultimate rebirth of the Czech nation. Because of his bold stance for independence in the way common people worship God, Hus was excommunicated and burned in Germany a century before the age of Martin Luther.

• *Standing by Jan Hus, get oriented with a...*

Spin-Tour: Whirl clockwise to get a look at Prague's diverse architectural styles: Gothic, Renaissance, Baroque, rococo, and Art Nouveau.

Start with the green domes of the Baroque **Church of St. Nicholas.** Originally Catholic, now Hussite, this church is a popular venue for concerts. (There's another green-domed Church of St. Nicholas—also popular for concerts—by the same architect across

Old Town Square

the Charles Bridge in the Little Quarter.) The Jewish Quarter (Josefov) is a few blocks behind the church, down the uniquely tree-lined Pařížská—literally, "Paris Street." (For more on the Jewish Quarter, see page 67.) Pařížská, an eclectic cancan of mostly Art Nouveau facades, leads to a bluff that once sported a 100-foot-tall stone Stalin. Demolished in 1962 after Khrushchev exposed Stalin's crimes, it was replaced in 1991 by a giant ticking **metronome**—partly to commemorate Prague's centennial exhibition (the 1891 exhibition is remembered by the Little Quarter's Eiffel-esque Petřín Tower), and partly to send the message that for every power, there's a time to go.

Spin to the right, past the Hus Memorial and the fine yellow Art Nouveau building. The large rococo palace on the right is part of the **National Gallery;** the temporary exhibits here are often the best in town.

To the right, you can't miss the towering, Gothic **Týn Church** (pronounced "teen"), with its fanciful spires flanking a solid-gold effigy of the Virgin Mary. For 200 years after Hus' death, this was Prague's leading Hussite church. Inside, black Baroque altars clash with the simple Gothic style. The narrow lane next to the church has the **Via Musica,** the most convenient ticket office in town (see page 145). Behind the Týn Church is a gorgeously restored medieval courtyard called **Ungelt** (see page 73). The row of pastel houses in front of Týn Church has a mixture of Gothic,

Renaissance, and Baroque facades. To the right of these buildings, shop-lined **Celetná street** leads to a square called Ovocný Trh (with the Estates Theater and Museum of Czech Cubism—see page 76), and beyond that, to the Powder Tower and Municipal House in the New Town (see page 88).

Continue spinning right—with more gloriously colorful architecture—until you reach the pointed 250-foot-tall spire marking the 14th-century **Old Town Hall** (which also encompasses the 5 houses to the left of the tower). Across the square from the Old Town Hall, touristy **Melantrichova street** leads directly to the New Town's Wenceslas Square (see page 82), passing the craft-packed Havelská Market (see page 66) along the way.

• *Now wander across the square, towards the Old Town Hall Tower. Embedded in the pavement at the base of the tower (near the snack stand), you'll see...*

Twenty-Seven Crosses: These white inlaid crosses mark the spot where 27 Protestant nobles, merchants, and intellectuals were beheaded in 1621 after rebelling against the Catholic Hapsburgs. The execution ended Czech independence for 300 years—and, for locals, it's still one of the grimmest chapters in their history. Until recently, Czechs walked around this sacred spot, avoiding stepping on it, and many would even stop to pay their respects. But today the sacred soil is home to a hot-dog vendor, and few notice the crosses in the pavement. Locals lament this transition: As the commercialized Old Town loses the power to evoke history, people here trample over their own past.

• *Looming behind the crosses is the...*

Old Town Hall: The main TI, to the left of the Astronomical Clock, contains a guides' desk and sells tickets for these two options: zipping up the only tower in town that has an elevator (40 Kč, fine views); or taking a 45-minute tour of the Gothic chapel and Town Hall, which includes a close-up of the inner guts of the Astronomical Clock (including its statues of the 12 apostles;

Havelská Market

Skinny, tourist-clogged Melantrichova street leads directly from Old Town Square's Astronomical Clock to the bottom of Wenceslas Square. But even along this most crowded of streets, a genuine bit of Prague remains: Havelská Market, offering crafts and produce.

The open-air market was set up in the 13th century for the German trading community. Though heavy on souvenirs these days, the market still keeps hungry locals and vagabonds fed cheaply. It's ideal for a healthy snack; merchants are happy to sell a single vegetable or piece of fruit, and you'll find a washing fountain and plenty of inviting benches midway down the street.

The market is also a fun place to browse for crafts. It's a home-grown, home-made kind of place; you'll often be dealing with the actual farmer or artist. The market is open daily from 9:00 to 18:00. It's better on weekdays for produce, but offers more puppets and toys on weekends.

50 Kč, 2/hr). A gallery inside the Town Hall features fine temporary exhibits (especially photography—check in the office for schedule). Notice the elaborate Renaissance window on the Town Hall house with the pink facade—the railings and the golden inscription *(Praga Caput Regni)* make it one of Prague's most beautiful windows.

• *The part of the Town Hall that visitors are generally most interested in is the iconic...*

Astronomical Clock: Ignore the ridiculous human sales racks, and join the gang for the striking of the hour on the Town Hall clock (daily 8:00–21:00, until 20:00 in winter). As you wait, see if you can figure out how the clock works.

With revolving disks, celestial symbols, and sweeping hands, this clock keeps several versions of time. Two outer rings show the hour: Bohemian time (Gothic numbers, counts from sunset—find the zero, next to 23...supposedly the time of tonight's sunset) and modern time (24 Roman numerals, XII at the top being noon, XII

at the bottom being midnight). Five hundred years ago, everything revolved around the earth (the fixed middle background).

To indicate the times of sunrise and sunset, arcing lines and moving spheres combine with the big hand (a sweeping golden sun) and the little hand (the moon showing various stages). Look for the orbits of the sun and moon as they rise through day (the blue zone) and night (the black zone).

If this seems complex to us, it must have been a marvel 500 years ago. Since the clock was heavily damaged during World War II, a lot of what you see today is a reconstruction.

The circle below (added in the 19th century) shows the signs of the zodiac, scenes from the seasons of a rural peasant's life, and a ring of saints' names—one for each day of the year, with a marker showing today's special saint.

Four statues flanking the clock represent the 15th-century outlook on time. A Turk with a mandolin symbolizes hedonism, a Jewish moneylender is greed, and the figure staring into a mirror stands for vanity. All these worldly goals are vain in the face of Death, whose hourglass reminds us that our time may soon run out.

At the top of the hour (don't blink—the show is pretty quick): First, Death tips his hourglass and pulls the cord, ringing the bell;

then the windows open and the 12 apostles parade by, acknowledging the gang of onlookers; then the rooster crows; and then the hour is rung. The hour is often off because of daylight saving time (completely senseless to 15th-century clockmakers). At the top of the next hour, stand under the tower—protected by a line of banner-wielding, powdered-wigged concert salespeople—and watch the tourists.

• *Now that you're oriented, you can use this delightful square as your launchpad for the rest of Prague's Old Town sights.*

Prague's Jewish Quarter (Josefov)

Prague's Jewish Quarter neighborhood and its well-presented, profoundly moving museum tell the story of the Jews of this region. For me, this is the most interesting Jewish sight in Europe (and worth ▲▲▲). The Jewish Quarter is an easy walk from Old Town

Prague's Jewish Quarter

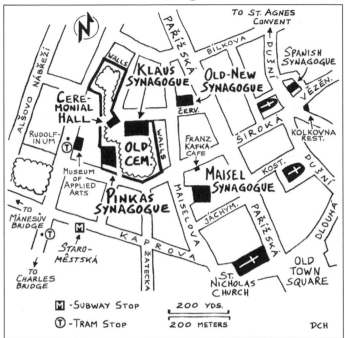

Square, up delightful Pařížská street (next to the green-domed St. Nicholas Church).

As the Nazis decimated Jewish communities in the region, Prague's Jews were allowed to collect and archive their treasures here. While the archivists ultimately died in concentration camps, their work survives. Seven sights scattered over a three-block area make up the tourists' Jewish Quarter. Six of the sights—all except the Old-New Synagogue—are called "the Museum" and are treated as one admission. Your ticket comes with a map locating the sights and listing admission appointments—the times you'll be let in if it's very crowded. (Without crowds, ignore the times.) You'll notice plenty of security (stepped up since 9/11).

Cost, Hours, Tours: To visit all seven sights, you'll pay 500 Kč (300 Kč for the six sights that make up the Museum and 200 Kč for the Old-New Synagogue; all sights open Sun–Fri 9:00–18:00, closed Sat—the Jewish Sabbath). There are occasional guided walks in English (40 Kč, 2.5 hrs, start at Maisel Synagogue, tel. 222-317-191). Most stops are described in English. The ticket lines at the cemetery and Pinkas Synagogue are longest. You'll likely save time if you buy your ticket at the Maisel Synagogue (the best place to start your visit, anyway).

Maisel Synagogue (Maiselova Synagóga)—This synagogue was built as a private place of worship for the Maisel family during the 16th-century Golden Age of Prague's Jews. Maisel was the financier of the Hapsburg king—and he had lots of money. The synagogue's interior is decorated neo-Gothic. In World War II, it served as a warehouse for the accumulated treasures of decimated Jewish communities that Hitler planned to use for his "Museum of the Extinct Jewish Race." The one-room exhibit (the upstairs "women's gallery" is closed for renovation) shows a thousand years of Jewish history in Bohemia and Moravia. Well-explained in English, the topics covered include the origin of the Star of David, Jewish mysticism, discrimination, and the creation of Prague's ghetto. Notice the eastern wall, with the holy ark containing the scroll of the Torah. The central case shows the silver ornamental Torah crowns that capped the scroll.

Spanish Synagogue (Španělská Synagóga)—This 19th-century, ornate, Moorish-style synagogue continues the history of the Maisel Synagogue, covering the 18th, 19th, and tumultuous 20th centuries. The upstairs is particularly intriguing (with c. 1900 photos of Josefov). The Spanish Synagogue is now used for classical concerts, often featuring the music of Jewish composers such as Felix Mendelssohn and Gustav Mahler (ticket desk just outside at the door). The building also contains the Jewish public library, the only one of its kind in Prague.

Pinkas Synagogue (Pinkasova Synagóga)—A site of Jewish worship for 400 years, today this is a poignant memorial to the victims of the Nazis. The walls are covered with the handwritten names of 77,297 Czech Jews who were sent from here to the gas chambers of Auschwitz and other camps. (You'll hear the somber reading of the names as you ponder this sad sight.) Hometowns are in gold and family names are in red, followed in black by the individual's first name, birthday, and last date known to be alive. Notice that families generally perished together. Extermination camps are listed on the east wall. Climb six steps into the women's gallery. The names in poor condition near the ceiling are from 1959. When the communists moved in, they closed the synagogue and erased everything. With freedom, in 1989, the Pinkas Synagogue was reopened and all the names rewritten. The synagogue closed briefly in 2003, as flood damage meant the names needed to be rewritten once again.

Prague's Jewish Heritage

The Jewish people of Palestine were dispersed by the Romans 2,000 years ago. Over the centuries, their culture survived in enclaves throughout the world: "The Torah was their sanctuary which no army could destroy." Jews first came to Prague in the 10th century. The main intersection of Josefov (Maiselova and Široká streets) was the meeting point of two medieval trade routes.

During the age of the Crusades in the 12th century, the pope declared that Jews and Christians should not live together. Jews had to wear yellow badges, and their quarter was walled in. It became a ghetto. In the 16th and 17th centuries, Prague had one of the biggest ghettos in Europe, with 11,000 inhabitants. Within its six gates, Prague's Jewish Quarter was a gaggle of 200 wooden buildings. It was said that "Jews nested rather than dwelled."

The "outcasts" of Christianity relied mainly on profits from moneylending (forbidden to Christians) and community solidarity to survive. While their money bought them protection (the kings highly taxed Jewish communities), it was often also a curse.

Upstairs is the **Terezín Children's Art Exhibit,** displaying art drawn by Jewish children who were imprisoned at Terezín Concentration Camp and later perished. Terezín is a powerful day trip from Prague, easily accessible by local bus (see page 164) or tour bus (see page 59). But the evocative power of the children's drawings is stronger than all of Terezín. Allow at least a half hour here.

Old Jewish Cemetery (Starý Židovský Hřbitov)—As you wander

among 12,000 evocative tombstones, remember that from 1439 until 1787, this was the only burial ground allowed for the Jews of Prague. Because of limited space, the Jewish belief that the body should not be moved once buried, and the sheer number of

Throughout Europe, when times got tough and Christian debts to the Jewish community mounted, entire Jewish communities were evicted or killed.

In the 1780s, Emperor Josef II, motivated more by economic concerns than by philanthropy, eased much of the discrimination against Jews. In 1848, the walls were torn down, and the neighborhood—named Josefov in honor of the emperor who provided this small measure of tolerance—was incorporated as a district of Old Town.

In 1897, ramshackle Josefov was razed and replaced by a new modern town—the original 31 streets and 220 buildings became 10 streets and 83 buildings. This is what you'll see today: an attractive neighborhood of pretty, mostly Art Nouveau buildings, with a few surviving historic Jewish structures. By the 1930s, Prague's Jewish community was hugely successful, thanks largely to their ability to appreciate talent—a rare quality in the small Central European countries whose citizens, as the great Austrian novelist Robert Musil put it, "were equal in their unwillingness to let one another get ahead."

Of the 120,000 Jews living in the area in 1939, just 10,000 survived the Holocaust to see liberation in 1945. Today only a couple of thousand Jews remain in Prague...but the legacy of their ancestors lives on.

graves, tombs were piled atop each other. With its many layers, the cemetery became a small plateau. And as things settled over time, the tombstones got crooked. The Jewish word for cemetery means "House of Life." Many Jews believe that death is the gateway into the next world. Pebbles on the tombstones are "flowers of the desert," reminiscent of the old days when a rock was placed upon the sand gravesite to keep the body covered. Wedged under some of the pebbles are scraps of paper containing prayers.

Ceremonial Hall (Obřadní Síň)—Leaving the cemetery, you'll find a neo-Romanesque mortuary house built in 1911 for the purification of the dead (on left). It's filled with a worthwhile exhibition, described in English, on Jewish burial traditions. A series of crude but instructive paintings show how the "burial brotherhood" took care of the ill and buried the dead. As all are equal before God, the rich and poor alike were buried in embroidered linen shrouds similar to the one you'll see on display.

Klaus Synagogue (Klauzová Synagóga)—This 17th-century synagogue (also at the exit of the cemetery) is the final wing

of a museum devoted to Jewish religious practices. On the ground floor, exhibits explain the Jewish calendar of festivals. The central case displays a Torah (the first 5 books of the Bible) and solid silver pointers used when reading—necessary since the Torah is not to be touched. Upstairs is an exhibit on the rituals of Jewish life (circumcision, bar and bat mitzvah, weddings, kosher eating, and so on).

Old-New Synagogue (Staronová Synagóga)—For more than 700 years, this has been the most important synagogue and the central building in Josefov. Standing like a bomb-hardened bunker, it feels like it has survived plenty of hard times. Stairs take you down to the street level of the 13th century and into the Gothic interior. Built in 1270, it's the oldest synagogue in Central Europe (separate 200-Kč admission includes worthwhile 10-minute tour—ask about it, Sun–Thu 9:30–18:00, Fri 9:30–17:00, closed Sat).

The lobby (where you show your ticket) has two fortified old lockers—where the most heavily taxed community in medieval Prague stored its money in anticipation of the taxman's arrival. As 13th-century Jews were not allowed to build, this was constructed by Christians. The builders were good at four-ribbed vaulting, but since that resulted in a cross, it wouldn't work for a synagogue. Instead, they made the ceiling using clumsy five-ribbed vaulting.

The interior is pure 1300s. The **Shrine of the Ark** in front is the focus of worship. The holiest place in the synagogue, it holds the sacred scrolls of the Torah. The old rabbi's chair to the right remains empty out of respect. The red banner is a copy of the one the Jewish community carried through town during medieval parades. Notice the yellow pointed hat, which the pope ordered all Jewish men to wear in 1215. Twelve is a popular number (e.g., windows) because it

symbolizes the 12 tribes of Israel. The horizontal slit-like windows are an 18th-century addition allowing women to view the men-only services.

The synagogue displays strikingly similar architectural features to the Convent of St. Agnes of Bohemia, a few blocks away (described below).

Non-Jewish Sights in Josefov

These sights are closer to the river than the Jewish sights described above.

Convent of St. Agnes of Bohemia (Klášter Sv. Anežky České)— Princess Agnes founded this convent in the 13th century as the first hospital in Prague. The building dates from the same era as the Old-New Synagogue. (Apparently, difference of faith was no problem for Gothic builders.) Agnes was canonized by Pope John Paul II (who loved to promote the Slavic faithful) in 1989. Since local celebrations of her sainthood on November 26 coincided with the Velvet Revolution, Agnes has since been regarded as the patron of the renascent Czech democracy (you'll see her on the 50-Kč bill).

Today the convent houses the **Museum of Medieval Art in Bohemia and Central Europe** (1200–1550). The 14th century was Prague's Golden Age, and the religious art displayed in this Gothic space is a testament to the rich cultural life of the period. It's one of the best collections of Gothic art in the world. The various Madonnas and saints were gathered here from churches all over Central Europe (100 Kč, free first Wed of the month 15:00–20:00; open Tue–Sun 10:00–18:00, closed Mon, 2 blocks northeast of Spanish Synagogue, along the river at Anežská 12). The convent garden has a pleasant café inside that serves a stylish lunch.

Museum of Applied Arts (Uměleckoprůmyslové Muzeum)— This museum shows off beautiful Czech arts and crafts: glass, ceramics, porcelain, furniture, metalwork, fashion, jewelry, books, and posters (Tue 10:00–20:00, Wed–Sun 10:00–18:00, closed Mon, near the Pinkas Synagogue, toward the river at 17 Listopadu #2, tel. 251-093-111).

Ungelt Courtyard, behind Týn Church

Ever since the Old Town was established, the Ungelt courtyard—located directly behind the Old Town Square's Týn Church—has served as a hostel for foreign merchants. Here the merchants (usually German) would store their goods and pay taxes before setting up a stall on the Old Town Square. Notice there are only two entrances into the complex—this way, safety of goods and merchants could be guaranteed. After decades of disuse, the courtyard had fallen into such disrepair in the 1980s that authorities were considering demolishing it. Recently marvelously restored, the Ungelt courtyard (a.k.a. Týnský Dvůr) is now the most pleasant area in the Old Town for an outdoor coffee (such as at Ebel Café—see page 140), sorting through wooden crafts, and paging through English books (at Anagram and Big Ben bookshops, described on page 143). Although Prague has undoubtedly lost some of its dreamy character to the booming tourist industry, places like Ungelt stand testimony

Prague's Charles University

Back in the 1300s, students studied the arts first, and only then proceeded to one of the other three faculties (medicine, law, and theology), of which theology was the most prestigious. Teaching was done in Latin, and the student body was cosmopolitan—Czechs made up only a fourth of the student body.

In the early 1400s, during the chaotic period of Hussite reforms, the university's policies were changed to give more power to the Czechs. In protest, many foreign students and professors left Prague and founded the first German university in Leipzig. Celebrated by Czech nationalists as a victory over foreigners, the new policies in fact reduced Charles University from a European center of learning to a provincial institution.

In the 1700s, German replaced Latin, and in the 1880s, Czechs won the freedom to study in their own language.

Today the Old Town continues to live a double life as both a commercial center and a university campus. Many of the buildings—lined with souvenir stalls outside—have classrooms that have been animated by lecturers for centuries, and some of the most hidden of the Old Town's courtyards have provided Czech scholars with their two most essential needs: good beer and a space for an inspiring conversation.

Charles University, always a center of Czech political thinking, has incited trouble and uprisings. Jan Hus initiated the reform of the Church here; the revolutions of 1618 and 1848 were sparked by university minds; and in the modern era, students rose up against totalitarian regimes in 1939, 1948, and 1968. The Germans closed down all Czech universities for the duration of World War II. Later, the communists fired professors unwilling to follow the party line and replaced them with applicants chosen on the basis of class background rather than ability. The Velvet

to the miracles money can work—had the communists stayed in for a few more years, Ungelt would have been a black hole by now. Ungelt also reminds us that Prague, for most of its history, has been a cosmopolitan center quite alien to the rest of the country.

The 16th-century Renaissance townhouse (left of the entry into Ungelt) is the **House of the Golden Ring** (Dům u Zlatého Prstenu), which displays a delightful collection of 20th-century Czech art. Its exterior has rectangular sgraffiti etchings (designs scratched out of one layer, revealing a different-colored layer beneath). Look up Boudník, Váchal, and Teige to understand why Prague in the 1930s and 1960s was considered to be at the forefront of European artistic development (Tue–Sun 10:00–18:00, closed Mon, Týnská 6).

Revolution that swept communists out of power in November 1989 started as a student demonstration.

Although many professors returned to the classrooms after 1989, the education system itself has yet to escape the legacy of the authoritarian regimes. From an early age, students are taught to memorize rather than to think independently, knowledge is measured by facts rather than by the ability to use them, and even at the university level few students dare to challenge the professor's view.

Charles University still attracts the best Czech and Slovak students. University education is, as in most of Europe, free in the Czech Republic, and student housing is heavily subsidized. You would expect that free admission would make education more accessible to students from poorer backgrounds. This is not always true. Since there is not enough money in the education system, the state does not have the means to build more schools. The demand exceeds the supply, so only a third of the people who apply to high school ("gymnasium") are accepted, and only half of university applicants are admitted. Students from better-educated backgrounds tend to do better in a system that begins selecting students from the age of 10.

Teachers are poorly paid (even a tenured university professor barely gets by) and libraries are underfunded. Consequently, even students have campaigned for the introduction of moderate fees that would improve access to education and allow professors to spend less time on side jobs and more time on lecture preparation and research. The final verdict on school fees lies with the politicians, who pay more attention to public opinion than to students and teachers.

Facing the other entrance into Ungelt is the Baroque facade of the **Church of St. James** (Kostel Sv. Jakuba), the most beautiful church in the Old Town. The Franciscan Order has occupied this church and the adjacent monastery nearly as long as the merchants occupied Ungelt. A medieval city was a complex phenomenon: side-by-side, there existed commerce, brothels, and a life of contemplation. Artistically, St. James (along with the Church of the Ascension of St. Mary at Strahov Monastery—see page 105) is a stunning example of how simple Gothic spaces could be transformed into sumptuous feasts of Baroque decoration. Contrast these elegant Baroque churches to the nearly nauseating, overblown illusory Baroque you'll see in churches such as St. Nicholas in the Little Quarter (see page 96). The blue light in the altar highlights one of Prague's most precious jewels, Madonna Pietatis. According to legend, a thief attempted to rob the piece from the altar, but his hand was frozen the moment he touched the statue. The monks had to cut off the arm in order for it to let go. The dried-up arm hangs from the wall to the right of the entrance as a warning.

Along Celetná Street, towards the New Town

Celetná, a pedestrian-only street, is a fine place to do some shopping (see page 142). It's also a convenient and relatively untouristy way to get from the Old Town Square to the New Town (specifically the Powder Tower and Municipal House, described on page 88). Along the way, at the square called Ovocný Trh, you'll find these two sights.

Museum of Czech Cubism in the Black Madonna House (Dům u Černé Matky Boží)—This is my favorite piece of 20th-century architecture in the Old Town. Cubism was a potent force in Prague, as this fascinating museum documents. On three floors, you'll see paintings, furniture, graphics, and architectural drafts by Czech Cubists. On the outside, the architect Gočár (who also designed several successful functionalist structures in the city) managed to scale the Cubist facade to fit with the surrounding buildings. Notice how from the third floor up, the Cubist shapes are much less accentuated, allowing the house to flow with the surrounding roofs. This is an example of what over centuries has been considered the greatest virtue of Prague's architects: the ability to adapt their grandiose plans to the existing context (100 Kč, Tue–Sun 10:00–18:00, closed Mon, Ovocný Trh 19, corner of Celetná and Ovocný Trh, tel. 224-301-003). If you're not interested in touring the museum itself, consider a drink in the similarly decorated upstairs Grand Café Orient (see page 140).

Estates Theatre (Stavovské Divadlo)—Built by a nobleman in 1770s, this classicist building—gently opening its greenish walls into Ovocný Trh—was the prime opera venue in Prague in times when an Austrian prodigy was changing the course of music. Wolfgang Amadeus Mozart premiered *Don Giovanni* in this building, and personally directed many of his works here. Prague's theater-goers would whistle arias from Mozart's works on the streets the morning after they premiered here. Today part of the National Theatre group, the Estates Theatre, continues to produce *The Marriage of Figaro, Don Giovanni* (playing through May 2006), and occasionally *The Magic Flute*. For a more intimate encounter with Mozart, go to Villa Bertramka (see page 148).

By the fountain on the side of the theater, combining Gothic with 1970s red brick, is the central building of **Charles University** (Karlova Univerzita; see sidebar). Small graduation ceremonies are held here throughout the year, which is why you'll likely see people with flowers.

If you continue up Celetná, you'll go through the **Powder Tower** and find yourself in front of the Art Nouveau **Municipal House** (described on page 88).

Bethlehem Square (Betlémská Náměstí)

These sights sit on charming, relatively quiet Bethlehem Square (Betlémská Náměstí)—a pleasantly untouristy chunk of Old Town real estate.

Bethlehem Chapel (Betlémská Kaple)—Emperor Charles IV founded the first university in Central Europe, and this was the university's chapel. Around the year 1400, priest and professor Jan Hus preached from the pulpit here (see sidebar on page 63). While meant primarily for students and faculty, Hus' Masses were open to the public. Standing-room-only crowds of more than 3,000 were the norm when Hus preached. Hus proposed that the congregation should be more involved in worship (e.g., actually drink the wine at Communion) and have better access to the word of God through services and scriptures written in the people's language, not in Latin. The stimulating, controversial ideas debated at the university spread throughout the city and, after Hus' death at the stake, sparked off the bloodiest civil war in Czech history.

Each subsequent age has interpreted Hus to its liking: For the Protestants, Hus was the founder of the first Protestant church (though he was actually an ardent Catholic); for the revolutionaries, this critic of the power of the Church was a proponent of social equality; for the nationalists, this Czech preacher was the defender of the language; and for the communists, Hus was the first communist ideologue.

Today's chapel is a 1950s reconstruction of the original. Try the unbelievably bad acoustics inside—it demonstrates the sloppy work sponsored by the communists (tiny upstairs exhibit and big chapel with English-info sheets available; entry-35 Kč; April–Oct daily 10:00–18:30; Nov–March Tue–Sun 10:00–17:30, closed Mon and during university functions; Betlémská Náměstí, tel. 224-248-595).

Klub Architektů, across from the entry, has a cavernous atmosphere inside, straw-chair seating outside, and good food in both places (see page 131).

At the other end of the square from the chapel is...

Náprstek's Museum of Asian, African, and American Cultures (Náprstkovo Muzeum Asijských, Africkych a Americkych Kultur)—A 19th-century philanthropist named Vojta Náprstek assembled one of Prague's most fascinating collections, focusing on the culture of Native Americans. Look for the actual attire of the Lakota chief Sitting Bull (Tue–Sun 10:00–17:00, closed Mon, Betlémská Náměstí 1, tel. 224-497-500, www.aconet.cz/npm).

Czechs are obsessed with Native Americans. Most kids spend

summers in camps (as Boy Scouts and Girl Scouts), where they learn about the American Indians' respect for nature, survival skills in the wilderness, courage, and the idealized noble spirit. A song celebrating the Little Big Horn victory is one of the most popular tales sung at campfires around the country. When Lance Armstrong, the famous cancer survivor, visited Prague's oncology ward in July of 2004—just days after his unprecedented sixth consecutive victory in the rigorous Tour de France—child cancer patients rewarded their idol with the Indian name "Fast Wind."

Along Karlova Street, to the Charles Bridge

Karlova street winds through medieval Prague from the Old Town Square to the Charles Bridge (it zigzags...just follow the crowds). This is a commercial gauntlet, and it's here that the touristy feeding-frenzy of Prague is most ugly. Street signs keep you on track, and *Karlův most* signs point to the bridge. Obviously, you'll find few good values on this drag.

The exception is the colorful pub **U Tygra**, where you can rest your feet, enjoy a cheap Pilsner beer, and watch locals (venture off 20 steps to the left, along Husova street). Bohumil Hrabal, the best modern Czech writer (best known for *I Served the King of England*), heard many of his famous stories from the regulars *(štamgast)* right here.

After 50 more yards along Karlova, at the intersection with Liliová street, turn right through an archway into the Baroque courtyard of the second-largest building in Prague, the...

Klementinum—This is the Czech Republic's massive national library. The contrast could not be starker—out of the most souvenir-packed stretch of Eastern Europe, you step into the meditative silence of Eastern Europe's biggest library. The Klementinum was built to house a college in the 1600s by the Jesuits, who had been invited to Prague by the Catholic Hapsburgs to offset the influence of the predominantly Protestant Charles University. The building was transformed into a library in the early 1700s, when the Jesuits had firmly taken control of the university. Their books, together with the collections of several noble families (written in all possible languages...except Czech), form the nucleus of what is now the six-million-volumes-strong National and University Library. (Note that the Klementinum's Chapel of Mirrors is a popular venue for evening concerts.)

The unassuming entrance to the stacks of this marvelous public library is by the archway to the left of where you entered the courtyard. To return from the timeless silence of books to the buzzing clamor of the 21st century, go through the archway into a smaller courtyard, then step through a small wooden gate. In front of you on the left is the start of the Charles Bridge.

Charles Bridge (Karlův Most)

One of Prague's defining landmarks, and easily worth ▲▲▲, this much-loved bridge offers one of the most pleasant and entertain-

ing 500-yard strolls in Europe. Be on the Charles Bridge at dawn, when it's magical, or any time before 9:00 to have the place to yourself.

At the Old Town end of the bridge, in a little square, is a statue of the bridge's namesake, **Charles IV.** This Holy Roman Emperor (*Karlo Quatro*—the guy on the 100-Kč bill) ruled his vast empire from Prague in the 14th century. He's holding a contract establishing Prague's university (see sidebar on page 74), the first in Northern Europe. This statue was erected in 1848 to celebrate the university's 500th birthday. The women around Charles' pedestal symbolize the university's four faculties: the arts, medicine, law, and theology.

Bridges were built on this spot before, as the remnant tower

from the Judith Bridge (the smaller of the two bridge towers at the far end) testifies. All were washed away by floods. After a major flood in 1342, Emperor Charles IV decided to commission an entirely new structure rather than repair the old one. Until the 19th century, this was Prague's only bridge crossing the river.

How do you make a bridge last seven centuries? Back in the 1300s, they believed in the magic of time and numbers. The founding stone was laid in 1357, on the 9th of July at 5:31 (it's a palindrome: 135797531). On the Old Town bank, a spot was chosen for the ending of the bridge that lined up perfectly with the

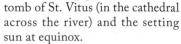

tomb of St. Vitus (in the cathedral across the river) and the setting sun at equinox.

This magical spot is now occupied by the **bridge tower,** considered one of the finest Gothic gates anywhere. Contemplate the fine sculpture on the Old Town side of the tower, showing the 14th-century hierarchy of kings, bishops, and angels. Climb the tower for a fine view...but nothing else (40 Kč, daily 10:00–19:00, as late as 22:00 in summer). The other side of the tower lacks decoration. Instead, a plaque commemorates the Swedish siege of 1648, when the bridge turned into a major battleground and the tower was heavily damaged (but the invading Swedes never made it across).

In the days of the Swedish siege, there were no statues on the bridge—only a **cross,** which you can still see as part of the third sculpture on the right. The gilded Hebrew inscription celebrating Christ was paid by a fine imposed on a Jew for mocking the cross.

The bronze Baroque statue depicting **John of Nepomuk**—a saint of the Czech people—draws a crowd (look for the guy with the 5 golden stars around his head, near the Little Quarter end of the bridge on the right). John of Nepomuk was a 14th-century priest to whom the queen confessed all her sins. According to a 17th-century legend, the king wanted to know his wife's secrets, but Father John dutifully refused to tell. He was tortured and eventually killed by being tossed off the bridge. When he hit the water, five stars appeared. The shiny plaque at the base of the statue depicts the heave-ho.

Devout pilgrims—from Mexico and Moravia alike—touch the engraving to make a wish come true. You get only one chance in life for this wish, so think carefully before you touch the saint. Do not touch the dog, which is said to bring bad luck. Notice the date on the inscription: This oldest statue on the bridge was unveiled in 1683, on the supposed 300th anniversary of the martyr's death. In times when the Czechs were being forcibly converted to Catholicism, John of Nepomuk became the rallying national symbol—"We will convert, but our patron must be Czech." John of Nepomuk was canonized three centuries after his death. You'll find a statue like this one on nearly every square and bridge in the country.

Most of the other Charles Bridge statues date from the late 1600s and early 1700s. Today half of them are replicas—the originals are in city museums, out of the polluted air.

At the far end of Charles Bridge, you reach the **Little Quarter.** For sights in this neighborhood, see page 94.

North of the Old Town, Outside the City Center

These three sights are all north of central Prague. The first two are roughly across the river from the Jewish Quarter; the third is closer to the center but farther east, near the Florenc bus station.

Museum of Modern and Contemporary Art (Museum Moderního a Současného Umění)—This fine collection of Czech and some European art from the 20th and 21st centuries is displayed on large, open floors in what was originally designed as Prague's Trade Palace. The works are arranged by content rather than chronology: art, architecture, industrial design (a field in which Czechs have traditionally been strong), and scenography (with superb theater and cinema stage decorations). The exhibition dedicates a section to every significant Czech artist. This can be a downside, as an outstanding artist has the same number of works displayed as a less notable one. Choose only a section of the museum to visit, as it's easy to get overwhelmed here (various tickets ranging from 100–300 Kč, depending on how much of the enormous exhibition you want to see; Tue–Sun 10:00–18:00, closed Mon, Dukelských Hrdinů 47, Praha 7, just across the river from the Jewish Quarter, take trams #12 or #17 from the center, tel. 224-301-111). The neighboring streets provide an appropriate setting for the museum, dating from the same period as the art.

Troja Castle (Trojský Zámek)—On a sunny day, you can spend a pleasant afternoon in this castle and the Prague Zoo (beautifully revamped after the 2002 flood) next door. The castle itself, built in 1679–1685, is a Baroque masterpiece with an extravagant interior. The frescoes in the central hall celebrate the Hapsburg dynasty. The castle's collection of 19th-century Czech art, with a focus on history, has a portrait gallery of city mayors. You can stroll the castle grounds, through the French-style garden and a fruit orchard (100 Kč; April–Oct Tue–Sun 10:00–18:00, closed Mon; Jan–March Sat–Sun 10:00–17:00 only, closed Mon–Fri; closed Nov–Dec; U Trojského Zámku 1, Praha 7, tel. 233-540-739).

Prague Municipal Museum (Museum Hlavního Města Prahy)—You'll learn about the history of Prague from prehistoric times to 1784, with particularly good displays on the city's development in the Middle Ages and Early Modern times (Tue–Sun 9:00–18:00, closed Mon, northeast of Main Train Station at Na Poříčí 52, near Metro: Florenc, tel. 224-816-772).

THE NEW TOWN

(Nové Město)

Enough of pretty, medieval Prague—let's leap into the modern era. The New Town, with Wenceslas Square as its focal point, is today's urban Prague. This part of the city offers bustling boulevards and interesting neighborhoods. The New Town is the best place to view Prague's remarkable Art Nouveau art and architecture and to learn more about its recent communist past.

Wenceslas Square (Václavské Náměstí)

More a broad boulevard than a square (until recently, trams rattled up and down its parklike median strip), this ▲▲ city landmark is named for King Wenceslas—featured both on the 20-Kč coin and the equestrian statue that stands at the top of the boulevard. This square functions as a stage for modern Czech history: The creation of the Czechoslovak state was celebrated here in 1918; in 1968, the Soviets put down huge popular demonstrations here; and, in 1989, more than 300,000 Czechs and Slovaks converged here to claim their freedom.

Starting near the Wenceslas statue at the top (Metro: Muzeum), stroll down the square:

The **National Museum** (Národní Muzeum) stands grandly at the top. While the museum is dull, the building offers a powerful view, and the interior is richly decorated in the Czech Revival neo-Renaissance style that heralded the 19th-century rebirth of the Czech nation (80 Kč, daily May–Sept 10:00–18:00, Oct–April 9:00–17:00, halls of Czech fossils and animals). The light-colored patches

Prague's New Town

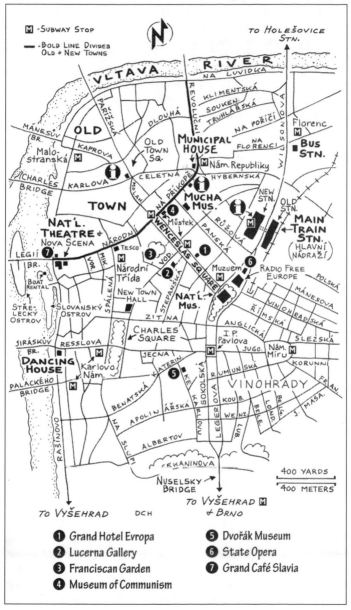

M –Subway Stop

— –Bold Line Divides Old + New Towns

TO HOLEŠOVICE STN.

VLTAVA RIVER

NA LUVIDKA

KLIMENTSKÁ

SOUKEN-

TRUHLÁŘSKÁ

NA POŘÍČÍ

Florenc

OLD

MÁNESŮV BR.

PAŘÍŽSKÁ

KAPROVA

DLOUHÁ

OLD TOWN SQ.

MUNICIPAL HOUSE

NA FLORENCI

Bus STN.

Malo-stranská

REVOLUČNÍ

Nám. Republiky

CHARLES BRIDGE

KARLOVA

CELETNA

NA PŘÍKOPĚ

HYBERNSKÁ

TOWN

MELAN...

MUCHA MUS.

NEW STN.

OLD STN.

MAIN TRAIN STN.

NAT'L. THEATRE

Nova Scena

NÁRODNÍ

Můstek

PANSKÁ

RŮŽOVÁ

(HLAVNÍ NÁDRAŽÍ)

LEGIÍ

BR.

MIK.

VOR.

TESCO

VOD.

WENCESLAS SQUARE

ŠTĚPÁNSKÁ

Muzeum

RADIO FREE EUROPE

POLSKÁ

BOAT RENTAL

SPÁLENÁ

Národní Třída

New Town HALL

NAT'L. MUS.

MÁNESOVA

STŘE- LECKÝ OSTROV

Slovanský Ostrov

ZITNA

ŘÍMSKÁ

VINOHRADSKÁ

JIRÁSKŮV BR.

RESSLOVA

CHARLES SQUARE

ANGLICKÁ

I.P. Pavlova

SLEZSKÁ

DANCING HOUSE

Karlovo Nám.

JEČNÁ

KATEŘIN...

KE KARLOVU

SOKOLSKÁ

RUMUNSKÁ

JUGO.

Nám. Míru

KORUNNÍ

PALACKÉHO BRIDGE

BENÁTSKÁ

APOLINÁŘSKÁ

LEGEROVA

WENZ.

KOU B.

BĚLE.

LOND.

BELG.

VINOHRADY

FRAN.

J. MASA.

RAŠÍNOVO

NA SLUPI

ALBERTOV

ČEKANINOVA

NUSELSKÝ BRIDGE

400 YARDS

400 METERS

TO VYŠEHRAD

DCH

TO VYŠEHRAD & BRNO

❶ Grand Hotel Evropa
❷ Lucerna Gallery
❸ Franciscan Garden
❹ Museum of Communism
❺ Dvořák Museum
❻ State Opera
❼ Grand Café Slavia

in the museum's columns fill holes where Soviet bullets hit during the crackdown against the 1968 "Prague Spring" uprising. Lowly masons—defying their communist bosses, who wanted the damage to be forgotten—showed their Czech spirit by intentionally mismatching their patches.

The nearby Metro stop (Muzeum) is the crossing point of two Metro lines built with Russian know-how in the 1970s.

The ugly **communist-era building** to the left of the National Museum housed the rubber-stamp Parliament back when they

voted with Moscow. A Social Realist statue showing triumphant workers still stands at its base. It's now home to Radio Free Europe. After communism fell, RFE lost its funding and could no longer afford its Munich headquarters. In gratitude for its broadcasts—which kept the people of Eastern Europe in touch with real news—the current Czech government now rents the building to RFE for 1 Kč a year. (As RFE energetically beams its American message deep into Islam from here, it has been threatened recently by Al-Qaeda, and a plan is underway to relocate it to an easier-to-defend locale in the suburbs.)

St. Wenceslas (Václav), commemorated by the statue, is the "good king" of Christmas-carol fame. He was the wise and benevo-

lent 10th-century duke of Bohemia. A rare example of a well-educated and literate ruler, he was credited by his people for Christianizing his nation and lifting up the culture. Wenceslas astutely allied the Czechs with Saxony, rather than Bavaria, giving the Czechs a vote when the Holy Roman Emperor was selected (and therefore more political clout). After his murder in 929, Wenceslas became a symbol of Czech nationalism and statehood—and remains an icon of Czech unity whenever the nation has to rally. Supposedly, when the Czechs face their darkest hour, Wenceslas will come riding out of Blaník Mountain (east of Prague) with an army of knights to rescue the nation. In 1620, when Austria stripped Czechs of their independence, many people went to Blaník Mountain to see whether it had opened up. They did the same at other critical points in their history (in 1938, 1948, and 1968)—but Wenceslas never emerged. Although now safely part of NATO and the EU, Czechs remain realistic: If Wenceslas hasn't come out yet, the worst times must still lie ahead....

Study the statue. Wenceslas is surrounded by the four other Czech patron saints. Notice the focus on books. A small nation without great military power, the Czech Republic chose national heroes who enriched the culture by thinking, rather than fighting. This statue is a popular meeting point. Locals say, "I'll see you under the horse's... tail."

Thirty yards below the big horse is a small garden with a low-key **memorial** "to the victims of communism"—such as Jan

Palach. In 1969, a group of patriots decided that an act of self-immolation would stoke the fires of independence. Jan Palach, a philosophy student who loved life, but wanted it with freedom, set himself on fire on the steps of the National Museum for the cause of Czech independence and died a few days later in a hospital ward. Czechs are keen on anniversaries. Huge demonstrations swept the city on the 20th anniversary of Palach's death. These led, 10 months later, to the overthrow of the Czech communist government.

This grand square is a gallery of modern **architectural styles**. As you wander downhill, notice the fun mix, all post-1850: Romantic neo-Gothic, neo-Renaissance, and neo-Baroque from the 19th century; Art Nouveau from around 1900; ugly functionalism from the mid-20th century (the "form follows function" and "ornamentation is a crime" answer to Art Nouveau); Stalin Gothic from the 1950s "communist epoch" (a good example is the Jalta building, halfway downhill on the right); and the glass-and-steel buildings of the 1970s.

Walk a couple of blocks downhill through the real people of Prague (not tourists) to **Grand Hotel Evropa,** with its hard-to-miss, dazzling Art Nouveau exterior and plush café interior full of tourists.

In **November of 1989,** this huge square was filled every evening with more than 300,000 ecstatic Czechs and Slovaks believing freedom was at hand. Assembled on the balcony of the building opposite Grand Hotel Evropa (look for the *Marks & Spencer* sign) were a priest, a rock star (famous for his unconventional style, which constantly unnerved the regime), Alexander Dubček (hero of the 1968 revolt), and Václav Havel (the charismatic playwright, newly released from prison, who was every freedom-loving Czech's Mandela). Through a sound system provided by the rock star, Havel's voice boomed over the gathered masses, announcing the resignation of the politburo and saying that the Republic of Czechoslovakia's freedom was imminent. Picture that cold November evening, with thousands of Czechs jingling their keychains in solidarity, chanting at the government, "It's time to go now!" (To quell this revolt, government tanks could have given it the Tiananmen Square treatment—which spilled lots of patriotic blood in China just 6 months earlier. Locals believe Gorbachev must have made a phone call recommending that blood not be shed over this.) For more on the events leading up to this climactic rally, see "Národní Třída and the Velvet Revolution" on page 90.

Immediately opposite Grand Hotel Evropa is the **Lucerna Gallery** (use entry marked *Divadlo Rokoko* and walk straight in). This is a grand mall from the 1930s, with shops, theaters, a ballroom in the basement, and the fine Lucerna Café upstairs. You'll see a sculpture—called *Wenceslas Riding an Upside-Down Horse*—hanging like a swing from a glass dome. David Černý, who created the statue in 1999, is the Czech Republic's most original contemporary artist. Always aspiring to provoke controversy, Černý has painted a legendary Russian tank pink, attached crawling babies to the rocket-like Žižkov TV tower, defecated inside the National Gallery to protest the policies of its director, and sunk a shark-like Saddam Hussein inside an aquarium for a 2005 exhibition. The Lucerna building (which also includes luxury apartments and offices) was built and until recently owned by Václav Havel's family. Inside are also a **Ticketpro box office** (with all available tickets, daily 9:30–18:00), a lavish 1930s Prague cinema (which shows artsy films in Czech with English subtitles, or vice versa, 110 Kč), and the popular **Lucerna Music Bar** in the basement (disco themes from the '70s, '80s, and '90s, 100 Kč, nightly from 21:00—see page 150).

Directly across busy Vodičkova street (with a handy tram stop) is the Světozor mall. Inside you'll find the **World of Fruit Bar Světozor**; it's every local's favorite ice-cream joint. True to its name, the bar tops its ice cream with every species of fruit. They sell cakes and milkshakes, too. Ask at the counter for an English menu.

Farther down the mall on the left is the entrance to a peaceful **Franciscan Garden** (Františkánská Zahrada). Its white benches and spreading rosebushes are a universe away from the fast beat of the city that throbs behind the buildings surrounding the garden.

Back on Wenceslas Square, if you're in the mood for a mellow hippie teahouse, consider a break at **Dobrá Čajovna** (literally, "Good Teahouse") near the bottom of the square (#14—see page 141). Or, if you'd like an old-time wine bar, pop into the plain

Šenk Vrbovec (nearby at #10); it comes with a whiff of the communist days, embracing the faintest bits of genteel culture from an age when refinement was sacrificed for the good of the working class. They serve traditional drinks, Czech keg wine, Moravian wines (listed on blackboard outside), *becherovka* (the 13-herb liqueur), and—only in autumn—*burčák* (this young wine tastes like grape juice halfway to wine).

The bottom of Wenceslas Square is called **Můstek,** which means "Bridge"; a bridge used to cross a moat here, allowing entrance into the Old Town (you can still see the original Old Town entrance down in the Metro station).

Running to the right from the bottom of Wenceslas Square is the street called **Na Příkopě** (meaning "On the Moat"). This busy boulevard follows the line of the Old Town wall, leading to one of the wall's former gates, the Powder Tower. Along the way, it passes the Museum of Communism (see page 89) and several of Prague's top Art Nouveau sights (see below). City tour buses (see page 59) leave from along this street, which offers plenty of shopping temptations (such as these malls: Slovanský Dům at Na Příkopě 22, and Černá Růže at Na Příkopě 12, next door to Mosers, with a crystal showroom upstairs).

Na Příkopě: Art Noveau Prague

Stroll up Na Příkopě to take in two of Prague's best Art Nouveau sights. The first one is on the street called Panská (turn right up the first street you reach as you walk up Na Příkopě from Wenceslas Square); the second is two blocks farther up Na Příkopě, next to the big, Gothic Powder Tower.

▲▲**Mucha Museum** —This is one of Europe's most enjoyable little museums. I find the art of Alfons Mucha (MOO-kah, 1860–1939) insistently likeable. See the crucifixion scene he painted as an eight-year-old boy. Read how this popular Czech artist's posters, filled with Czech symbols and expressing his people's ideals and aspirations, were patriotic banners that aroused the national spirit. And check out the photographs of his models. With the help of this abundant supply of slinky models, Mucha was a founding father of the Art Nouveau movement. Prague isn't much on museums, but, if you're into Art Nouveau, this one is great. Partly overseen by Mucha's grandson, it's two blocks off Wenceslas Square and wonderfully displayed on one comfortable floor (120 Kč, daily 10:00–18:00, Panská 7, tel. 224-233-355, www.mucha.cz). While the exhibit is well-described in English, the 30-Kč English brochure on the art is a good supplement. The included 30-minute video is definitely worthwhile (in English, ask for the starting time upon entry); it describes the main project of Mucha's life—the *Slavic Epic,* now on display in Moravský Krumlov (see page 237).

Art Nouveau

Prague is the best Art Nouveau town in Europe, with fun-loving facades gracing streets all over town. Art Nouveau, born in Paris, is "nouveau" because it wasn't inspired by Rome. It's

neo-nothing...a fresh answer to all the revival styles of the later 19th century and an organic response to the Eiffel Tower art of the Industrial Age. The style liberated the artist in each architect. Notice the unique curves and motifs on each Art Nouveau facade, which express originality. Artists such as Alfons Mucha believed that the style should include all facets of daily life. They designed everything from buildings and furniture to typefaces and cigarette packs.

Prague's three top Art Nouveau architects are Jan Koula, Josef Fanta, and a guy (Osvald Polivka) whose last name means "soup" in Czech (think "Cola, Fanta, and Soup"—easy to remember and impress your local friends).

Prague's Art Nouveau highlights include the facades lining the streets of the Jewish Quarter, the Mucha window in St. Vitus Cathedral, and Grand Hotel Evropa on Wenceslas Square. The top two places for Art Nouveau fans are the Mucha Museum and the Municipal House.

Coming back to Na Příkopě and continuing toward the Powder Tower, notice the neo-Renaissance **Živnostenská Banka** building on the corner of Nekázanka. It houses a modern bank with classy 19th-century ambience (enter and peek into the main hall upstairs).

At the end of Na Příkopě, you'll arrive at the...

▲**Municipal House (Obecní Dům)**—The Municipal House is the "pearl of Czech Art Nouveau" (built 1905–1911). It features Prague's largest concert hall, a great Art Nouveau café, and two other restaurants. Pop in and wander around the lobby of the concert hall. Walk through to the ticket office on the ground floor. Most days, there are guided tours through the Municipal

House that show you all the halls worth seeing. Then choose your place for a meal or drink (for suggestions, see page 134).

Standing in front of the Municipal House, you can survey four different styles of architecture. First,  enjoy the pure Art Nouveau of the Municipal House itself. Featuring a goddess-like Praha presiding over a land of peace and high culture, the *Homage to Prague* mosaic on the building's striking facade stoked cultural pride and nationalist sentiment. Across the street, the classical fixer-upper from 1815 was the customs house (soon to be renovated). The stark national bank building (Česká Národní Banka) is textbook functionalism from the 1930s. And the big, black Powder Tower (not worth touring inside) was the Gothic gate of the town wall, built to house the city's gunpowder. The decoration on the tower, portraying Czech kings, is the best 15th-century sculpture in town. If you go through the tower, you'll reach Celetná street, which leads past a few sights to the Old Town Square (see page 61).

Národní Třída: Communist Prague

From Můstek at the bottom of Wenceslas Square, you can head west (in the opposite direction from Na Příkopě and the Art Nouveau sights) for an interesting stroll through urban Prague to the National Theatre and the Vltava River. Before starting the walk, consider dropping into the Museum of Communism, a few steps down Na Příkopě (on the right).

▲**Museum of Communism**—This museum traces the story of communism in Prague: the origins, dream, reality, and nightmare; the cult of personality; and finally, the Velvet Revolution. Along the way, it gives a fascinating review of the Czech Republic's 40-year stint with Soviet economics. You'll find propaganda posters, busts of communist All-Stars (Marx, Lenin, Stalin), a photograph of the massive stone Stalin that overlooked Prague until 1962, and re-created slices of communist life—from a bland store counter to a typical classroom (with a poem on the chalkboard extolling the virtues of the tractor). Don't miss the 20-minute video (which plays continuously) showing how the Czech people chafed under the big red yoke from the 1950s through 1989 (180 Kč, daily 9:00–21:00, Na Příkopě 10, above a McDonald's and next to a casino—Lenin would turn over in his grave, tel. 224-212-966, www.museumofcommunism.com).

Prague: Pre-1989

It's hard to imagine the gray and bleak Prague of the communist era. Before 1989, the city was a wistful jumble of possibility. Cobbled lanes were shadowed by sooty, crusty buildings. Timbers—strung across the lanes like laundry lines—held crumbling buildings apart. Consumer goods were plain and uniform, stacked like Legos on the thin shelves in shops where customers waited in line for a tin of ham or a bottle of ersatz Coke. The Charles Bridge was as black as its statues, with no commerce except for a few shady characters trying to change money. Hotels had two price schedules: one for people of the Warsaw Pact nations and another (6 to 8 times as expensive) for capitalists. This made the run-down, Soviet-style hotels as expensive as fine Western ones. At the train station, frightened but desperate characters would meet arriving foreigners to rent them a room in their flat, in order to get enough hard Western cash to buy batteries or Levis at one of the hard-currency stores.

Now head for the river (with your back to Wenceslas Square, go left down 28 Října to Národní Třída). Along the way, Národní Třída has a story to tell.

Národní Třída and the Velvet Revolution—Národní Třída, the street that connects Wenceslas Square with the National Theatre and the river, is a busy thoroughfare running through the heart of urban Prague. In 1989, this unassuming boulevard played host to the first salvo of a Velvet Revolution that would topple the communist regime.

Make your way down Národní Třída until you hit the tram tracks (just beyond the Tesco department store). On the left, look for the photo of Bill Clinton playing saxophone, with Václav Havel on the side (this is the entrance to Reduta, Prague's best jazz club—see page 150). Just beyond that, you'll come to a short corridor with white arches. Inside this arcade is a simple memorial to the hundreds of students injured here by the police on November 17, 1989. That afternoon, 30,000 students gathered in Prague's New Town to commemorate the 50th anniversary of the suppression of student protests by the Nazis, which had led to the closing of Czech universities through the end of World War II. The 1989 demonstration—initially planned by the Communist Youth as a celebration of the communist victory over fascism—spontaneously turned into a protest *against* the communist regime. "You are just like the Nazis!" shouted the students. The demonstration was planned to end in the National Cemetery at Vyšehrad (the hill just south of the New Town). But when the planned events concluded in Vyšehrad, the students decided to march on towards Wenceslas Square to make history.

As they worked their way north along the Vltava River towards the New Town's main square, the students were careful to keep their demonstration peaceful. Any hint of violence, the demonstrators knew, would incite brutal police retaliation. In fact, as the evening went on, the absence of police became conspicuous. (In the 1980s, the police never missed a chance to participate in any demonstration... preferably outnumbering the demonstrators). At about 20:00, as the students marched down this very stretch of street towards Wenceslas Square, three rows of policemen suddenly blocked the demonstration at the corner of Národní and Spálená streets. A few minutes later, military vehicles with fences on their bumpers (having crossed the bridge by the National Theatre) appeared behind the marching students. This new set of cops compressed the demonstrators into the stretch of Národní Třída between Voršilská and Spálená. The end of Mikulandská street was also blocked, and policemen were hiding inside every house entry. The students were trapped.

At 21:30, the "Red Hats" (a special anti-riot commando force known for its brutality) arrived. The Red Hats lined up on both sides of this corridor. To get out, the trapped students had to run through the passageway as they were beaten from the left and right. Police trucks ferried students around the corner to the headquarters of the secret police (on Bartolomějská) for interrogation.

The next day, university students throughout Czechoslovakia decided to strike. Actors from theaters in Prague and Bratislava joined the student protest. Two days later, the students' parents—shocked by the attacks on their children—marched into Wenceslas Square. The wave of peaceful demonstrations sparked by the events of November 17, 1989, ended later that year on December 29 with the election of Václav Havel as the president of a free Czechoslovakia.

Along the Vltava River

I've listed these sights from north to south, beginning at the grand, neo-Renaissance National Theatre, which is five blocks south of Charles Bridge and stands along the riverbank at the end of Národní Třída.

National Theatre (Národní Divadlo)—Opened in 1883 with Smetana's opera *Libuše*, this theater was the first truly Czech venue in Prague. From the very start, it was nicknamed

the "Cradle of Czech Culture." The building is a key symbol of the Czech national revival that began in the late 18th century. In 1800, "Prag" was predominantly German. The Industrial Revolution brought Czechs from the countryside into the city, their new urban identity defined by patriotic teachers and priests. By 1883, most of the city spoke Czech, and the opening of this theater represented the birth of the modern Czech nation. It remains an important national icon: The state annually pours more subsidies into this theater than into all of Czech film production. It's the most beautiful venue in town for opera or ballet, often with world-class singers on stage (see page 148).

Next door (just inland, on Národní Třída) is the boxy, glassy facade of the **Nová Scéna**. This "New National Theatre" building, dating from 1983 (the 100th anniversary of the original National Theatre building), reflects the bold and stark communist aesthetic.

Across the street from the National Theatre is the former haunt of Prague's intelligentsia, **Grand Café Slavia,** a Viennese-style coffeehouse fine for a meal or drink with a view of the river.

Just south of the National Theatre in the Vltava, you'll find...

Prague's Islands—From the National Theatre, the Legions' Bridge (Most Legií) leads across the island called **Střelecký Ostrov.** Covered with chestnut trees, this island boasts Prague's best beach (on the sandy tip that points north to Charles Bridge). You might see a fisherman pulling out trout from a river that's now much cleaner than it used to be. Bring a swimsuit and take a dip just a stone's throw from Europe's most beloved bridge. In summer, the island hosts open-air movies (most in English or with English subtitles, nightly mid-July–early Sept at around 21:00, www.strelak.cz).

In the mood for boating instead of swimming? On the next island down, **Slovanský Ostrov,** you can rent a paddleboat (bring a picture ID as deposit). You'll also find a 19th-century palace that houses the fancy Restaurant Žofín (see page 135).

A 10-minute walk (or one stop on tram #17) from the National Theatre, beyond the islands, is Jirásek Bridge (Jiráskův Most), where you'll find the...

Dancing House (Tančící Dům)—If ever a building could get your toes tapping, it would be this one, nicknamed "Fred and Ginger" by American architecture buffs. This metallic samba is the work of Frank Gehry (who designed the equally striking Guggenheim

Museum in Bilbao, Spain, and Seattle's Experience Music Project). Eight-legged Ginger's wispy dress and Fred's metal mesh head are easy to spot. The building's top-floor restaurant, La Perle de Prague, is a fine place for a fancy meal (see page 136).

Of course, most Czechs have never heard of Fred and Ginger. They prefer to think that the two "figures" represent the nation's greatest 20th-century heroes, the WWII paratroopers Gabčík and Kubiš. Their 1942 assassination of Reinhard Heydrich, who controlled the Nazi-occupied Czech lands, was the most significant act of Czech resistance. German retaliation was violent. Hundreds of Czechs were executed and two villages—Lidice and Ležáky— were summarily razed to the ground. In the weeks following the assassination, the two paratroopers hid along with other freedom fighters in the crypt of the **Greek Orthodox Church** on Resslova street, one block up from the Dancing House. One soldier betrayed the others. Gestapo surrounded the church. To escape capture, each of the men inside the church saved his last bullet for himself. Today, the crypt of that church shelters a modest exhibition on the history of the Czech resistance movement.

Three blocks up Resslova street is...

Charles Square (Karlovo Náměstí) —Prague's largest square is covered by lawns, trees, and statues of Czech writers. It's a quiet antidote to the bustling Wenceslas and Old Town Squares. The Gothic New Town Hall at the top-left corner of the square has excellent views and labeled panoramic photographs that help you orient yourself to what you see. The little parlor across the street has the best Italian ice cream in town.

THE LITTLE QUARTER
(Malá Strana)

This charming neighborhood, huddled under the castle on the west bank of the river, is low on blockbuster sights but high on ambience. The most enjoyable approach from the Old Town is across Charles Bridge. From the end of the bridge (TI in tower), Mostecká street leads two blocks up to the Little Quarter Square (Malostranské Náměstí) and the huge Church of St. Nicholas. But before you head up there, consider a detour to Kampa Island (all described below).

Between Charles Bridge and Little Quarter Square

Kampa Island—One hundred yards before the castle end of the Charles Bridge, stairs on the left lead down to the main square

of Kampa Island (mostly created from the rubble of the Little Quarter, which was destroyed in a 1540 fire). The island features relaxing pubs, a breezy park, a new art gallery, and river access. From the main square, Hroznová lane (on the right) leads to a bridge. To the left of the bridge, notice the high-water marks from

the flood of August 2002. The water mill is the last survivor of many that once lined the canal here. Each mill once had its own protective water spirit *(vodník)*. Today only one wheel—and one spirit (Mr. Kabourek)—remain.

Fifty yards beyond the bridge is the...

Lennon Wall (Lennonova Zeď)—While the ideas of Lenin hung like a water-soaked trench coat upon the Czech people, the ideas

Prague's Little Quarter

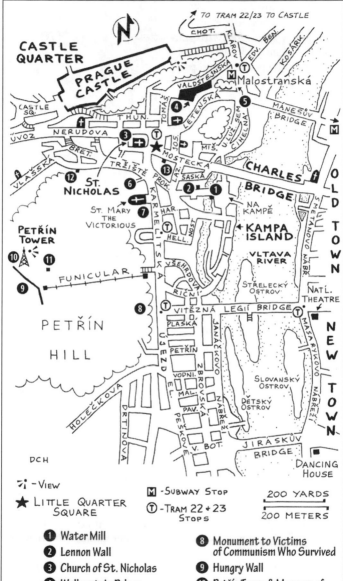

Map labels:

TO TRAM 22/23 TO CASTLE

CASTLE QUARTER

PRAGUE CASTLE

CHOT.

KLAROV

EDV. BEN.

KOSARK.

Malostranská

VALDŠTEJNSKÁ

MÁNESŮV BRIDGE

CASTLE SQ.

THUN.

NERUDOVA

UVOZ

BRET.

VLASSKA

TRŽIŠTĚ

St. NICHOLAS

St. MARY THE VICTORIOUS

KARMELITSKA

TOMÁŠ.

LETENSKÁ

U LUŽ SEM.

CIHELNÁ

MOSTECKÁ

ŠASKÁ

PROK.

LÁZ.

CHARLES BRIDGE

NA KAMPĚ

KAMPA ISLAND

VLTAVA RIVER

OLD TOWN

PETŘÍN Tower

FUNICULAR

HAR.

HELL.

VŠEHRDOVA

ŘIČNÍ

STŘELECKÝ OSTROV

SMETANOVO NÁBŘ.

NÁTL. THEATRE

PETŘÍN HILL

VÍTĚZNÁ

PLASKÁ

LEGIÍ BRIDGE

NEW TOWN

HOLEČKOVA

DRTINOVA

ÚJEZD

PETŘÍN

JANÁČKOVO

VODNI.

MAL.

PAV.

ZBROVSKA

PESKOVE

 V. BOT.

SLOVANSKÝ OSTROV

DĚTSKÝ OSTROV

MASARYKOVO NÁBŘEŽI

JIRÁSKŮV BRIDGE

DANCING HOUSE

DCH

Legend:

⛰ – VIEW

★ LITTLE QUARTER SQUARE

Ⓜ – SUBWAY STOP

Ⓣ – TRAM 22 + 23 STOPS

200 YARDS

200 METERS

1. Water Mill
2. Lennon Wall
3. Church of St. Nicholas
4. Wallenstein Palace
5. Wallenstein Garden
6. Vrtba Garden
7. Church of St. Mary the Victorious
8. Monument to Victims of Communism Who Survived
9. Hungry Wall
10. Petřín Tower & Museum of Jára Cimrman
11. Mirror Maze
12. U. S. Embassy
13. Torture Museum

of rock singer John Lennon gave many locals hope and a vision. When Lennon was killed in 1980, a memorial wall covered with graffiti spontaneously appeared. Night after night, the police would paint over the "All You Need Is Love" and "Imagine" graffiti. And day after day, it would reappear. Until  independence came in 1989, travelers, freedom-lovers, and local hippies gathered here. Silly as it might seem, this wall is remembered as a place that gave hope to locals craving freedom. Even today, while the tension and danger associated with this wall is gone, people come here to imagine.

From here, you can continue up to Little Quarter Square. Just before the square, on Mostecká street, is Prague's...

Torture Museum—This gimmicky moneymaker is similar to other European torture museums, but is interesting nevertheless, showing models of 60 gruesome medieval tortures with well-written English descriptions (120 Kč, daily 10:00–22:00, just below Little Quarter Square at Mostecká 21, tel. 224-215-581).

On or near Little Quarter Square (Malostranské Náměstí)

The focal point of this neighborhood, Little Quarter Square (Malostranské Náměstí), is dominated by the huge Church of St. Nicholas.

Church of St. Nicholas (Kostel Sv. Mikuláše)—When the Jesuits came to Prague in the 18th century, they found the perfect piece of real estate for their church and its associated school—right on Little Quarter Square. The church (built 1703–1760) is the best example of High Baroque in town (50 Kč, daily 9:00–17:00, opens at 8:30 for prayer). It's giddy with curves and illusions. The altar features a lavish gold-plated Nicholas flanked by the two top Jesuits: the founder, St. Ignatius Loyola and his missionary follower, St. Francis Xavier. Climb up the **gallery** through the staircase in the right transept to look at a collection of large canvases by Karel Škréta, the greatest Czech Baroque painter. Notice that at first glance, the canvases are utterly dark. But as sunbeams shine through the window, various parts of the painting brighten up. Like a looking-glass, it reflects the light, creating a play of light and darkness. This painting technique reflects a central Baroque belief: The world is full of darkness, and the only hope that makes it come alive comes from God. The walls seem to nearly fuse with the sky, suggesting that happenings on earth are closely connected to heaven.

For a good look at the city and the church's 250-foot dome, climb the **bell tower** (30 Kč, April–Oct daily 10:00–18:00, closed Nov–March, tower entrance is outside the right transept). The Little Quarter residents prized their ancient church bells, which they believed carried the soul of their neighborhood. So before the Jesuits were given permission to build, they had to promise the Little Quarter councilmen that the bell tower standing in the middle of the square would remain untouched, or that a new one would be built. The new bell tower had to be as prominent as the church's dome. That's why this tower can be seen before the dome from any of the streets approaching the square—and why it offers such commanding views over the Little Quarter.

The church is also a **concert** venue in evenings; 400-Kč tickets are generally on sale at the door (www.psalterium.cz).

From here, you can hike 10 minutes uphill to the castle (and 5 more min to the Strahov Monastery). For information on these sights, see the next chapter. If you're walking up to the castle, consider going via...

Nerudova Street—This steep, cobbled street, leading from Little Quarter Square to the castle, is named for Jan Neruda, a gifted 19th-century journalist (and somewhat less talented fiction writer). It's lined with old buildings still sporting the characteristic doorway signs (e.g., the lion, 3 violinists, house of the golden suns) that once served as street addresses. The surviving signs are carefully restored and protected by law. They represent the family name, the occupation, or the various passions of the people who once inhabited the houses. In 1777, in order to collect taxes more effectively, Hapsburg empress Maria Theresa decreed that numbers be used instead of these quaint house names. This neighborhood is filled with old noble palaces, now generally used as foreign embassies and offices of the Czech parliament.

North of Little Quarter Square, near Malostranská Metro Station

Near the Malostranská Metro station, a few blocks north of Little Quarter Square, is this fine mansion and garden. If you want to reach Little Quarter Square from here, follow Valdštejnská street.

Wallenstein Palace (Valdštejnský Palác)—Of the neighborhood's many impressive palaces, this one is by far the largest and most beautiful. Commissioned by the Hapsburg general and Czech nobleman Albrecht z Valdštejna (or, in German, Albrecht von Wallenstein) during the Thirty Years' War, the complex is a testimony to what a great business war can be for an unscrupulous individual. For 21 years (1618–1639), the mercenary Albrecht conspired with all sides involved in the war. He was the banker of the Czech Estates Uprising until he ran off to Vienna with the money

Jára Cimrman:
When Optimists Should Be Shot

"I am such a complete atheist that I am afraid God will punish me." Such is the pithy wisdom of Jára Cimrman, the man overwhelmingly voted the "Greatest Czech of All Time" in a nationwide poll in 2005. Who is Jára Cimrman? A philosopher? An explorer? An inventor? He is all of these things, yes, and much more.

Born in the mid-19th century to a Czech tailor of Jewish descent and an Austrian actress, Cimrman studied in Vienna before starting off on his journeys around the world. He traversed the Atlantic by a steamboat he designed himself, taught drama to peasants in Peru, and drifted across the Arctic Sea on an iceberg. Other astounding feats soon followed. Cimrman was the first to come within 20 feet of the North Pole. He was the first to invent the light bulb (unfortunately, Edison beat him to the patent office by 5 minutes). It was he who suggested to the Americans the idea for a Panama Canal, though, as usual, he was never credited. Indeed, Cimrman surreptitiously advised many of the world's greats: Eiffel on his tower, Einstein on his theories of relativity, Chekhov on his plays. ("You can't just have *two* sisters," Cimrman told the playwright. "How about three?") In 1886, long before the world knew of Sartre or Camus, Cimrman was writing tracts such as *The Essence of the Existence*, which would become the foundation for his philosophy of "Cimrmanism," also known as "Non-Existentialism." (Its central premise: "Existence cannot not exist.")

This man of unmatched genius would have won the honor of "Greatest Czech of All Time" if not for the bureaucratic narrow-mindedness of the poll's sponsors, who had a single objection to Cimrman's candidacy: "He's not real." Jára Cimrman is the brainchild of two Czech humorists—Zdeněk Svěrák and Jiří Šebánek—who brought their patriotic Renaissance man to life in 1967 in a satirical radio play. So, even though Cimrman handily won the initial balloting in January, Czech TV officials—blatantly biased against his non-existentialism—refused to let him into the final rounds of the competition.

How should we interpret the fact that the Czechs would

to join the Hapsburgs. Plundering territories in the name of the Catholic faith, Albrecht followed his own simple rule: half for the emperor, half for myself. When Hapsburg favors waned, Albrecht secretly negotiated with the Swedes. When desperate Hapsburgs put him in charge of their armies once again, he continued to play both sides. Finally, somebody had enough: Albrecht was murdered in his bedroom in 1639.

rather choose a fictional character as their greatest countryman over any of their flesh-and-blood national heroes—say, Charles IV (the 14th-century Holy Roman Emperor who established Prague as the cultural and intellectual capital of Europe), Jan Hus (the 15th-century religious reformer who challenged the legitimacy of the Catholic Church), Comenius (the 17th-century educator and writer considered one of the fathers of modern education), or Martina Navrátilová (someone who plays a sport with bright green balls)? The more cynically inclined—many Czechs among them—might point out that the Czech people have largely stayed behind their mountains for the past millennia, with little interest in, or influence on, happenings elsewhere in the world. Perhaps Cimrman is so beloved because he embodies that most prickly of ironies: a Czech who was greater than all the world's greats, but who for some hiccup of chance has never been recognized for his achievements.

Personally, I like to think that the vote for Cimrman says something about the country's rousing enthusiasm for blowing raspberries in the face of authority. Throughout its history—from the times of the Czech kings who used crafty diplomacy to keep the German menace at bay, to the days of Jan Hus and his questioning of the very legitimacy of any ruler's power, to the flashes of anti-communist revolt that at last sparked the Velvet Revolution in 1989—the Czechs have maintained a healthy disrespect for those who would tell them what is best or how to live their lives. Other countries soberly choose their "Greatest" from musty tomes of history, but the Czechs won't play this silly game. Their vote for a fictional personage, says Cimrman's co-creator Svěrák, says two things about the Czech nation: "That it is skeptical about those who are major figures and those who are supposedly 'the Greatest.' And that the only certainty that has saved the nation many times throughout history is its humor."

Cimrman would agree. A man of greatness, he was always a bit skeptical of those who saw themselves as great, or who marched forward under the banner of greatness. As Cimrman liked to say, "There are moments when optimists should be shot."

The inconspicuous entry to the palace's **Wallenstein Garden** (Valdštejnská Zahrada) is by the Malostranská Metro station (free, April–Oct daily 10:00–18:00, closed Nov–March). The garden, renovated in the late 1990s, features a large pool surrounded by peacocks. The statues that line the central walkway, inspired by Greek mythology, were done by the Danish artist Adrian de Vries—arguably the best Renaissance sculptor outside Italy. Notice the elegant classical shapes, a sharp contrast to the chubbiness of the Baroque figures on the Charles Bridge and elsewhere in the city. The original statues were stolen by invading Swedish armies in 1648, and are still in Sweden; the present replicas were cast in the early 1900s.

The Renaissance garden and the palace were built by Italian architects, just like most of the Little Quarter. The *sala terena* is a drama and music stage inspired by Greek amphitheaters. Notice the unusual pairing of columns—at the time, a trendy invention of the Italian architect Palladio. The gory depictions of the Trojan War inside tell you about the taste and character of the owner. The bizarre wall on the left was an expression of an uncertain age. It creates the illusion of caves and holes, stalagmites and stalactites. Look for the sculpted elves, snakes, chameleons, and frogs. The wall continues into a cage with live owls that completes the transition from dead to living nature. The twisted cries of the owls deepen the surreal sensation of the place. Exit through the door in the right corner of the garden by the *sala terena.* You'll pass into a small courtyard surrounded by what once was the residential part of the palace. Today the upper chamber of the Czech parliament meets inside.

For a terraced Baroque garden to compare to this Renaissance one, visit the **Vrtba Garden** (Vrtbovská Zahrada, 100 Kč, daily 10:00–18:00; just south of Little Quarter Square, on Karmelitská before the Church of St. Mary the Victorious—see below).

South of Little Quarter Square, to Petřín Hill

Karmelitská street, leading south (along the tram tracks) from Little Quarter Square, is home to these sights.

Church of St. Mary the Victorious (Kostel Panny Marie Vítězné)—This otherwise ordinary Carmelite church displays Prague's most precious jewel, the Infant of Prague (Pražské Jezulátko). Brought to the Czech lands during the Hapsburg era by a Spanish noblewoman who came to marry a Czech nobleman, the Infant has become a focus of worship and miracle tales in Prague and Spanish-speaking countries. South Americans come on pilgrimage to Prague just to see this one statue (free, Mon–Sat 10:00–17:30, Sun 13:00–17:00, Karmelitská 9, www.pragjesu.com).

Continue a few more blocks down Karmelitská to the south end of the Little Quarter (where the street is called Újezd, roughly across the Legions' Bridge from the National Theatre). Here you find yourself at the base of...

Petřín Hill—This hill, topped by a replica of the Eiffel Tower, features several offbeat sights.

The figures walking down the steps in the hillside make up the **Monument to Victims of Communism Who Survived.** These figures are gradually atrophied by the totalitarian regime. They do not die, but gradually disappear. To the left of the monument is the **Hungry Wall,** the 14th-century Charles IV's equivalent of FDR's work-for-food projects. On the right is the base of a handy **funicular**—hop on to reach Petřín Tower (uses 20-Kč tram/Metro ticket, runs daily, every 10–15 min from 8:00–22:00).

The summit of Petřín Hill is considered the best place in Prague to take your date for a romantic city view. Built for an exhibition in 1891, the 200-foot-tall **Petřín Tower** is a fifth the height of its Parisian big brother built two years earlier. But, thanks to this hill, the top of the tower sits at the same elevation as the real Eiffel Tower. You can take the spiral stairs (on the left) leading up to several rooms with painted coats of arms and no English explanations, or better, climb the 400 steps for amazing views over the city.

In the basement of the tower is the funniest sight in Prague, the **Museum of Jára Cimrman, Genius Who Did Not Become Famous.** The museum traces Cimrman's (fictional) life, including pictures and descriptions of the thinker's overlooked inventions (50 Kč, daily 10:00–22:00). For more on the mysterious Cimrman, see the sidebar on page 98.

The **mirror maze** next door is nothing special, but fun to quickly wander through since you're already here (50 Kč, daily 10:00–22:00).

THE CASTLE QUARTER

(Hradčany)

Looming above Prague, dominating its skyline, is the Castle Quarter. Prague Castle and its surrounding sights are packed with Czech history as well as with tourists. In addition to the castle itself, I enjoy visiting the nearby Strahov Monastery—with a fun old library and beautiful views over all of Prague.

Castle Square (Hradčanské Náměstí)—right in front of the castle gates—is at the center of this neighborhood. Stretching along the promontory away from the castle is a regal neighborhood that ends at the Strahov Monastery. Above the castle are the Royal Gardens, and below the castle are more gardens and lanes leading down to the Little Quarter.

Getting to Prague Castle

If you're not up for a hike, the tram offers a sweat-free ride to the castle.

By Foot: Begin in the Little Quarter (see page 94), just across Charles Bridge from the Old Town. Hikers can follow the main cobbled road (Mostecká) from Charles Bridge to Little Quarter Square, marked by the huge, green-domed Church of St. Nicholas. (The nearest Metro stop is Malostranská, from which Valdštejnská street leads down to Little Quarter Square.) From Little Quarter Square, hike uphill along Nerudova street (described on page 97). After about 10 minutes, a steep lane on the right leads to the castle. (If you continue straight, Nerudova becomes Úvoz and climbs to the Strahov Monastery.)

By Tram: Trams #22 and #23 take you up to the castle. While you can catch the tram in various places, these three stops are particularly convenient: at the Národní Třída Metro stop (between Wenceslas Square and the National Theatre in the New Town); in front of the National Theatre (Národní Divadlo, on the riverbank

Prague's Castle Quarter

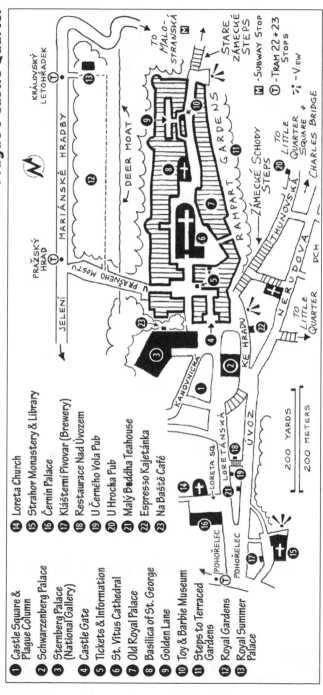

1. Castle Square & Plague Column
2. Schwarzenberg Palace
3. Sternberg Palace (National Gallery)
4. Castle Gate
5. Tickets & Information
6. St. Vitus Cathedral
7. Old Royal Palace
8. Basilica of St. George
9. Golden Lane
10. Toy & Barbie Museum
11. Steps to Terraced Gardens
12. Royal Gardens
13. Royal Summer Palace
14. Loreta Church
15. Strahov Monastery & Library
16. Černín Palace
17. Klášterní Pivovar (Brewery)
18. Restaurace Nad Úvozem
19. U Černého Vola Pub
20. U Hrocha Pub
21. Malý Buddha Teahouse
22. Espresso Kajetánka
23. Na Baště Café

M - Subway Stop
T - Tram 22 + 23 Stops
🔆 - View

in the New Town); and at Malostranská (the Metro stop in the Little Quarter). After rattling up the hill, these trams make three stops near the castle: Get off at **Královský Letohrádek** for the scenic approach to the castle (through the Royal Gardens—see below); or stay on one more stop to get off at **Pražský Hrad** (most direct but least interesting—simply walk along U Prašného Mostu over the bridge into Castle Square); or go yet one more stop to **Pohořelec** to visit the Strahov Monastery (from the stop, go uphill and through the gate toward the twin spires) before hiking down to the castle.

Tram Tips: When you're choosing which of the castle's three tram stops to get off at, consider the time of day. The castle is plagued with crowds. If visiting in the morning, use the Pražský Hrad tram stop for the quickest commute to the castle. Be at the door of St. Vitus Cathedral when it opens at 9:00 (just 10–15 minutes later, it's swamped with tour groups). See the castle sights quickly, then move on to the Strahov Monastery. I'd avoid the castle entirely mid-morning, but by mid-afternoon, the tour groups are napping and the grounds are (relatively) uncrowded. If going in the afternoon, take the tram to the Pohořelec stop, see the Strahov Monastery, then wander down to the castle.

Above the Castle, near the Královský Letohrádek Tram Stop

These sights, above Prague Castle, are only worth visiting if you get off tram #22 or #23 at Královský Letohrádek (the palace is across the street from this stop).

Royal Summer Palace (Královský Letohrádek)—This love gift is like a Czech Taj Mahal, given by Emperor Ferdinand I to his beloved Queen Anne. It's the finest Renaissance building in town. You can't go inside, but the building's detailed reliefs are worth a close look. In good Renaissance style, they're based on classical, rather than Christian, stories. The one depicted here is Virgil's *The Aeneid*. The fountain in front of the palace features the most elaborate bronzework in the country. (If you stick your head under the bottom of the fountain, you'll find out why it's called the "Singing Fountain.")

From here, you can reach the cathedral by strolling through the...

Royal Gardens (Královská Zahrada)—Once the private grounds and residence (you'll see the building) of the communist presidents, these were opened to the public with the coming of freedom under Václav Havel (April–Oct daily 10:00–18:00, closed Nov–March). Walk through these gardens (with fine views of St. Vitus Cathedral) to the gate, which leads you over the moat and into Castle Square.

Strahov Monastery and Library (Strahovský Klášter Premonstrátů a Strahovská Knihovna)

Twin Baroque domes high above the castle mark the Strahov Monastery (a 15-min hike uphill from Little Quarter, or a 5-min walk from castle). Worth ▲, this complex is best reached from the Pohořelec stop on tram #22 or #23 (from the stop, go uphill 200 yards and through the gate into the monastery grounds). After seeing the monastery, hike down to the castle.

Monastery: The monastery had a booming economy of its own in its heyday, with vineyards and the biggest beer hall in town—still open. Its main church, dedicated to the Assumption of St. Mary, is an originally Romanesque structure decorated by the monks in textbook Baroque (usually closed, but look through the window inside the front door to see its interior).

Library: The adjacent library offers a peek at how enlightened thinkers in the 18th century influenced learning (60 Kč, daily 9:00–12:00 & 13:00–17:00). Cases in the library gift shop show off illuminated manuscripts. Some are in old Czech, but these are rare. Because the Enlightenment believed in the universality of knowledge, there was  little place for vernaculars—therefore, there are few books in the Czech language. Two rooms are filled with 17th-century books under elaborately painted ceilings. The theme of the first and bigger hall is philosophy, with the history of man's pursuit of knowledge painted on the ceiling. The other hall focuses on theology. Notice the gilded locked case containing the *libri prohibiti* (prohibited books) at the end of the room. Only the abbot had the key, and you had to have his blessing to read these books—by writers such as Nicolas Copernicus and Jan Hus, even including the French encyclopedia. As the Age of Enlightenment began to take hold in Europe in the end of 18th century, monasteries still controlled the books. The hallway connecting these two library rooms was filled with cases illustrating the new practical approach to natural sciences. Find the baby dodo bird (which became extinct in the 17th century).

Nearby Views: Just downhill from the monastery and through the gate, the views from the **monastery garden** are among the best in Prague. From the public perch below the tables, you can see St. Vitus Cathedral (the heart of the castle complex), the green dome of the Church of St. Nicholas (marking the center of the Little Quarter), the two dark towers fortifying the Charles Bridge, and the fanciful black spires of the Týn Church (marking the Old Town Square). On the horizon is the modern **Žižkov TV and radio tower** (conveniently marking the liveliest nightlife zone in town—see page 151). Begun in the 1980s, it was meant to jam Radio Free Europe's broadcast from Munich. By the time it was finished, Radio Free Europe's headquarters had actually moved to Prague.

To reach the castle from Strahov Monastery, take Loretánská (the upper road, passing Loreta Square—see below); this is more interesting than going on the lower road, Úvoz, which takes you steeply downhill, below Castle Square.

On Loreta Square, between Strahov Monastery and Castle Square

Loreta Square (Loretánské Náměstí) is on Loretánská street, between the Strahov Monastery and Castle Square. As you wander this road, you'll pass several mansions and palaces, and an important pilgrimage church.

Loreta Church—This church has been a hit with pilgrims for centuries, thanks to its dazzling bell tower, peaceful yet plush cloister, sparkling treasury, and much-venerated "Holy House" (90 Kč, Tue–Sun 9:00–12:15 & 13:00–16:30, closed Mon).

The central **Santa Casa** (Holy House) was considered by some pilgrims to be part of Mary's home in Nazareth. Because many pilgrims returning from the Holy Land docked at the Italian port of Loreto, it's called the Loreta Shrine. The Santa Casa is the "little Bethlehem" of Prague. It is the traditional departure point for Czech pilgrims setting out on the long, arduous journey to Europe's most important pilgrimage site, Santiago de Compostela, in northwest Spain.

The small Baroque church behind the Santa Casa is one of the most beautiful in Prague. The frescoes on the ceilings of the ambulatory illustrate a prayer to St. Mary. The Santa Casa itself, with only a few 15th-century frescoes and an old statue of Mary, might seem like a bit of a letdown, but consider that you're entering the holiest spot in the country for generations of believers. Upstairs, the highlight is a room full of jeweled worship aids in the treasury (well-described in English). Behind vault doors, you'll squint at a monstrance (Communion wafer holder) from 1699, with over 6,000 diamonds. Enjoy the short carillon concert at the top of the hour; from the lawn in front of the main entrance, you can see the racks of bells being clanged.

European Flags Fly in the Czech Republic

Today the blue flag of the European Union flies alongside the Czech flag on the roof of government buildings, such as the Ministry of Foreign Affairs. The Czech Republic entered the EU along with nine other countries on May 1, 2004. Most Czechs are disappointed they weren't admitted much earlier.

The former president of the Czech Republic, Václav Havel, said the EU offers Europe the historic chance to finally get together and resolve issues over a table rather than on the battlefield. But there are Euro-skeptics, including the right wing, the communists, and the current Czech president, Václav Klaus, who argues that the country is surrendering too much of its autonomy to Brussels. Still, most Czechs are optimistic about their future in the EU, and the majority of the government feels that membership will benefit the country. The year following Czech entry into the EU saw the largest GDP growth since 1989, as well as growing foreign investment. Japanese and Korean companies now find it advantageous to produce in the Czech Republic, since they're exempted from EU tariffs.

On the opposite side of the square is the...

Černín Palace—This palace once belonged to one of the most cosmopolitan Czech families, and so in 1918, it was turned into the Ministry of Foreign Affairs. In May of 2005, a memorial to the first secretary of state of Czechoslovakia, Edvard Beneš, was unveiled in front of the Ministry. This second president of Czechoslovakia, who led the country from London exile during World War II, is highly controversial these days (see page 180). The tiny size of the statue expresses the nation's present uncertainty about the legacy of the man.

Notice the bust of Hana Benešová, Edvard's wife, on the nearby house where she lived for a brief period. Czechs measure their statesmen through their wives.

Castle Square (Hradčanské Náměstí)

This is the central square of the Castle Quarter. Enjoy the awesome city view and the two entertaining bands that play regularly at the gate. (If the Prague Castle Orchestra is playing, say hello to friendly, mustachioed Josef, and consider getting the group's terrific

CD.) A tranquil café called Espresso Kajetánka hides a few steps down, immediately to the right as you face the castle (see page 138). From here, stairs lead into the Little Quarter.

Castle Square was a kind of medieval Pennsylvania Avenue—the king, the most powerful noblemen, and the archbishop lived here. Look uphill from the gate. The Renaissance **Schwarzenberg Palace** (on the left, with the big rectangles scratched on the wall, now under renovation) was where the Rožmberks "humbly" stayed when they were in town from their Český Krumlov estates. The Schwarzenberg family (marvel at their coat of arms, made of human bones, in the ossuary in Kutná Hora) inherited the Krumlov estates and aristocratic prominence in Bohemia, and stayed in the palace until the 20th century.

The archbishop still lives in the yellow rococo **palace** across the square (with the 3 white goose necks in the red field—the coat of arms of Prague's archbishops).

Through the portal on the left-hand side of the palace, a lane leads to the **Sternberg Palace** (Šternberský Palác), filled with the National Gallery's skippable collection of European paintings—mostly minor works by Albrecht Dürer, Peter Paul Rubens, Rembrandt, and El Greco (100 Kč, Tue–Sun 10:00–18:00, closed Mon).

The Baroque sculpture in the middle of the square is a **plague column**, erected as a token of gratitude to the saints who saved the population from the epidemic, and an integral part of the main square of any Hapsburg town.

The statue marked *TGM* honors **Tomáš Garrigue Masaryk** (1850–1937), a university prof and a pal of Woodrow Wilson. At the end of World War I, Masaryk united the Czechs and the Slovaks into one nation and became its first president (see sidebar on page 110).

Prague Castle (Pražský Hrad)

For more than a thousand years, Czech leaders have ruled from Prague Castle. Today Prague's Castle is, by some measures, the biggest on earth. A visit here is worth ▲▲. Four stops matter, and all are explained here: St. Vitus Cathedral, Old Royal Palace, Basilica of St. George, and the Golden Lane.

Hours: Castle sights are open daily April–Oct 9:00–17:00, Nov–March 9:00–16:00, last entry 15 min before closing; the

grounds are open daily 5:00–23:00. St. Vitus Cathedral is closed Sunday mornings for Mass. Be warned that St. Vitus Cathedral can be unexpectedly closed due to special services—consider calling ahead to confirm.
Tel. 224-373-368 or 224-372-434, www.hrad.cz.

Tickets: You can choose from four different types of tickets.

Route A costs 350 Kč and includes everything: the cathedral sights (apse, crypt, and tower—note that just looking around the front part of the cathedral is free), Old Royal Palace, Basilica of St. George, Powder Tower, Golden Lane (during peak sightseeing hours—it's free in the morning and evening), and an exhibition on the castle's building history. For the thorough visit described below, opt for Route A.

Route B (220 Kč) includes the cathedral sights and Old Royal Palace.

Route C (50 Kč) gets you into the Golden Lane only, and **Route D** (50 Kč) into the Basilica of St. George only. If you want to save time and money, take Route D—tour the Basilica of St. George, wander the grounds, and explore the front half of the cathedral and peek into the tomb of Prince Wenceslas (this part of cathedral is free).

Tours: Hour-long tours in English depart from the main ticket office about three times a day, but cover only the cathedral and Old Royal Palace (80 Kč; reserve a week in advance if you want a private guide-400 Kč for up to 5 people, then 80 Kč per additional person, tel. 224-373-368). If you rent the worthwhile **audioguide** (200 Kč/2 hrs, 250 Kč/3 hrs), you won't be able to exit the castle from the bottom since you need to backtrack uphill to return the audioguide where you got it.

Crowd-Beating Tips: Huge throngs of tourists turn the castle grounds into a sea of people during peak times (9:15–15:00). St. Vitus Cathedral is the most crowded part of the castle complex. If visiting in the morning, ideally be at the cathedral entrance promptly at 9:00, when the doors open. For 10 minutes, you'll have the sacred space for yourself (after about 9:15, tour guides shouting over each other turn the church into a hawkers' square). Late afternoon is least crowded.

Tomáš Garrigue Masaryk
(1850–1937)

Masaryk was the George Washington of Czechoslovakia. He founded the first democracy in Eastern Europe at the end of World War I, uniting the Czechs and the Slovaks to create Czechoslovakia. Like Václav Havel 70 years later, Masaryk was a

politician whose vision extended far beyond the mountains enclosing the Bohemian basin.

Masaryk was born into a poor servant family in southern Moravia. After finishing high school, the village boy set off to attend university in Vienna. Masaryk earned his Ph.D. in sociology just in time for the opening of the Czech-language university in Prague. By that time, he was already married to an American music student named Charlotta Garrigue, who came from a prominent New York family. Charlotta opened the doors of America's high society to Masaryk. Among the American friends he made was a young Princeton professor named Woodrow Wilson.

Masaryk was greatly impressed with America, and his admiration for its democratic system became the core of his gradually evolving political creed. He traveled the world and went to Vienna to serve in the parliament. By the time World War I broke

Castle Gate and Courtyards—Begin at Castle Square. From here, survey the castle—the tip of a 1,500-foot-long series of courtyards, churches, and palaces. The guard changes on the hour (5:00–23:00), with the most ceremony at noon.

Walk under the fighting giants, under an arch, through the passageway, and into the courtyard. The modern green awning with the golden winged cat (just past the ticket office) marks the offices of the Czech president.

As you walk through another passageway, you'll find yourself facing...

▲▲▲St. Vitus Cathedral (Katedrála Sv. Víta)—The Roman Catholic cathedral symbolizes the Czech spirit—it contains the tombs and relics of the most important local saints and kings, including the first three Hapsburg kings.

Before entering, check out the **facade**. What's up with the guys in suits carved into the facade below the big round window? They're the architects and builders who finished the church. Started out in 1914, Masaryk was 64 years old and—his friends thought—ready for retirement. But while most other Czech politicians stayed in Prague and supported the Hapsburg Empire, Masaryk went abroad in protest and formed a highly original plan: to create an independent, democratic republic of Czechs and Slovaks. Masaryk and his supporters recruited an army of 100,000 Czechs and Slovak soldiers willing to fight with the Allies against the Hapsburgs...establishing a strong case to put on his friend Woodrow Wilson's Oval Office desk.

On the morning of October 28, 1918, news of the unofficial capitulation of the Hapsburgs reached Prague. Local supporters of Masaryk's idea quickly took control of the city and proclaimed the free republic. As the people of Prague tore down double-headed eagles (a symbol of the Hapsburgs), Czechoslovakia was born.

On November 11, 1918, four years after he had left the country as a political nobody, Masaryk arrived in Prague as the greatest Czech hero since the revolutionary priest Jan Hus. The dignified old man rode through the masses of cheering Czechs on a white horse. He told the jubilant crowd, "Now go home—the work has only started." Throughout the 1920s and 1930s, Masaryk was Europe's most vocal defender of democratic ideals against the rising tide of totalitarian ideologies.

In 2001, the U.S. government honored Masaryk's dedication to democracy by erecting a monument to him in Washington, D.C.— he is one of only three foreign leaders (along with Gandhi and Churchill) to have a statue in the American capital.

in 1344, construction was stalled by wars and plagues. But, fueled by the 19th-century rise of Czech nationalism, Prague's top church was finished in 1929 for the 1,000th anniversary of the death of St. Wenceslas. While it looks all Gothic, it's actually two distinct

halves: modern neo-Gothic and the original 14th-century Gothic. For 400 years, a temporary wall sealed off the unfinished cathedral.

Go inside and find the third **stained-glass window** on the left. This masterful 1931 Art Nouveau window is by Czech artist Alfons Mucha (if you like this, you'll love the Mucha Museum in the New Town—see page 87). Notice Mucha's stirring nationalism: Methodius and Cyril (leaders in Slavic-style Christianity) are top and center. Cyril is baptizing the

The Catholic Church in Prague

In stark contrast to Poland, the powerful Catholic Church—traditionally closely allied with the Hapsburgs and Austria—was never the favorite institution of the freedom-loving Czechs. The communists took advantage of this popular sentiment, and in their Marxist zeal did everything short of banning the Church to uproot the faith of the relatively few practicing Catholics. In the early 1950s, most monks and priests, including the archbishop,  were arrested and sent to prisons, from which they were not released until the thawing of Khrushchev era. A wise old priest remembers his 13 years in a labor camp as "a fascinating, well-spent time in the company of some truly great minds."

During the communist era, Church property was confiscated, churches quickly deteriorated, churchgoers were persecuted, and many priests had to become confidants of the secret police in order to continue their service. Ironically, by persecuting Catholics, the communists gave the Church the opportunity to improve its reputation with the Czechs. In the 1980s, the charismatic Prague archbishop Cardinal Tomášek managed to do exactly that by frequently standing up to the regime. By 1989, Tomášek was a main symbol of anti-communist opposition (along with Václav Havel).

After 1989, many Czechs returned to the Catholic faith. The trend peaked in 1992 when Tomášek died (now buried under the Mucha window in St. Vitus Cathedral). Since then, the Church's hold has steadily declined, for various reasons. The media depicts the Church as greedy; questions have arisen about the status of former church property; and the new archbishop—named Vlk (Wolf), which his critics find fitting—is uninspiring.

These days, "new" and fashionable spiritual movements, such as Buddhism, are drawing Czechs in increasing numbers. The Dalai Lama is now one of Prague's most frequent visitors.

mythic, lanky, long-haired Czech man. In the center is a kneeling boy and a prophesying elder—that's young St. Wenceslas and his grandmother, St. Ludmila. In addition to being specific historical figures, these characters are also symbolic: The old woman, with closed eyes, stands for the past and memory, while the young boy, with a penetrating stare, represents the hope and future of a nation. Notice how master designer Mucha draws your attention to these two figures through the use of colors—the dark blue on the outside gradually turns into green, then yellow, and finally the gold of the woman and the crimson of the boy in the center. In Mucha's color language, blue stands for the past, gold for the mythic, and red for  the future. Besides all the meaning, Mucha's art is simply a joy to behold.

Show your ticket and circulate around the **apse.** You'll pass a carved wood relief of Prague in 1620, depicting the victorious Hapsburg armies entering the castle after the Battle of White Mountain, while the Protestant king Frederic escapes over the Charles Bridge (before it had any statues). The second part of this Counter-Reformation wood relief, on the other side from the altar, captures the "barbaric" Protestant nobles destroying the Catholic icons in the cathedral after the Prague defeat.

A fancy roped-off chapel (right transept) houses the **tomb of St. Wenceslas,** surrounded by precious 14th-century murals showing scenes of his life (see description on page 84), and a locked door leading to the crown jewels. The Czech kings used to be crowned right here in front of the coffin, draped in red.

You can climb 287 steps up the **spire** for one of the best views of the whole city (included in Route A or B ticket, or pay 20 Kč at the cathedral ticket window, April–Oct daily except Sun morning, 9:00–17:00, last entry 16:15, closes at 16:00 in winter).

Back Outside the Cathedral: Leaving the cathedral, turn left (past the public WC). The **obelisk** was erected in 1928—a single piece of granite celebrating the 10th anniversary of the establishment of Czechoslovakia. It was originally much taller, but broke in transit—an inauspicious start for a nation destined to last only 70 years. Up in the fat, green tower of the cathedral is the Czech Republic's biggest bell, nicknamed "Zikmund." In June of 2002, it cracked—and two months later, the worst flood in recorded history hit the  city. As a nation sandwiched between great powers, Czechs are deeply superstitious. Often feeling unable to influence the course of their own history, they helplessly look at events as we might look at the weather and other natural phenomena—trying to figure out what fate has in store for them next.

Find the 14th-century **mosaic** of the Last Judgment outside on the right transept. It was commissioned Italian-style by King Charles IV, who was modern, cosmopolitan, and ahead of his time. Jesus oversees the action, as some go to heaven and some go to hell. The Czech king and queen kneel directly below Jesus and the six patron saints. On coronation day, they would walk under this arch, which would remind them (and their subjects) that even those holding great power are not above God's judgment. The royal crown and national jewels are kept in a chamber (see the grilled windows) above this entryway, which was the cathedral's main entry for centuries when the church was incomplete.

Across the square and 20 yards to the right, a door leads to the...

Old Royal Palace (Starý Královský Palác)—This was the seat of the Bohemian princes starting in the 12th century. While extensively rebuilt, the **large hall** is late Gothic, designed as a

multipurpose hall for the old nobility. It's big enough for jousts—even the staircase was designed to let a mounted soldier gallop in. It was filled with market stalls, giving nobles a chance to shop without actually going into town. In the 1400s, the nobility met here to elect their king. This tradition survived until modern times, as the parliament crowded into this room until the late 1990s to elect the Czechoslovak (and later Czech) president. (The last two elections happened in another, far more lavish hall in the castle.) Look up at the flower-shaped, vaulted ceiling—much more elaborate than the simple cross ceiling in the cathedral.

On the right, enter the two small Renaissance rooms known as the "**Czech Office**." From these rooms, two governors used to oversee the Czech lands for the Hapsburgs in Vienna. In 1618, angry Czech Protestant nobles poured into these rooms and threw the two Catholic governors out of the window, sparking the Thirty Years' War. This was the second of Prague's many "defenestrations" (see the pictures), a uniquely Czech solution to political discord, where offending politicians are literally tossed out of a window. The two governors landed—fittingly—in a pile of horse manure... so despite the height, they suffered only broken arms.

Look down on the chapel from the end, and go out on the balcony for a fine Prague view. Is that Paris' Eiffel Tower in the distance? No, it's Petřín Tower—a fine place for a relaxing day at the park, offering sweeping views over Prague (see page 100).

Across from the palace exit is the...

Basilica of St. George (Bazilika Sv. Jiří)— Step into the beau-

tifully lit Basilica of St. George to see Prague's best-preserved Romanesque church. St. Wenceslas' mother, St. Ludmila, was reburied here in 973. The first Bohemian convent was established here near the palace.

Today, the **convent** next door houses the National Gallery's Collection of Old Masters, featuring the best Czech paintings from the Mannerist and Baroque periods (100 Kč, Tue–Sun 10:00–18:00, closed Mon).

Continue walking downhill through the castle grounds. Turn left on the first street, which leads into the...

Golden Lane (Zlatá Ulička)—During the day, this street of old

buildings, which origi-nally housed goldsmiths, is jammed with tourists and lined with overpriced gift shops. Franz Kafka lived briefly at #22. There's a deli/ bistro at the top and a conve-nient public WC at the bot-tom. In the morning and at night, the tiny street is free, empty, and romantic.

Toy and Barbie Museum (Muzeum Hraček)—At the bottom of the castle complex, just after leaving the Golden Lane, a long, wooden staircase leads to two entertaining floors of old toys and dolls thoughtfully described in English. You'll see a century of teddy bears, 19th-century model train sets, and an incredible Barbie collection (the entire top floor). Find the buxom 1959 first edition, and you'll understand why these capitalistic sirens of material discontent weren't allowed here until 1989 (50 Kč, not included in any castle tickets, daily 9:30–17:30).

After Your Castle Visit: Tourists squirt slowly through a fortified door at the bottom end of the castle. From there, you can follow the steep lane directly back to the riverbank (and the Malostranská Metro station).

Or you can take a hard right and stroll through the long, delightful park. Along the way, notice the modernist design of the

Na Valech Garden, which was carried out by the "court architect" of the 1920s, Jože Plečnik of Slovenia.

Halfway through the long park is a viewpoint overlooking **terraced gardens;** you can zigzag down through these gardens into the Little Quarter (120 Kč, April–Oct daily 10:00–18:00, closed Nov–March).

If you continue through the park all the way to Castle Square, you'll find two more options: a staircase leading down into the Little Quarter, or a cobbled street taking you to historic Nerudova street (described on page 97).

SLEEPING

Peak time is during the months of April, May, June, September, and October. During Christmas and Easter, the prices are a bit higher still. July and August are not too bad. I've listed peak-time prices. If you're traveling in July or August, you'll find rates generally 15 percent lower, and during November-March, 30 percent lower.

Room-Booking Services

Prague is awash with fancy rooms on the push list; private, small-time operators with rooms to rent in their apartments; and roving agents eager to book you a bed and earn a commission. You can save about 30 percent by showing up in Prague without a reservation and finding accommodations upon arrival. It is, however, a hustle and you will not necessarily get your choice. If you're driving, you'll see booking agencies as you enter town. Generally, if you book at one of these, your host can come and lead you to their place.

Athos Travel, run by Filip Antoš, will find the right room for you from among 140 properties (ranging from hostels to 5-star hotels), 90 percent of which are in the historical center. To book a room, call them or use their handy Web site, which allows you to search for a room based on various criteria (best to arrange in advance during peak season, can also help with last-minute booking off-season, tel. 241-440-571, fax 241-441-697, www.athos.cz, info@athos.cz).

AVE, at the Main Train Station (Hlavní Nádraží), is a less personable but still helpful booking service (daily 6:00–23:00, tel. 251-551-011, fax 251-555-156, www.avetravel.cz, ave@avetravel.cz). With the tracks at your back, walk down to the orange ceiling and past the "Meeting Point" (don't go downstairs)—their office is

Sleep Code

(25 Kč = about $1, country code: 420)
S = Single, **D** = Double/Twin, **T** = Triple, **Q** = Quad, **b** = bathroom, **s** = shower only. Unless otherwise noted, credit cards are accepted and breakfast is included. Everyone listed here speaks English.

To help you sort easily through these listings, I've divided the rooms into three categories based on the price for a standard double room with bath:

$$$ **Higher Priced**—Most rooms 4,000 Kč or more.
 $$ **Moderately Priced**—Most rooms between
              3,000–4,000 Kč.
  $ **Lower Priced**—Most rooms 3,000 Kč or less.

in the left corner by the exit to the rip-off taxis. AVE has several other offices—at Holešovice Train Station, the airport, Wenceslas Square, and Old Town Square. Their display board shows discounted hotels. They have a slew of hotels and small pensions available ($80/2,000-Kč pension doubles in old center, $40/1,000-Kč doubles a Metro ride away). You can reserve by e-mail (using your credit card as a deposit) or just show up at the office and request a room. Many of AVE's rooms are not very convenient to the center; be clear on the location before you make your choice. They sell taxi vouchers for those who want the convenience of a ride from the station's taxi stand, though they cost double the fair rate.

For a more personal touch, contact Lída at **Magic Praha** for help with accommodations (Spálená 21, 1st floor, tel. & fax 224-931-674, mobile 604-207-225, www.magicpraha.cz, magicpraha@magicpraha.cz; see "Helpful Hints," page 54).

Central Prague

You'll pay a premium to sleep in the heart of romantic old Prague—but many travelers figure it's worth the expense. I've listed my hotels by neighborhood (see "Prague's Four Towns," page 50). All of these listings are in the very central "Praha 1" district.

Old Town Hotels and Pensions

You'll pay higher prices to stay in the Old Town, but for many travelers, the convenience is worth the expense. These places are all within a 10-minute walk of the Old Town Square.

$$$ Hotel Central is a sentimental favorite—I stayed there in the communist days. Like the rest of Prague, it's now changing with the times: Its 69 rooms have been renovated, leaving it fresh and bright. It's well-run, and the location—three blocks east of the Old Town Square—is excellent (Sb-3,990 Kč, Db-4,650 Kč, Tb-5,150 Kč, 5 percent discount with cash, ask for a "Rick Steves discount" with your e-mail request in 2006, elevator, Rybná 8, Metro: Náměstí Republiky, tel. 224-812-041, fax 222-328-404, central@orfea.cz).

$$$ Cloister Inn is well-located, with 75 modern rooms. The exterior is more concrete than charm—the building used to be shared by a convent and a secret-police prison—but inside, it's newly redone and plenty comfortable (Sb-4,000 Kč, Db-4,200 Kč, Tb-4,700 Kč, elevator, free Internet in lobby, Konviktská 14, tel. 224-211-020, fax 224-210-800, www.cloister-inn.com, cloister@cloister-inn.com).

$$ Hotel Haštal, on a quiet, hidden square in the Old Town, was a popular hotel back in the 1920s. Renovated and re-opened in 2002, it's decorated with Art Nouveau posters that complement the neighborhood's vibrant circa-1900 architecture (Sb-2,900 Kč, Db-3,600 Kč, extra bed-550 Kč, 20 percent discount when booking online, thin walls, Haštalská 16, tel. 222-314-335, www.hastal .com, info@hastal.com). The hotel's small restaurant has excellent beer and food—try the beefsteak with bleu-cheese sauce, or the lunch specials (popular with the local crowd).

$$ Dům u Krále Jiřího (literally, "House by King George") is situated in a 14th-century palace that once belonged to the Hussite king. More rooms are gradually being added, as the owners buy and refurbish more of the surrounding apartments, fitting stylishly furnished rooms into historic spaces. The upper floors have romantic views over the crooked roofs of the Old Town, while some of the lower-floor rooms open into a private courtyard (Sb-1,950 Kč, Db-3,100 Kč, extra bed-1,000 Kč, Liliová 10, tel. 221-466-100, www.kinggeorge.cz).

$$ Pension u Medvídků has 31 comfortably renovated rooms in a big, rustic, medieval shell with dark wood furniture. Upstairs, you'll find lots of beams to smack into (Sb-2,300 Kč, Db-3,500 Kč, Tb-4,500 Kč, extra bed-500 Kč, "historical" rooms 10 percent more, apartment 20 percent more, Internet in lobby, Na Perštýně 7, tel. 224-211-916, fax 224-220-930, www.umedvidku.cz, info@umedvidku.cz). The pension runs a popular beer-hall restaurant that has live music most Fridays and Saturdays until 23:00.

$$ Hotel u Klenotníka, with 11 modern, comfortable rooms in a plain building, is three blocks off the Old Town Square (Sb-2,500 Kč, Db-3,300–3,800 Kč, Tb-4,500 Kč, 10 percent off when booking direct with this book in 2006, Rytířská 3, tel. 224-211-699, fax 224-221-025, www.uklenotnika.cz, info@uklenotnika.cz).

$$ Hotel u Tří Bubnů (literally, "Three Drums") fills one of the oldest buildings in town, 50 yards toward the river from

Hotels in Prague's Old Town

★ **OLD TOWN SQUARE**

Ⓜ – SUBWAY STOP

Ⓣ – TRAM 22 + 23 STOP

¼ MILE / 400 METERS

❶ Hotel Central
❷ Cloister Inn
❸ Hotel Haštal
❹ Dům u Krále Jiřího
❺ Pension u Medvídků
❻ Hotel u Klenotníka
❼ Hotel u Tří Bubnů

❽ Expres Hotel
❾ To Hotel Salvator
❿ Pension Unitas & Art Prison Hostel
⓫ Pension Accord
⓬ Old Prague Hostel
⓭ Hostel Týn
⓮ To Magic Praha Room-Booking Office

DCH

the Old Town Square. Its 18 rooms are spacious, with high ceilings and wooden beams (Db-3,900 Kč, extra bed-1,000 Kč, U Radnice 8, tel. 224-214-855, fax 224-236-100, www.utribubnu.cz, utribubnu@volny.cz).

$$ Expres Hotel rents 29 simple rooms and brings a continental breakfast to your room (S-1,000 Kč, Sb-3,000 Kč, D-1,400 Kč, Db-3,200 Kč, Tb-3,600 Kč, 5 percent discount with cash, elevator, Skořepka 5, tel. 224-211-801, fax 224-223-309, www .pragueexpreshotel.cz, info@pragueexpreshotel.cz). While a good value, it's in a red-light zone and comes with late-night music from nearby clubs on weekends.

$$ Hotel Salvator rents 30 comfortable rooms on a quiet street above a fun South American restaurant (D-2,100 Kč, Db-3,100 Kč, Qb-4,200 Kč, extra bed-500 Kč, elevator, Truhlářská 10, 3 min from Metro: Náměstí Republiky, tel. 222-312-234, fax 222-316-355, www.salvator.cz, hotel@salvator.cz).

$ Pension Unitas rents 35 small, tidy, youth hostel–type rooms with plain, minimalist furnishings and no sinks (S-1,260 Kč, D-1,580 Kč, T-1,900 Kč, Q-2,200 Kč, T and Q are cramped with bunks in D-sized rooms, easy reservations without a deposit, non-smoking, quiet hours 22:00–7:00, Bartolomějská 9, tel. 224-221-802, fax 224-217-555, www.unitas.cz, unitas@unitas.cz). They run a fine little youth hostel in the former prison downstairs (see "Old Town Hostels," below).

$ Pension Accord, which opened in an apartment building in 2005, offers simple, clean rooms. Since they're new, this place is still figuring things out: Breakfast is served in a nearby restaurant, which doesn't open until 9:00 (as an alternative, eat in the friendly neighborhood bakery shop U Lucerny next door, or ask hotel clerk to have food brought to your room). Still, given the location, the value is unbeatable (Sb-2,200 Kč, Db-2,900 Kč, Tb-3,500 Kč, extra bed-600 Kč, Rybná 9, tel. 222-328-816, fax. 222-324-406, www.accordprague.com, info@accordprague.com).

Old Town Hostels

$ Old Prague Hostel, open since just 2005, is a small and very friendly place on the second and third floors of an apartment building on a back alley near the Powder Tower. The spacious rooms were once apartment bedrooms, so it feels less institutional than most hostels. The TV lounge/breakfast room was once the living room (S-1,180 Kč, D-1,360 Kč, bunk in 3- to 8-person room-440–530 Kč; includes breakfast, sheets, towels, and lockers; reserve ahead, Benediktská 2, tel. 224-829-058, fax 224-829-060, www.oldpraguehostel.com, oldpraguehostel@seznam.cz).

$ Hostel Týn, hidden in a silent courtyard two blocks from the Old Town Square, is the ultimate find. The management is aware of its value, so they don't bother being too friendly (D-1,100 Kč, T-450 Kč per person, bunk in 4- to 5-bed room-400 Kč, reserve ahead, Týnská 19, tel. 224-828-519, mobile 776-122-057, www.hostel-tyn.web2001.cz, backpacker@razdva.cz).

$ Art Prison Hostel fills a former prison in the basement of Pension Unitas (see above). With tiny, high windows and no plumbing, the rooms are stark—but not as stark as when Václav Havel did time here (64 beds, S-1,100 Kč, D-1,260 Kč, bunk in 4- to 5-bed cell-370–510 Kč, includes sheets and breakfast, easy reservations without deposit if arriving by 17:00, no curfew, non-smoking, shared modern facilities, lockers, Bartolomějská 9, tel. 224-221-802, www.unitas.cz, unitas@unitas.cz).

In the New Town, on Wenceslas Square

To locate these hotels, see the map on page 127.

$$$ Hotel Adria, with a prime Wenceslas Square location, cool Art Nouveau facade, and 88 completely modern and business-class rooms, is your big-time, four-star, central splurge (Sb-3,900 Kč, Db-4,650 Kč, these prices only if you reserve online, air-con, elevator, minibars...the works, Václavské Náměstí 26, tel. 221-081-111, fax 221-081-300, www.adria.cz, accom@adria.cz).

$$ Grand Hotel Evropa is in a class by itself. This landmark hotel, famous for its wonderful 1903 Art Nouveau facade, is the centerpiece of Wenceslas Square. But someone pulled the plug on the hotel about 50 years ago, and it's a mess. It offers haunting beauty in all of its public spaces, 92 dreary and ramshackle rooms, and a weary staff. They're waiting for a billion-crown investor to come along and rescue the place, but for now, they offer some of the cheapest rooms  on Wenceslas Square (S-1,600 Kč, Sb-3,000 Kč, D-2,600 Kč, Db-4,000 Kč, T-3,100 Kč, Tb-5,000 Kč; some rooms have been very slightly refurbished, some remain in unrefurbished old style, they cost the same either way; every room is different, elevator, Václavské Náměstí 25, tel. 224-228-117, fax 224-224-544, www.evropahotel.cz, info@evropahotel.cz).

In the Little Quarter

$$$ Dům u Velké Boty (literally, "House at the Big Boot"), in front of the German Embassy, is the quintessential family hotel in Prague. Each room is uniquely decorated, most in the tasteful Biedermeier style of the 19th century (tiny S-1,800 Kč, two D rooms that share a bathroom-3,000 Kč each, Db-4,160 Kč,

Hotels and Restaurants in the Little Quarter

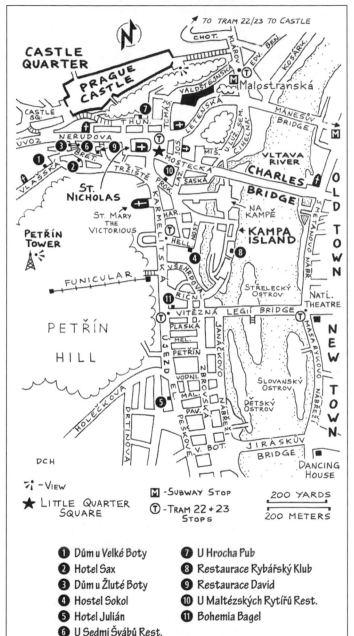

Legend:

🔏 – View

★ Little Quarter Square

Ⓜ – Subway Stop

Ⓣ – Tram 22 + 23 Stops

200 Yards

200 Meters

1. Dům u Velké Boty
2. Hotel Sax
3. Dům u Žluté Boty
4. Hostel Sokol
5. Hotel Julián
6. U Sedmi Švábů Rest.
7. U Hrocha Pub
8. Restaurace Rybářský Klub
9. Restaurace David
10. U Maltézských Rytířů Rest.
11. Bohemia Bagel

extra bed-500 Kč, lavish breakfast-200 Kč extra, Vlašská 30, tel. 257-532-088, www.dumuvelkeboty.cz). The owners, Mr. and Mrs. Rippl, treat every one of their guests as a friend, and the wellspring of their stories never runs dry. Ask Mrs. Rippl about her great uncle (the bishop who once owned the house), or Mr. Rippl about how he served soup to East Germans arriving in the thousands at the German Embassy in October 1989 to obtain exit visas out of the Communist Bloc. There's no sign on the house—find it by the splendid geraniums that Mr. Rippl nurtures in the windows.

$$$ Hotel Sax, on a quiet corner a block below the Little Quarter action, will delight the artsy yuppie with its 22 rooms, fruity atrium, and modern, stylish decor (Sb-4,100 Kč, Db-4,400 Kč, Db suite-5,100 Kč, extra bed-1,000 Kč, elevator, near Church of St. Nicholas, 1 block below Nerudova at Jánský Vršek 3, reserve long in advance, tel. 257-531-268, fax 257-534-101, www.sax.cz, hotel@sax.cz).

$$$ Dům u Žluté Boty (literally, "House at the Yellow Boot") is the most charming small hotel in Prague, hiding on a small lane in the Little Quarter. Each of its seven rooms has a completely different feel: Some preserve the 16th-century wooden ceilings, some feel like mountain lodges, and others are a bit marred by an insensitive 1970s adaptation. The manager's husband is a distinguished artist whose paintings (for sale) embellish the dining room and halls. The only drawback of this hotel is its thin walls—you'll know exactly what your neighbors are arguing about (Sb-3,800 Kč, Db-4,300 Kč, Tb-5,000 Kč, extra bed-900 Kč, Jánský Vršek 11, tel. 257-532-269, fax 257-534-134, www.zlutabota .cz, hotel@zlutabota.cz).

$ Hostel Sokol, plain and institutional, with 100 beds, is peacefully located just off parklike Kampa Island in the Tryš House buildings (the seat of the Czech Sokol Organization). Big WWI hospital-style rooms are lined with single beds and lockers (8–14 per room, 350 Kč per bed, D-900 Kč, cash only, no breakfast, easy to reserve by phone or e-mail without deposit, open 24/7, members' kitchen, Nosticova 2, tel. 257-007-397, fax 257-007-340, hostel@sokol-cos.cz). From the Main Train Station, ride tram #9 to Újezd. From the Holešovice station, take tram #12 to Újezd.

In the Castle Quarter
$$$ Residence Domus Henrici, just above Castle Square, is a quiet retreat that charges—and gets—top prices for its eight smartly appointed rooms, some of which include good views (Ds-5,100 Kč, Db-5,600–6,200 Kč depending on size, extra bed-900 Kč, less off-season, pleasant terrace, Loretánská 11, tel. 220-511-369, fax 220-511-502, www.domus-henrici.cz, henrici@hidden-places.com).

This is a five-minute walk above the castle gate in a quiet, elegant area.

Away from the Center

Moving just outside central Prague saves you money—and gets you away from the tourists and into some more workaday residential neighborhoods. The following listings (great values compared to the downtown hotels listed above) are all within a 5- to 15-minute tram or Metro ride from the center.

Beyond Wenceslas Square

These hotels are in urban neighborhoods on the outer fringe of the New Town, northeast of Wenceslas Square, but still within several minutes' walk of the sightseeing zone.

$$$ Hotel Sieber, with 20 rooms, is a quality, four-star, business-class hotel in an upscale residential neighborhood near the former royal vineyards (Vinohrady). They do a good job of being homey and welcoming (Sb-4,480 Kč, Db-4,780 Kč, extra bed-990 Kč, 4th night free, 30 percent discount for last-minute reservations, air-con, elevator, 3-min walk to Metro: Jiřího z Poděbrad, or tram #11, Slezská 55, Praha 3, tel. 224-250-025, fax 224-250-027, www.sieber.cz, reservations@sieber.cz).

$$ Hotel Anna, with 24 bright, pastel, and classically charming rooms, is a bit closer in—just 10 minutes by foot east of Wenceslas Square (Sb-2,400 Kč, Db-3,300 Kč, Tb-4,000 Kč, non-smoking rooms, elevator, Budečská 17, Praha 2, Metro: Náměstí Míru, tel. 222-513-111, fax 222-515-158, www.hotelanna .cz, reception@hotelanna.cz). The hotel runs a cheaper but similarly pleasant annex, the **Dependence,** two blocks away (Sb-1,860 Kč, Db-2,560 Kč, no elevator but all rooms on the 1st floor, reception and breakfast at main hotel).

$$ Hotel Luník, with 35 rooms, is dignified and no-nonsense, but friendly. It's out of the medieval faux-rustic world in a normal, pleasant business district. It's two Metro stops from the Main Train Station (Metro: I. P. Pavlova) or a 10-minute walk south of Wenceslas Square (Sb-2,400 Kč, Db-3,300 Kč, Tb-3,800 Kč, extra bed-500 Kč, 10 percent discount if you reserve online, some street noise, elevator, Londýnská 50, Praha 2, tel. 224-253-974, fax 224-253-986, www.hotel-lunik.cz, recepce@hotel-lunik.cz).

$$ Hotel 16, a stately little place with an intriguing Art Nouveau facade, high ceilings, and a clean, sleek interior, rents 14 fine rooms (Sb-2,600 Kč, Db-3,500 Kč, Db suite-4,000 Kč, Tb-4,700 Kč, back/quiet rooms face the garden, front/noisier rooms face the street, air-con, elevator, 10-min walk south of Wenceslas Square, Metro: I. P. Pavlova, Kateřinská 16, Praha 2, tel. 224-920-636, fax 224-920-626, www.hotel16.cz, hotel16@hotel16.cz).

$ Hostel Elf is close to the Main Train Station and Florenc bus station (a 10-min walk from each). It's fun-loving, ramshackle, and covered with noisy, self-inflicted graffiti. They offer cheap, basic beds, a helpful staff, and lots of creative services—kitchen, free luggage room, laundry, no lockout, free tea, cheap beer, a terrace, and lockers (dorm beds-260–340 Kč, D-820 Kč, includes sheets and breakfast, Husitská 11, Praha 3, tel. 222-540-963, www.hostelelf.com, info@hostelelf.com).

South of the Charles Bridge, near the Vltava River

These hotels are listed from north to south.

$$ Hotel Julián, an oasis of professional, predictable decency in a quiet, untouristy neighborhood, is just south of the Little Quarter on the castle side of the river. Its 32 spacious, fresh, well-furnished rooms and big, homey public spaces hide behind a noble neoclassical facade. The staff is friendly and helpful (Sb-3,680 Kč, Db-3,980 Kč, Db suite-4,800 Kč, extra bed-900 Kč, discount for booking online, 5 percent discount off best quoted rate with this book in 2006, free tea and coffee in room, elevator, Internet in lobby, parking lot, Elišky Peškové 11, Praha 5, reservation tel. 257-311-150, reception tel. 257-311-145, fax 257-311-149, www.julian.cz, casjul@vol.cz). Free lockers and a shower are available for those needing to check out early but stay until late (e.g., for an overnight train). Mike's Chauffeur Service, based here, is reliable and affordable (see page 154).

$ Dům u Šemíka, a friendly hotel named for a heroic mythical horse, offers 25 rooms in a residential neighborhood just below Vyšehrad Castle, a 10-minute tram ride south of the Old Town (Sb-2,150 Kč, Db-2,700 Kč, apartment-2,950–5,300 Kč depending on size, extra bed-790 Kč; from the center, take tram #18 to Albertov, then walk 2 blocks uphill; or take tram #7 to Výtoň, go under rail bridge, and walk 3 blocks uphill to Vratislavova 36; Praha 2, tel. 224-920-736, fax 224-911-602, www.usemika.cz, usemika@usemika.cz).

$ Guest House Lída, with 12 homey and spacious rooms, fills a big house in a quiet residential area farther inland, a 15-minute tram ride from the center. Jan and Jiří Prouza, who run the place, are a wealth of information and know how to make people feel at home (Sb-1,380 Kč, small Db-1,440 Kč, Db-1,760 Kč, Tb-2,110 Kč, cash only, family rooms, top-floor family suite with kitchenette, garage parking-200 Kč/day, Metro: Pražského Povstání; exit Metro and turn left on Lomnicka between the Metro station and big blue-glass ČSOB building, follow Lomnicka for 500 yards, then turn left on Lopatecka, go uphill and ring bell at Lopatecká #26, no sign outside; Praha 4, tel. & fax 261-214-766, http://sweb.cz/pensionlida, lidabb@seznam.cz). The Prouza brothers also rent

Hotels and Restaurants in the New Town and Beyond

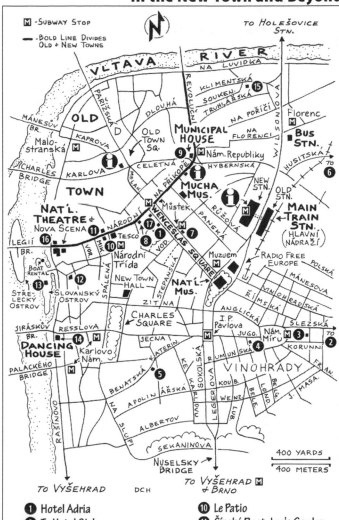

1 Hotel Adria
2 To Hotel Sieber
3 Hotel Anna
4 Hotel Luník
5 Hotel 16
6 To Hostel Elf
7 Grand Hotel Evropa
8 Restaurace u Pinkasů
9 Kavárna Obecní Dům, Francouzská Rest. & Plzeňská Rest.

10 Le Patio
11 Čínská Rest. Lee's Garden
12 Hospoda u Nováka
13 Restaurant Žofín
14 La Perle de Prague
15 Rest. Club Des Vins Červená Tabulka
16 Grand Café Slavia
17 Dobrá Čajovna Teahouse & Šenk Vrbovec Wine Bar

four apartments across the river, equally far away (Db-1,500 Kč, Tb-1,920 Kč, Qb-2,100 Kč).

In Praha 6, beyond the Castle

The Praha 6 district is a quiet and very local-feeling neighborhood west of the castle. These hotels are well-connected to the center by trams.

$$ Hotel Adalbert occupies an 18th-century building, a part of the Czech Republic's oldest monastery, the Břevnov Monastery (Břevnovský Klášter; founded by St. Adalbert in 993). Built by the prolific Baroque architect Kryštof Ditzenhoffer, and brilliantly restored after the return of the Benedictine monks in the 1990s, the monastery complex is the ultimate retreat for those who come to Prague soul-searching or just wanting a quiet place away from the bustle. Join the monks for morning and evening prayers in the St. Margaret Basilica, a large and elegant Baroque church executed with unusual simplicity. Feed yourself in the monastery fruit orchard that rises in terraces up the hill above the monastery (Sb-2,600 Kč, Db-3,600 Kč, extra bed-1,050 Kč, Markétská 1, Praha 6, tram #22 or #23 to Břevnovský Klášter; 5 min by tram from the castle, 10 min from the Little Quarter, 15 min from Old and New Towns; tel. 220-406-170, fax 220-406-190, www.hoteladalbert.cz, info@hoteladalbert.cz). Individual tours of the monastery can be reserved in the visitors' office. The church is always open one hour before Mass (daily 18:00), and often also during the day. The meditative **Klášterní Šenk** (Monastery Beerhall)—set up in 2005 like a village pub, complete with coarse wooden floors, furnishings, and, on cold rainy days, a cherry-wood fire in the central fireplace—is becoming a hit with monks and locals alike for its excellent Czech food for Czech prices. Although the restaurant alone isn't worth the trip from downtown Prague, it's the perfect choice for people staying at the monastery (daily 11:30–23:00, tel. 220-406-294).

$ Pension Větrník is situated in a former 17th-century windmill in one of Prague's most popular residential areas, halfway between the airport and the city. It's owned and run by Mr. Opatrný, a legendary Czech chef who sailed the world feeding cruise-ship passengers and won gold medals in cooking competitions. The six rooms here are the pride of the Opatrný family, who live on the upper floors. With a day's notice, Mr. Opatrný can prepare you a feast you'll never forget. The garden has a bear-like, good-hearted dog and a tennis court—rackets and balls are provided (four Db-2,100 Kč, two suites-3,150 Kč, U Větrníku 4, Praha 6; the airport bus #179 stops right in front of the house, tram #18 goes straight to the Charles Bridge, both take 20 min; tel. 220-612-404, fax 235-361-406, www.pensionvetrnik.wz.cz).

EATING

A big part of Prague's charm is found in wandering aimlessly through the city's winding old quarters, marveling at the architecture, watching the people, and sniffing out fun restaurants. You can eat well here for very little money. What you'd pay for a basic meal in Vienna or Munich will get you a feast in Prague. In addition to meat-and-potatoes Czech cuisine (see "Czech Food," page 31), you'll find trendy, student-oriented bars and lots of fine ethnic eateries. For ambience, the options include traditional, dark Czech beer halls; elegant Art Nouveau dining rooms; or hip and modern.

Watch out for scams. Many restaurants put more care into ripping off green tourists (and even locals) than in their cooking. Tourists are routinely served cheaper meals than what they ordered, given a menu with a "personalized" price list, charged extra for things they didn't get, or shortchanged. Speak Czech. Even saying "Hello" in Czech (see phrases on page 23) will get you better service. Avoid any menu without clear and explicit prices. Be careful of waiters padding the tab. Carefully examine your itemized bill and understand each line (a 10 percent service charge is sometimes added—in that case, there's no need to tip extra). Tax is always included in the price, so it shouldn't be tacked on later. Part with very large bills only if necessary, and deliberately count your change. Never let your credit card out of your sight. Make it a habit to get cash from an ATM to pay for your meals. You will make waiters infinitely happier. Remember, there are two parallel worlds in Prague: the tourist town and the real city. Generally, if you walk two minutes away from the tourist flow, you'll find better value, ambience, and service.

RESTAURANTS

I've listed these eateries by neighborhood (see "Prague's Four Towns," page 50). The most options—and highest prices—are in the Old Town. If you want a memorable splurge, see "Dining with Style" on page 135. For a light meal, consider one of Prague's many memorable cafés (see "Cafés in the Old Town" on page 139).

In the Old Town

With the inevitable closing of cheap student pubs (replaced by shops and hotels that make more money), it's getting difficult to find a truly Czech pub in the historic city center. Most Czechs no longer go to "traditional" eateries, preferring the cosmopolitan taste of the world to the mundane taste of sauerkraut.

To meet Czechs, head to a trendy bar in the Old Town (see page 131), the New Town (page 134), or in Žižkov and Vinohrady (see page 138).

Characteristically Czech Places

Ancient institutions with "authentic" Czech ambience have become touristy—but they're still great fun and a good value.

Plzeňská Restaurace u Dvou Koček (literally, "By the Two Cats") is a typical Czech pub with cheap, no-nonsense, hearty Czech food and beer, and—once upon a time—a local crowd. Sandwiched between the two red-light-district streets, the restaurant has a name that's a bit ambiguous (200 Kč for 3 courses and beer, serving original Pilsner Urquell with accordion music nightly until 23:00, under an arcade, facing a tiny square between Perlová and Skořepka streets).

Restaurace u Pinkasů, with a menu that reads like a 19th-century newspaper, is a Prague institution (founded in 1843). Recent renovation has added convenience to past glory, while tactfully preserving traditional spaces. In the summer, sit in the garden behind the building in the shade of the Gothic arches of the St. Mary of the Snows Church. The cellar, spanned by Renaissance vaults, prepares excellent smoked meats (restaurant—daily 9:00–24:00, cellar—16:00–4:00 in the morning, tucked in a courtyard near the bottom of Wenceslas Square, on border between Old and New Towns, see location on map on page 125, Jungmannovo Náměstí 16, tel. 221-111-150).

Restaurace u Provaznice (literally, "By the Ropemaker's Wife") has all the Czech classics peppered with the story of a once-upon-a-time-faithful wife. (Check the menu for details of the gory story.) Natives congregate here for the best "pig leg" in town (daily 11:00–24:00, a block into the Old Town from the bottom of

Wenceslas Square at Provaznická 3, tel. 224-232-528).

U Medvídků, which started out as a brewery in 1466, is now a flagship beer hall of the Czech Budweiser. The ambience of the one large room is bright, noisy, and a bit smoky (daily 11:30–23:00, a block toward Wenceslas Square from Bethlehem Square at Na Perštýnì 7, tel. 224-211-916). The small beer bar next to the restaurant (daily 16:00–3:00 in the morning) is used by university students during emergencies—such as after most other pubs have closed.

Česká Kuchyně (literally, "Czech Kitchen") is a blue-collar cafeteria serving steamy old Czech cuisine to a local clientele. There's no English inside, so—if you want apple charlotte, but not tripe soup—be sure to review the small English menu in the window outside before entering. Note the numbers of the dishes you'd like that correspond to the Czech menu you'll see inside. Pick up your tally sheet as you enter, grab a tray, point liberally to whatever you'd like, and keep the paper to pay as you exit. It's extremely cheap...unless you lose your paper (daily 9:00–20:00, across from Havelská Market at Havelská 23, tel. 224-235-574).

Havelská Market, surrounded by colorful little eateries, offers picnic fixings (see page 66).

Hip Restaurants and Bars

Restaurace Mlejnice is a fun little pub strewn with farm implements and happy eaters, tucked away just out of the tourist crush two blocks from the Old Town Square (order carefully and understand your itemized bill, daily 11:00–24:00, between Melantrichova and Železná at Kožná 14, reservations smart in evening, tel. 224-228-635).

Country Life Vegetarian Restaurant is a bright, easy, non-smoking cafeteria with a well-displayed buffet of salads and hot veggie dishes. It's midway between the Old Town Square and the bottom of Wenceslas Square. They're serious about their vegetarianism, serving only plant-based, unprocessed, and unrefined food (Mon–Thu 8:30–19:00, Fri 8:30–18:00, Sun 11:00–18:00, closed Sat, through courtyard at Melantrichova 15/Michalská 18, tel. 224-213-366).

Kozička Bar, hiding in a brick-walled modern cellar, is popular with local yuppies drawn here by the Krušovice beer and late opening hours. They also have good food that ranges from Czech beef tongue to pasta and exotic fish (Mon–Fri 12:00–4:00 in the morning, Sat 18:00–4:00 in the morning, Sun 18:00–3:00 in the morning, Kozí 1, tel. 224-818-308).

On Bethlehem Square (Betlémské Náměstí): **Klub Architektů** is a modern student hangout with a medieval cellar serving cheap vegetarian meals, hearty salads, and a few "gourmet entrées" next

Prague Restaurants

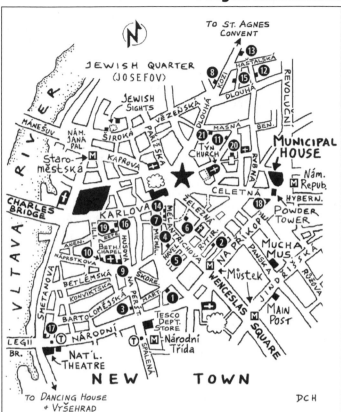

OLD TOWN SQUARE

Ⓜ -Subway Stop
Ⓣ -Tram 22 + 23 Stop

¼ MILE
400 METERS

❶ Plzeňská Rest. u Dvou Koček
❷ Restaurace u Provaznice
❸ U Medvídků Beerhall
❹ Česká Kuchyně
❺ Havelská Market
❻ Restaurace Mlejnice
❼ Country Life Vegetarian Rest.
❽ Kozička Bar
❾ Klub Architektů
❿ Restaurace u Betlémské Kaple
⓫ Beas

⓬ Dahab
⓭ Molly Malone's Irish Pub
⓮ Restaurant u Prince Terrace
⓯ Orange Moon
⓰ U Zlatého Tygra Pub
⓱ Grand Café Slavia
⓲ Grand Café Orient
⓳ Café Montmartre & Café at the Palace of King George
⓴ Ebel Coffee House
㉑ Bohemia Bagel

to Bethlehem Chapel (daily, Betlémské Náměstí 169, tel. 224-401-214). **Restaurace u Betlémské Kaple**, on the other side of the chapel, has light wooden decor, a cheap lunch menu, and fish specialties that attract natives and visitors in search of a good Czech bite for Czech prices (daily 11:00–23:00, Betlémské Náměstí 2, tel. 222-221-639).

Ethnic Eateries on or near Dlouhá Street

Dlouhá, the wide street leading away from the Old Town Square behind the Jan Hus monument (left of Týn Church), is lined with ethnic restaurants catering mostly to local yuppies. Within the space of a couple of blocks, you can eat your way around the world. These places are all within a few steps of Dlouhá street.

Beas is a cheap vegetarian restaurant ruled by a Punjabi chef who concocts bland *thalis* (mixed platters) in the style of North Indian plains and *dosas* of the south Indian variety. Tucked away in a courtyard behind the Týn Church, this place is popular with university students (Mon–Sat 9:30–20:00, Sun 10:00–18:00, Týnská 19).

Orange Moon specializes in Thai curries, but you'll also find dishes from Myanmar (Burma) and India served in a space delightfully decorated with artwork from Southeast Asia. This restaurant attracts a mixture of locals, expats, and occasionally tourists (daily 11:30–23:30, reservations recommended, Rámová 5, tel. 222-325-119).

Dahab has a cheap Moroccan buffet in the front, and a dim hall with metal chandeliers and comfy chairs in the back. This popular hang-out specializes in couscous, teas, and Turkish coffee. Try their goat cheese, chicken couscous, and the "Moroccan whisky" mint tea. There's belly dancing every Friday night (daily 12:00–24:00, Dlouhá 33, tel. 224-827-375).

Dining with an Old Town Square View

Restaurant u Prince Terrace, in the five-star U Prince Hotel facing the Astronomical Clock, is designed for foreign tourists. A sleek elevator takes you to its rooftop, where every possible inch is used to serve good food (fish, Czech, and international) to its guests. The view is arguably the best in town—especially at sunset, when a reservation is smart. The menu is a fun but overpriced mix, with photos to make ordering easy (daily until 24:00, brusque staff, Staroměstské Náměstí 29, tel. 224-213-807).

In the Jewish Quarter

To locate the first two eateries, see the map on page 68.

Kolkovna is big and woody, yet modern, serving a fun mix of Czech and international cuisine—ribs, salads, cheese plates, and good beer (daily 11:00–24:00, across from Spanish Synagogue at V Kolkovně 8, tel. 224-819-701, www.kolkovna.cz). Kolkovna is now a chain, with branches on Republic Square (Restaurant Celnice, daily 11:00–2:00 in the morning, near Náměstí Republiky at V Celnici 4), and near the castle, at the viewpoint by Strahov Monastery (Restaurant Bellavista, daily 10:00–24:00, Strahovské Nádvoří 1).

Franz Kafka Café is a handy spot to break up a demanding tour of the Jewish Quarter with a snack or drink (daily 10:00–21:00, a block from the cemetery at Široká 12).

Molly Malone's Irish Pub has been the expat and local favorite for Guinness ever since the Velvet Revolution enabled the Celts to return to one of their homelands. Worn wooden floors, dingy walls, and the Irish manager transport you right into the heart of blue-collar Dublin (which is, after all, a popular place for young Czechs to find jobs in the high-tech industry). Hidden in a forgotten corner of Josefov, Molly Malone's is a destination for those who have adopted Prague, and are not just passing through (Sun–Thu 11:00–1:00 in the morning, Fri–Sat 11:00–2:00 in the morning, U Obecního Dvora 4, tel. 224-818-851). There's another, less local-feeling location opposite the Irish and American embassies in the Little Quarter (Tržiště 4).

In the New Town

Art Nouveau Splendor in the Municipal House

For location, see map on page 127.

The **Municipal House** (Obecní Dům), the sumptuous Art Nouveau concert hall, has three special restaurants: a café, a French restaurant, and a beer cellar (Náměstí Republiky 5). The dressy café, **Kavárna Obecní Dům,** is drenched in chandeliered, Art Nouveau elegance (light, pricey meals and drinks with great atmosphere and bad service, 250-Kč hot meal special daily, open daily 7:30–23:00, live piano or jazz trio 16:00–20:00, tel. 222-002-763). **Francouzská Restaurace,** the fine and formal French restaurant, is in the next wing (700- to 1,000-Kč meals, daily 12:00–16:00 & 18:00–23:00, tel. 222-002-777). **Plzeňská Restaurace,** downstairs, brags it's the most beautiful Art Nouveau pub in Europe (cheap meals, great atmosphere, daily 11:30–23:00, tel. 222-002-780).

Trendy Eateries on or near Národní Třída

Along Národní Třída, the street linking Wenceslas Square with the National Theatre and the Vltava River, you'll find fun, memorable restaurants. For locations, see map on page 127.

At **Le Patio,** the first thing you'll notice are the many lanterns suspended from the ceiling—and the big ship moored out back (okay, just its hulking facade). Le Patio has a hip, continental feel to it, but for a place that also sells furniture (head straight back and down the stairs), they definitely need comfier dining chairs. The food is French with some Czech highlights, and actually worth the high prices you'll pay. Plunk down 150 Kč for some freshly squeezed juice that will send a shiver down your tongue. The atmosphere is as pleasant and carefully designed as the dishes (daily 8:00–23:00, Národní 22, tel. 224-934-375). There's another location in the Old Town, at Haštalská 18 (tel. 224-819-767).

Čínská Restaurace Lee's Garden combines red carpet, dark-wood furniture, and excellent food into the best Chinese value in the area. With prices at traditional Czech eateries shooting up due to tourist demand, once-upon-a-time exotic and expensive Chinese food is becoming the thrifty local's favorite. They also sell swords, knives, and sport guns on the first floor (daily 10:30–22:30, on 2nd floor above Chinese shop at Národní 23, tel. 224-221-888).

Hospoda u Nováka, behind the Nová Scéna (the glass annex next door to the National Theatre), takes the treatment of its "patients" seriously—notice the regulars' beer taps filed into the wooden case to the right of the door as "medication taken" reports. A red-and-white sign above the bar (reading *Border area, entry strictly prohibited*) is reminiscent of the 1980s, when these placards, spaced every 20 yards, lined the Czech barbed-wire side of the Iron Curtain. Nostalgic of the communist era, in which pubs were close-knit communities where regulars escaped from the depression of daily life, U Nováka is a bright and smoky paradise where you can happily curse whatever regime you happen to live under— just like the natives have always done. The waiter will eventually bring the English menu that consists of well-executed Czech classics, but doesn't list the cheap daily specials (daily 10:00–23:00, V Jirchářích 2, tel. 224-930-639).

Dining with Style

In Prague, a fancy candlelit dinner with fine wines and connoisseur dishes costs more than most locals can afford—but it's still a bargain in comparison to similar restaurants in Paris or Dallas. Even here, they're willing to accept credit cards, but prefer cash. Remember that ATMs are everywhere. My first two listings are south of the sightseeing action; the last one is tucked away northeast of the Old Town. For locations, see map on page 127.

Restaurant Žofín is a Prague institution, taking you back to the era of waltzing elegance. Nicknamed for Franz Josef's mother,

Sofia, it shares a circa-1880 palace with a famous ballroom on a small island south of Charles Bridge (mostly traditional 3-course *menus* range from simple/310 Kč to gourmet/990 Kč, huge and reasonable wine list, plain garden tables or sumptuous reserve-in-advance indoor tables, Slovanský Island, reach island by bridge south of National Theatre, tel. 224-934-548).

La Perle de Prague fills the seventh and eighth floors of Frank Gehry's wild and modern Dancing House building with Prague's high society and top-end visitors enjoying a fine river view and gourmet French cuisine. It's white-tablecloth dressy, and offers terrace seating in good weather. While few tables are actually by the window, be sure to enjoy a pre-dinner drink or sip your last glass of wine upstairs, next to Fred Astaire's wire-mesh head, on the roof terrace (500-Kč business lunch, 900-Kč dinner *menu*, daily 12:00–14:00 & 19:00–22:30, reservations required to even get in the elevator, 15-min walk south of Charles Bridge, Tancící Dům, Rašínovo Nábřeží 80, tel. 221-984-160, www.laperle.cz).

Restaurant Club Des Vins Červená Tabulka (literally, "Red Chalkboard") is in a low, beautifully reconstructed town house in a quiet neighborhood that exists outside of the tourist circus. Sit indoors, next to a 1930s motorcycle, or outdoors, in a court-yard under a wooden staircase and balcony. The delicate dishes, served on ironed tablecloths, cater to Prague's yuppies. The wines are excellent and a great value (daily 11:30–23:00; from Municipal House, go up Revoluční and turn right on Truhlářská, which you'll follow to Petrské Náměstí—restaurant is up the street across the square at Lodecká 4; tel. 224-810-401).

In the Little Quarter

These characteristic eateries are handy for a bite before or after your Prague Castle visit. My first three listings are nicely affordable; the last two are splurges. For locations, see map on page 123.

U Sedmi Švábů (literally, "By the Seven Roaches") is a cool medieval den a world apart from the tacky theme restaurants around town. Since America was not yet discovered in the Middle Ages, you won't find any corn, potatoes, or tomatoes on the menu. The salty yellow things that come with the Krušovice beer are chickpeas. Carnivores thrive here: Try the skewered meats *(špíz u Sedmi Švábů)*, flaming beef *(flambák)*, or pork knuckle (daily 11:00–23:00, Janský Vršek 14, tel. 257-531-455).

U Hrocha (literally, "By the Hippo"), a very authentic little pub packed with beer-drinkers and smoke, serves simple, traditional meals—basically meat starters with bread. Just below the castle near Little Quarter Square, it's actually the haunt of many members of Parliament—located just around the corner (daily 12:00–23:00, chalkboard lists daily meals in English, Thunovská 10).

Restaurace Rybářský Klub, on Kampa Island, is run by the Society of Czech Fishermen and serves the widest and tastiest selection of freshwater fish in Prague at reasonable prices. Dine on fish-cream soup, pike, trout, carp, or catfish under the imaginative artwork of Little Quarter painter Mr. Kuba (3-course meal for around 300 Kč, daily 12:00–23:00, U Sovových Mlýnů 1, tel. 257-534-200).

Restaurace David, with two little 18th-century rooms hiding on a small cobblestone street opposite the American Embassy in the Little Quarter, is the best place in town for an elegant meal. The exquisite cuisine—a mix of Czech and European styles, ranging from game to roasted duck and liver—is served in the most artistic of arrangements, and the waiters move around with the grace of the 19th century (most meals 600–1,000 Kč, open daily, reservations highly recommended, Tržiště 21, tel. 257-533-109).

U Maltézských Rytířů (literally, "By the Maltese Knights"— named after the nearby church and monastery) dates back a millennium... and the cavernous basement sure smells like it. But the cuisine is top-notch, whether pheasant or fish, and for 500 Kč you'll get a full meal to round out your midsection. If you're into history, you'll also like the wall tapestries and ancient iconography relating to knightly orders of ages past. The candlelit non-smoking section down below (way below) can be romantic, but avoid it if you're very claustrophobic (daily 13:00–23:00, Prokopská 10, tel. 257-530-075, www.umaltezskychrytiru.cz).

In the Castle Quarter

To locate the following restaurants, see the map on page 103.

Klášterní Pivovar (literally, "Monastery Brewery") was founded by an abbot in 1628. The brewery closed down in 1907, but it finally re-opened in 2004 after meticulous restoration in two large rooms and a pleasant courtyard. The wooden decor and circa-1900 newspaper clippings (including Hapsburg emperor Franz Josef's "Proclamation to My Nations," announcing the beginning of the First World War), bring you to the heart of the best in Czech pub dining. Beer cheese served on a toasted black-yeast bread is a must starter for any meal here. Both locally brewed beer and Czech Budweiser flows through the piping (daily 10:00–22:00, Strahovské Nádvoří 301, tel. 233-353-155, www.klasterni-pivovar .cz). It's directly across from the entrance to the Strahov library (not to be confused with the enormous, group-oriented Klášterní Restaurace next door).

Restaurace Nad Úvozem is hidden in the middle of a staircase that connects Loretánská and Úvoz streets. This secret spot, which boasts super views of Petřín Hill and the Little Quarter, offers excellent food for surprisingly low prices given its location. Try the roast beef in plum sauce. The service is slower when the restaurant is full, as the kitchen has limited space (daily 12:00–21:00; as you go down Loretánská watch for pans, scoops, and spoons hanging on chains on your right at #15; tel. 220-511-532). To discourage pub-goers from mingling with diners, the beer here is terribly overpriced (69 Kč). Instead, have a Kozel (traditional "goat" brand with excellent darks) before or after lunch in the dingy pub called **U Černého Vola** (literally, "By the Black Ox"), located two houses above the staircase (no sign outside, sniff for cigarette smoke and look for the only house on the block without an arcade, daily 10:00–22:00, no English menu).

Malý Buddha (literally, "Little Buddha") serves delightful food—especially vegetarian—and takes its theme seriously. You'll step into a mellow, low-lit escape of bamboo and peace to be served by people with perfect complexions and almost no pulse (Tue–Sun 13:00–22:30, closed Mon, non-smoking, between the castle and Strahov Monastery at Úvoz 46, tel. 220-513-894).

Cafés near the Castle: **Espresso Kajetánka,** just off Castle Square, is the best place to finish up a castle visit. To escape the sun and the bustle of tour groups, go down the staircase to the outside seating in a serene garden, or inside the bird room (all kinds of flying species painted on the walls). The views from below are as good as from the benches on top. The restroom is in the basement, 70 winding steps below the level of the Castle Square (daily 10:00–20:00, Ke Hradu, tel. 257-533-735). **Na Baště Café,** more convenient but not as scenic, is in a garden through the gate to the left of the main castle entry. The outdoor seating, among Jože Plečnik's ramparts and obelisks, is the castle at its most peaceful.

Rubbing Elbows with Hip Locals Away from the Center, in Vinohrady and Žižkov

Café Medúza (literally, "Jellyfish"), an authentic between-the-world-wars café with plush sofas and pictures of 1930s movie stars, draws a crowd of dreamy young Czechs enjoying coffee, cigarettes, dark Svijany beer, and cheap lunch specials (Mon–Fri 11:00–1:00 in the morning, Sat–Sun 12:00–1:00 in the morning, Belgická 17, Metro: Náměstí Míru; from Metro stop, walk a bit down and look for Belgická on your left; tel. 222-515-107).

At **Hlučná Samota** (literally, "Too Loud a Solitude"), the wooden floor and brick walls are dedicated to the great Czech writer Bohumil Hrabal. Though he never visited here, Hrabal would surely be delighted by some of the most beautiful waitresses in Prague, as well as the rich mix of Czech and Italian cuisine (including honey duck, spinach salmon, and Prague's own Staropramen beer to wash it all down). An outdoor lunch—under the shade of linden trees on a quiet, circa-1900 Zagreb street—can easily stretch into an all-afternoon affair (daily 11:00–23:00, Záhřebská 14, tel. 222-522-839, www.hlucnasamota.cz).

Restaurace u Sadu, on Škroupa square below the Žižkov TV Tower, is popular with young Czechs in the summer. An outdoor lunch on this quiet square under a futuristic monument must be one of the most atmospheric eating options in Prague (daily 10:00–2:00 in the morning, Škroupovo Náměstí 5, tel. 222-727-072). The restaurant up in the TV tower itself is expensive, but gives you Neil Armstrong's perspective on Prague.

Hospůdka nad Viktorkou, named for this neighborhood's soccer team, is around the corner on Bořivojova street. This quintessential blue-collar Žižkov pub features occasional live performances by local bands, a warm glass terrace in the winter, and a little courtyard with a shady canopy of chestnut trees in the summer. Sipping a beer while chatting with the natives in this purest of Prague institutions, you'll feel like you've really found the true Prague (daily 12:00–24:00, Bořivojova 79, tel. 222-722-557).

DRINKS

Beer

For many, *pivo*(beer) is the top Czech tourist attraction. Two classic pubs for enjoying a Pilsner are **U Zlatého Tygra** (literally, "By the Golden Tiger"), just south of Karlova on Husova (daily 15:00–23:00, often jam-packed), and **Hostinec u Pinkasů** (open daily), in the dead-end alley just off the bottom of Wenceslas Square. While you're sipping your brew, read the "Czech Beer" sidebar on page 33.

Cafés in the Old Town

These places—dripping with history—are as much about the ambience as they are about the coffee. Most cafés also serve sweets and light meals.

Grand Café Slavia, across from the National Theatre (facing the Legií Bridge on Národní street), is a fixture in Prague, famous as a hangout for its literary elite. Today, it's a bit tired, with an Art Deco interior, lousy piano entertainment, and celebrity photos on the wall. But its cheap and fun menu, filled with interesting traditional dishes (meals, sweets, coffees, liqueurs—including absinthe for 55 Kč), make it a fun stop (daily 8:00–23:00, sit nearest the river). Notice the *Drinker of Absinthe* painting on the wall (and on the menu)—with the iconic Czech writer struggling with reality.

Grand Café Orient, upstairs in the Black Madonna House (which also houses the Museum of Czech Cubism—see page 76), opened in 2005 after major renovations. With Cubist decor toned to dark green, this stylish space full of air and light is a surprisingly good value, with prices pitched to the local's pocket (Mon–Fri 9:00–22:00, Sat–Sun 10:00–22:00, Ovocný Trh 19—at the corner of Celetná near the Powder Tower, tel. 224-224-240).

Café Montmartre, on a small street parallel to Karlova, combines Parisian ambience with unbeatable Czech prices. Dreamy Czech minds have found their asylum here after Slavia (see above) and other long-time favorites have either closed down or got stuck in their grand past. The main room is perfect for discussing philosophy, while the intimate room behind the courtyard is where you recite poetry to your date (Mon–Fri 10:00–23:00, Sat–Sun 12:00–23:00, Řetězová 7, tel. 222-221-244). The courtyard at the end of the street belongs to one of most fascinating Old Town complexes, the **Palace of King George of Poděbrady (Dům pánů z Kunštátu a Poděbrad).** The restaurant, gallery, and museum located inside have erratic hours, but are well worth a peek if you're nearby (between Liliová and Husova at Řetězová 222). The three magnificent Romanesque rooms in the basement (once at street level) are the best-preserved traces of the layering of Prague's architectural history. The display also tells you about this 15th-century Hussite king, who is credited with being the first statesman in history to propose the idea of the United Nations (to protect European heritage from the destructive Turkish invasions).

Ebel Coffee House, in the Ungelt courtyard behind the Týn Church, prides itself on the wide assortment of fresh coffee grounds (from every coffee-growing country in the world), and a colorful decor that delights the mind as much as the caffeine does. The Jumbo Latte is double the size of a Starbucks' venti. Adopting the successful franchise's model, Ebel has opened five other branches in Prague, all of them catering primarily to tourists. But only the Ungelt location has a carefree atmosphere—the others feel cramped (daily 9:00–22:00, Týn 1, tel. 224-895-788).

Bohemia Bagel is hardly authentic—exasperated Czechs insist that bagels have nothing to do with Bohemia. Owned by an American, this trendy café caters mostly to youthful tourists, with good sandwiches (100–125 Kč), a little garden out back, and Internet access (1.50 Kč/min; daily

7:00–24:00; 2 locations: in the Old Town at Masná 2, tel. 224-812-560; and in the Little Quarter at Újezd 16, tel. 257-310-529).

Tea

Many Czech people are bohemian philosophers at heart and prefer the mellow, smoke-free environs of a teahouse to the smoky, traditional beer hall. Young Czechs are much more interested in traveling to exotic destinations like Southeast Asia, Africa, or Peru than to Western Europe, so the Oriental teahouses set their minds in vacation mode.

While there are teahouses all over town, a fine example in a handy locale is Prague's original one, established in 1991: **Dobrá Čajovna** (literally, "Good Teahouse"; Mon–Sat 10:00–21:30, Sun 14:00–21:30, near the base of Wenceslas Square, opposite McDonald's at Václavské Náměstí 14, www.cajovna.com). This teahouse, just a few steps off the bustle of Wenceslas Square, takes you into a very peaceful world that elevates tea to an almost religious ritual. At the desk you'll be given an English menu and a bell. Grab a seat and study the menu, which lovingly describes each tea. The menu lists a world of tea (very fresh, prices by the small pot), "accompaniments" (such as Exotic Miscellany), and light meals "for hungry tea drinkers." When you're ready to order, ring your bell to beckon a tea monk—likely a member of the "Lovers of Tea Society."

SHOPPING

Prague's entire Old Town seems designed to bring out the shopper in visitors. Puppets, glass, and ceramics are traditional. Shop your way from the Old Town Square up Celetná to the Powder Tower, then along Na Příkopě to the bottom of Wenceslas Square (Václavské Náměstí).

Celetná is lined with big stores selling all the traditional Czech goodies. Celetná Crystal, about midway down the street, offers the largest selection of affordable crystal. You can get the glass safely shipped home directly from the shop (for purchases over 1,000 Kč, you can get a refund of the VAT tax—see below).

Na Příkopě has a couple of good modern malls. The best is Slovanský Dům (Na Příkopě 22), where you wander deep past a 10-screen multiplex into a world of classy restaurants and designer shops surrounding a peaceful, parklike inner courtyard. Another modern mall is Černá Růže (Na Příkopě 12). Next door is Mosers, which has a museum-like crystal showroom upstairs.

My readers highly praise **České Kožené Zboží,** a leather store with products exclusively from Czech craftsmen (Mon–Fri 10:00–18:00, Sat 10:00–14:00, Truhlářská 10, from Municipal House go 2 blocks toward the river along Revoluční street and then turn right, mobile 603-787-175).

Bookstores

Globe Bookstore, a few blocks behind the National Theatre, is a mellow literati/expat café with regular poetry readings and lectures. The reader-friendly space features a wide selection of Czech literature in English, recent American releases, second-hand fiction, and also Internet access (daily 10:00–24:00, Pštrossova 6, www.globebookstore.cz).

Anagram Bookshop, in the Ungelt courtyard behind the Týn Church, professes that of all the ways of acquiring books, writing them yourself is the most praiseworthy method. While you won't be asked to leave a bit of yourself here, you will find books in English on a wide range of topics (Mon–Sat 10:00–20:00, Sun 10:00–19:00, Týn 4, tel. 224-895-737, www.anagram.cz).

Big Ben Bookshop, also part of Ungelt (entrance in front of St. James Church), is cramped into a smaller space but has a wider variety of guidebooks and Czech titles than Anagram (Malá Štupartská 5, tel. 224-826-565, www.bigbenbookshop.com).

V Ráji, next to Maisel Synagogue in the Jewish Quarter, is the flagship store of a small publishing house dedicated to books about Prague. They offer an assortment of photo publications, fairy tales, and maps (Maiselova 12, tel. 222-326-925).

Kiwi Map Store, near Wenceslas Square, is one of Prague's best sources for maps (Mon–Fri 9:00–19:00, Sat 9:00–14:00, closed Sun, Jungmanova street 23, tel. 224-948-455, www.kiwick .cz). For suggestions on specific maps to look for, see page 11.

Getting a VAT Refund

Wrapped into the purchase price of your Czech souvenirs is a Value Added Tax (VAT) of 19 percent. If you make a purchase of at least 1,000 Kč (about $40) at a store that participates in the VAT refund scheme, you're entitled to get most of that tax back (see chart for VAT rates and minimum amounts). Personally, I've never felt that VAT refunds are worth the hassle, but if you do, here's the scoop.

If you're lucky, the merchant will subtract the tax when you make your purchase (this is more likely to occur if the store ships the goods to your home). Otherwise, you'll need to do all this:

- **Get the paperwork.** Have the merchant completely fill out the necessary refund document, called a "cheque" (not to be confused with a "Czech"). You'll have to present your passport at the store.

- **Get your stamp at the border or airport.** Process your cheque(s) at your last stop in the country with the customs agent who deals with VAT refunds. It's best to keep your purchases in your carry-on for viewing, but if they're too large or dangerous (such as knives) to carry on, then track down the proper customs agent to inspect them before you check your bag. You're not supposed to use your purchased goods before you leave. If you show up at customs wearing your chic Czech shirt, officials might look the other way—or deny you a refund.

- **Collect your refund.** You'll need to return your stamped documents to the retailer or its representative. Many merchants work with services such as Global Refund or Premier

Tax Free, which have offices at major airports, ports, or border crossings. These services, which extract a 4 percent fee, can refund your money immediately in your currency of choice or credit your card (within 2 billing cycles). If you have to deal directly with the retailer, mail the store your stamped documents, and then wait. It could take months.

Customs Regulations

You can take home $800 in souvenirs per person duty-free. The next $1,000 is taxed at a flat 3 percent. After that, you pay the individual item's duty rate. You can also bring in duty-free a liter of alcohol (slightly more than a standard-size bottle of wine), a carton of cigarettes, and up to 100 non-Cuban cigars. As for food, anything in cans or sealed jars is acceptable. Don't bring back dried meats, cheeses, or fresh fruits and veggies. To check customs rules and duty rates, visit www.customs.gov.

ENTERTAINMENT

Prague booms with live and inexpensive theater, classical, jazz, and pop entertainment. Everything's listed in several monthly cultural events programs (free at TI) and in the *Prague Post* newspaper.

You'll be tempted to gather fliers as you wander through the town. Don't bother. To really understand all your options (the street Mozarts are pushing only their concerts), drop by the **Via Musica** box office at Týn Church on the Old Town Square. The event schedule posted on their wall clearly shows everything that's playing today and tomorrow, including tourist concerts, Black Light Theater, and marionette shows, with photos of each venue and a

map locating everything (daily 10:00–19:00, tel. 224-826-969).

Ticketpro, at Rytířská 31 (between the Havelská Market and the Estates Theatre), sells tickets for the serious concert venues and most music clubs (daily 8:00–12:00 & 12:30–16:30; also has a booth in the Tourist Center at Rytířská 12, daily 9:00–20:00).

Black Light Theater

A kind of mime/modern dance variety show, Black Light Theater has no language barrier and is, for many, more entertaining than a classical concert. Unique to Prague (though somewhat comparable to the Canadian Cirque du Soleil), Black Light Theater originated in the 1960s as a playful and mystifying theater of the absurd. The two main venues are **Ta Fantastika** (*Aspects of Alice* at 21:30, more poetic, more puppets, traditional, a little artistic nudity, 620 Kč, reserved seating, near east end of Charles Bridge at Karlova 8,

Entertainment in Prague's Old Town

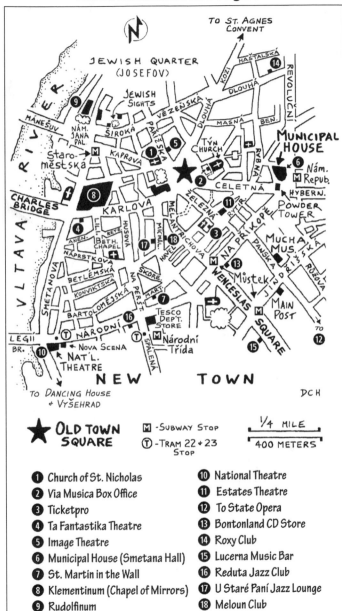

★ **OLD TOWN SQUARE**

Ⓜ – SUBWAY STOP

Ⓣ – TRAM 22 & 23 STOP

¼ MILE / 400 METERS

❶ Church of St. Nicholas
❷ Via Musica Box Office
❸ Ticketpro
❹ Ta Fantastika Theatre
❺ Image Theatre
❻ Municipal House (Smetana Hall)
❼ St. Martin in the Wall
❽ Klementinum (Chapel of Mirrors)
❾ Rudolfinum

❿ National Theatre
⓫ Estates Theatre
⓬ To State Opera
⓭ Bontonland CD Store
⓮ Roxy Club
⓯ Lucerna Music Bar
⓰ Reduta Jazz Club
⓱ U Staré Paní Jazz Lounge
⓲ Meloun Club

tel. 222-221-366, www.tafantastika.cz) and **Image Theatre** (more mime and absurd—"it's precisely the fact that we are all so different that unites us," shows at 18:00 and 20:00, 450 Kč, open seating—arrive early to grab a good spot, just off Old Town Square at Pařížská 4, tel. 222-314-448, www.imagetheatre.cz). Shows last about 90 minutes. Avoid the first four rows, which get you so close that it ruins the illusion. The other black light theaters advertising around town aren't as good.

Tourist Concerts

Each day, six or eight classical concerts designed for tourists fill delightful Old World halls and churches with music of the crowd-pleasing sort: Vivaldi, Best of Mozart, Most Famous Arias, and works by the famous Czech composer Antonín Dvořák. Concerts typically cost 400–1,000 Kč, start anywhere from 13:00 to 21:00, and last one hour. Common venues are two buildings on Little Quarter Square (the Church of St. Nicholas and the Prague Academy of Music in Liechtenstein Palace); in the Klementinum's Chapel of Mirrors; at the Old Town Square (in a different Church of St. Nicholas); and in the stunning Smetana Hall in the Municipal House (see page 88). The artists vary from excellent to amateur.

A sure bet is the jam session held every Monday at 17:00 at **St. Martin in the Wall**, where Prague's best professional musicians gather to tune in and chat with each other (400 Kč, Martinská street, just north of Tesco building in the Old Town).

Prague Castle Orchestra

One of Prague's most entertaining acts performs regularly on Castle Square. This trio—Josef on flute, Radek on accordion, and passionate Jarda on bass—plays a lively Czech mélange of Smetana, swing, old folk tunes, and 1920s cabaret songs. Look for them if you're visiting the castle (see page 107) and consider picking up their fun CD. They're also available for private functions (pay them 2,000 Kč apiece for a 45-min performance, mobile 603-552-448, josekocurek@volny.cz).

Serious Concerts

True music-lovers should consider Prague's top symphonic venue, the **Rudolfinum** (featuring the Prague Philharmonic, on Palachovo Náměstí, in Jewish Quarter on the Old Town side of Mánes Bridge). Concerts in the large Dvořák Hall or the small Suk Hall usually start at 19:30 (also afternoons on weekends). The ticket office is on the right side, under the stairs (250–1,000 Kč, open until few minutes before the show starts).

Mozart, Smetana, Dvořák, and More

The three major composers connected with Prague—Mozart, Smetana, and Dvořák—all have museums dedicated to their life and work in the city.

During his frequent visits to Prague, Austrian **Wolfgang Amadeus Mozart** (1756–1791) stayed with his friends in the beautiful, small, neo-classicist Villa Bertramka, now the Mozart Museum. Surrounded by a peaceful garden, the villa preserves the time when the Salzburg prodigy felt more appreciated in Prague than in Austria. Intimate concerts are held some afternoons and evenings, either in the garden or the small concert hall (110 Kč, daily April–Oct 9:30–18:00, Nov–March 9:30–17:00, Mozartova 169, Praha 5; from Metro: Anděl, it's a 10-min walk—head to Hotel Mövenpick and then go up alley behind hotel; tel. 257-317-465, www.bertramka.cz).

A statue of **Bedřich Smetana** (1824–1884), the father of Czech classical music, is seated in front of his museum, listening intently to the rapids of the Vltava River near the Charles Bridge (Tue–Sun 10:00–17:00, closed Mon, Novotného Lávka, Praha 1, tel. 224-229-075). Like Richard Wagner, Smetana aimed to stir the Romantic nationalist spirit. His finest work, the cycle of symphonic poems called *My Country (Má Vlast),* was inspired by places and myths important to the Czech people. *Vltava,* the most beautiful of the poems, will likely be the first sound of Prague you hear if you're flying Czech Airlines—the soft tune emanates from the loudspeakers upon arrival.

The **National Theatre** (Národní Divadlo, on the New Town side of Legií Bridge)—with a must-see neo-Renaissance interior (see page 91) —is best for opera and ballet (shows from 19:00, 300–1,000 Kč, tel. 224-912-673, www.nationaltheatre.cz). The **Estates Theatre** (Stavovské Divadlo) is where Mozart premiered and personally directed many of his most beloved works (see page 76). *Don Giovanni, The Marriage of Figaro,* and *The Magic Flute* are on the program a couple of times each month (shows from 20:00, 800–1,400 Kč, between the Old Town Square and the New Town on a square called Ovocný Trh, tel. 224-214-339, www .estatestheatre.cz). The ticket office for both of these theaters is in the little square (Ovocný Trh) behind the Estates Theatre.

The **State Opera** (Státní Opera) focuses on Verdi (shows at 19:00 or 20:00, 400–1,200 Kč, buy tickets at the theater, on 5. Května—the busy street between the Main Train Station and Wenceslas Square, tel. 224-227-693, www.opera.cz).

World-class musicians are in town during the **Prague**

Antonín Dvořák (1841–1904) is the Czech Republic's best-known composer. For three years, Dvořák directed the National Conservatory in New York, during which time he composed his most famous work, the *New World Symphony (Z Nového Světa)*. Dvořák's advice to his students was to look for inspiration in America's own authentic melodies (African American spirituals and Native American music) rather than in European models. Dvořák's gentle opera of a water nymph, *Rusalka*, is considered the best Czech opera and is often performed in Prague's National Theatre. The Dvořák Museum is located in Villa America, which was once the composer's home (Tue–Sun 10:00–17:00, closed Mon, Ke Karlovu 20, Praha 2, tel. 224-923-363).

Two other important composers from Czech lands are the moderns Mahler and Janáček. **Gustav Mahler** (1860–1911), a Jew from Jihlava (see page 199), was a pioneer of atonal music. His best works are *Symphony No. 1: Titan* and *The Song of the Earth*, both inspired by the sounds of the Moravian woods and fields. His *Symphony No. 1* is a traditional favorite of the Czech Philharmonic, which usually performs it with Dvořák's *New World Symphony* in the Rudolfinum.

Leoš Janáček (1854–1928), the most original and least accessible Czech composer, was stimulated by language—its flow and abrupt pauses. He's known for his *Symphonietta* and *Lachian Dances (Lašské Tance)*, as well as the opera *Cunning Little Vixen (Příhody Lišky Bystroušky)*, another perennial in the National Theatre's repertoire.

Spring (mid-May through the beginning of June, www.festival.cz) and **Prague Autumn** (mid-Sept through mid-Oct, www.pragueautumn.cz) music festivals.

For any of these concerts, locals dress up, but many tourists wear casual clothes—as long as you don't show up in sneakers and ripped jeans, you'll be fine.

Music Clubs

Young locals keep Prague's many music clubs in business. Most clubs are neighborhood institutions with decades of tradition, generally holding only 100–200 people. Live rock and Bob Dylan–style folk are what younger generations go for. A number of good jazz clubs attract a diverse audience, from ages 18 to 80. In the last decade, ethnic music has also become hugely popular: Roma (Gypsy) bands, Moravian poets, African drummers, Cuban boleros, and Moroccan divas often sell out even the largest venues. You can buy tickets at the club, or, for most places, at the Ticketpro

Buying Czech CDs

... e to get CDs is the huge **Bontonland** music and ... at the bottom of Wenceslas Square (enter from th... t has a big *Kenvelo* sign on the outside). In the classical mu... section, you'll find many interpretations of Czech works. For the best rendition, look for music performed by the Czech Philharmonic, conducted by Václav Neumann.

For contemporary, lighter music, get a CD by Čechomor (*Metamorphosis* is their best). This band, which began by playing traditional Czech music at weddings and funerals, synthesized the sound of folk ballads and has since become one of the most popular groups in the country. Jiří Pavlica and Hradišťán keep the music of Moravia alive, while Věra Bílá and Ida Kellarová capture the lively spirit of the Roma (Gypsies). Some cool Czech rock groups are Psí Vojáci, Neočekávaný Dýchánek, and Už Jsme Doma.

offices (see page 145). If you like jazz, I've listed some fine options; avoid the Jazzboat (advertised by commission-hungry hotels), which has mediocre musicians and high prices.

In the Old Town

Roxy, a few blocks from the Old Town Square, features live bands from outside the country twice a week—anything from Irish punk to Balkan brass. On other nights the floor is taken over by experimental DJs that will give you a healthy dose of Japanese pop (concerts start at 20:00, disco at 22:00, cover from 100 Kč, Mon free, easy to book online and pick up tickets at the door, Dlouhá 33, tel. 224-826-296, www.roxy.cz).

In the New Town

Lucerna Music Bar, at the bottom of Wenceslas Square, is popular for disco nights. Friday and Saturdays are the "1980s Party," featuring the silly pop songs of the last years under communism, when spineless Czech pop stars took the easy route to success instead of coming up with thoughtful lyrics that could have furthered the cause of freedom. The scene is a big, noisy dance hall with a giant video screen. Young and trendy, the Lucerna has cheap prices, and even older tourists mix in easily (music nightly from 21:00, around 100-Kč cover, in the basement of Lucerna Gallery, Vodičkova 36, tel. 224-217-108).

➤The small **Reduta Jazz Club,** with cushioned brown sofas stretching along mirrored walls, will launch you straight into the 1960s classic jazz scene. The top Czech jazzmen—Stivín and Koubková—regularly perform here. Even Bill Clinton played the sax here (live jazz every night from 21:00, on Národní street next to Café Louvre).

For more modern and Latin jazz, head to the nearby, less atmospheric **U Staré Paní Jazz Lounge** (shows start nightly at 21:00, Michalská street, tel. 603-551-680). Across the street is the laid-back café-disco **Meloun Club,** in a Gothic stone vault cellar (at #12, no gigantic TV screens or Ikea tables).

In the Little Quarter

These clubs are far more mellow than others (including the lively Roxy in the Old Town and Palác Acropolis in Žižkov).

Malostranská Beseda, on the Little Quarter Square, was known in the communist era for playing host to underground rock bands, semi-legal bards, and daring jazzmen—a stark contrast to the regime-pampered pop stars. Today Beseda is the only club in the center with daily live performances, and the crowd tends to be a bit older than in the other clubs (shows from 20:30, about 150-Kč cover, Malostranské Náměstí 21, tel. 257-532-092).

Baráčnická Rychta, with a gymnasium-like hall, saw many great polka parties in the 1920s. Since then, rock has replaced waltz, but the place still feels like a village dancehall, complete with flags of bakers' and butchers' guilds and black-and-white photos of the proud Austro-Hungarian landlords. It's a great scene if the hall is full, but less popular bands look a bit lost in the large space. Try the yeasty and strong Svijany beer here (3 shows weekly starting at 20:00 or 21:00, arrive earlier to get a seat at a table, 150-Kč cover, on Tržiště, tucked away from tourists and out-of-town Czechs in a small courtyard directly across from American Embassy, tel. 257-532-461).

In Žižkov

This hip neighborhood, below the Žižkov TV tower (Metro: Jiřího z Poděbrad), has Prague's highest concentration of cool pubs.

Palác Akropolis is *the* home of Czech independent music. Originally a 1920s movie theatre, in the 1990s it was turned into a chill-out lounge, a literary café, and two halls that offer a mix of concerts, disco, and theater (advance ticket sales at café, Mon–Fri 10:00–24:00, Sat–Sun 16:00–24:00, corner of Kubelíkova and Fibichova, under TV tower, Metro: Jiřího z Poděbrad, tel. 296-330-913, www.palacakropolis.cz).

Sports

Prague's top sports are soccer (that's "football" here) and hockey. Surprisingly, the Czechs are a world power in both.

You'll find the latest schedules for games in the *Prague Post* newspaper (soccer—usually late Sat, Sun, or Mon afternoon

Feb–May and Aug–Nov; hockey—Tue, Fri, Sun nights Sept–April). Both soccer and hockey games are rarely sold out—just show up at the stadium 15 minutes before the game starts.

Soccer

The Czech soccer team reached the finals and semifinals of the last three European Cups. Within the Czech Republic, the two oldest and by far most successful soccer clubs are the bitter Prague rivals, Sparta and Slavia. Slavia has always been the better team, while Sparta has merely harvested more trophies. Sparta's stadium at Letná (behind the metronome ticking above the river) is easier to get to.

Hockey

The Czech national hockey team won four out of last seven world championships, including 2005 (Canada won two, and Slovakia the remaining one). Think Jaromír Jágr, one of the NHL's leading scorers. There are more than a hundred Czech players in America's NHL.

Sparta and Slavia also have hockey teams, but the rivalry is less intense, as the teams from smaller towns are more than their equals. Slavia plays in the brand-new, state-of-the-art Sazka Arena built for the 2004 world hockey championships (right at the Českomoravská Metro stop).

Back in the old days, ice hockey was the only battleground on which Czechoslovaks could seek revenge on their Russian oppressors. To this day, the hockey rink is where Czechs are proudest about their nationality. If you are in town in May during the hockey championships, join locals cheering their team in front of a giant screen on the Old Town Square and other main squares around the country.

Ice hockey is also the most popular sport in Slovakia. To understand the friendly relationship between Czechs and Slovaks after their Velvet Divorce in 1989 (see sidebar on page 242), just walk into any Czech or Slovak pub during the hockey championships. Unless the two teams are playing each other, all Czechs passionately support the Slovak team, and vice versa.

TRANSPORTATION CONNECTIONS

Centrally located Prague is a logical gateway between Western and Eastern Europe. If you're coming from the West and using a Eurailpass, you must purchase tickets to cover the portion of the journey from the Czech border into Prague (buy at station before you board train for Prague). Or supplement your pass with a **Prague Excursion Pass**, giving you passage from any Czech border station into Prague and back to any border station within seven days (first class-€50, second class-€40, youth second class-€30). EurAide, a travel agency with offices in Berlin and Munich, also sells these passes for a bit less from their American office (U.S. tel. 941/480-1555, fax 941/480-1522, www.euraide.de/ricksteves). From the East, Prague has convenient night-train connections with Budapest, Kraków, and Warsaw (see below).

You'll find handy Czech train and bus schedules at www.vlak -bus.cz. Train info tel. 221-111-122 (little English spoken).

For rail travel tips, see page 16. Remember that for all train connections, it's important to confirm which of Prague's stations to use.

From Prague by Train to: Benešov (10-min walk from **Konopiště Castle**; hrly, 45 min), **Karlštejn** (from Prague's Smíchov station, hrly, 40 min, then a 20-min walk to castle), **Křivoklát** (from Prague's Smíchov station, 90 min, transfer in Beroun), **Kutná Hora** (7/day, 1 hr, more with change in Kolín), **Český Krumlov** (8/day, 1/day direct, 4 hrs), **Třeboň** (7/day, 2.5 hrs, transfer at Veselí nad Lužnicí), **Telč** (3/day, 4–5 hrs, requires 2 changes; bus is better—see below), **Třebíč** (nearly hrly, 4–5 hrs, transfer in Brno; bus is better—see below), **Slavonice** (bus to Telč—see below—then 1-hr train to Slavonice, 4 hrs total), **Olomouc** (hrly, 3.5 hrs; use Olomouc for connections to **Wallachia**), **Břeclav** (with connections on to **Mikulov Wine Region**—see page 226; every 2 hrs, 3.5 hrs direct, most from Prague's Holešovice station), **Brno** (every 2 hrs direct, 2.75 hrs; bus is better—see below), **Moravský Krumlov** (go to Brno, then take 45-min train; bus from Prague to Brno is faster), **Berlin** (5/day, 5 hrs), **Munich** (3/day with changes, 6 hrs; 1 direct night train), **Frankfurt** (4 direct/day, 6 hrs), **Vienna** (3/day, 5 hrs), **Budapest** (5 direct/day, 7 hrs; 1 direct night train, 9 hrs), **Kraków** (1 direct night train/day, 8.5 hrs; otherwise transfer in Katowice, Wrocław, or Ostrava-Svinov, 8–11 hrs), **Warsaw** (2/day direct, including 1 night train, 9–12 hrs; or 1/day, 9 hrs, with transfer in Ostrava-Svinov).

By Bus to: Terezín (hrly, 1 hr), **Český Krumlov** (7/day, 3.5 hrs, from Florenc station; an easy direct 3-hr bus leaves at about 9:00), **Třeboň** (2/day, 2.5 hrs), **Telč** (5 buses/day Mon–Fri, 3/day Sat–Sun, 2–3 hrs; more with a transfer in Jihlava, 3 hrs total), **Třebíč** (7/day, 2.5 hrs), **Brno** (2/hr from Florenc station, 2.5 hrs). Note that some buses from Prague to Telč and Třebíč go from the Roztyly station (on the red Metro line), not the main bus station, Florenc.

By Car with a Driver: Mike's Chauffeur Service is a reliable family-run company with fair and fixed rates around town and beyond. Friendly Mike's motto is, "We go the extra mile for you" (round-trip fares with waiting time included, guaranteed through 2006 with this book: Český Krumlov-3,500 Kč, Terezín-1,700 Kč, Karlštejn-1,500 Kč, minivan with plenty of room for up to 4 people, minibus also available, tel. 241-768-231, mobile 602-224-893, www.mike-chauffeur.cz, mike.chauffeur@cmail.cz). On the way to Krumlov, Mike will stop at no extra charge at Hluboká Castle or České Budějovice, where the original Bud beer is made. Mike offers a "Panoramic Transfer to Vienna" for 7,000 Kč (depart Prague at 8:00, arrive Český Krumlov at 10:00, stay up to 6 hrs, 1-hr scenic Czech riverside-and-village drive, then a 2-hr autobahn ride to your Vienna hotel, maximum 4 people). Mike also offers a similar "Panoramic Transfer to Budapest" for 10,000 Kč (2 hrs to Český Krumlov, then 1-hr scenic drive to Linz, followed by 5–6 hrs on expressway to Budapest).

BEYOND PRAGUE

DAY TRIPS

Prague has plenty to keep a traveler busy, but don't overlook the enjoyable day trips in the nearby Bohemian countryside. Within an hour of Prague (in different directions), you'll find a rich medieval town, a sobering concentration camp, and three grand castles.

Down-to-earth Kutná Hora was once home to the world's largest silver mine; it's now known for its opulent cathedral, built with riches from the mining bonanza. Terezín, a walled town, served as a containment camp for Jews during World War II. The charming nearby town of Litoměřice offers an opportunity to reflect on the camp. Two of the country's most popular castles—Konopiště (better interior) and Karlštejn (better exterior)—give you a good look at the Czech version of this European medieval architectural form. Křivoklát Castle is one of the purest Gothic structures in the country, and a less touristy alternative to the other two castles. The village of Lány is a pilgrimage site for Czech patriots.

Kutná Hora

Kutná Hora (KOOT-nah HO-rah) is a refreshingly authentic town of 20,000, on top of what was once Europe's largest silver mine. In its heyday, the mine was so productive that Kutná Hora was Bohemia's "second city" after Prague. The standard coinage of much of Europe was minted here. By about 1700, the mining and minting petered out, and the city slumbered. Once rich, then ignored, Kutná Hora is now newly appreciated by tourists looking for a handy side-trip from Prague. Visitors are charmed by its wonderfully preserved state and interesting sights: the fine St. Barbara's Cathedral, the fascinating silver mine, and the eerie Bone Church.

Start your visit at Hrádek (the Czech Museum of Silver), make an appointment for a tour, and then build your day around it.

Kutná Hora, unlike dolled-up Český Krumlov, is a typical Czech town. The shops on the main square cater to locals, and the factory between the Bone Church and the train station—since the 1930s, the biggest tobacco processor in the country—is now Philip Morris' headquarters for Central Europe. After touristy Prague, Kutná Hora is about as close to quintessential Czech life as you can get.

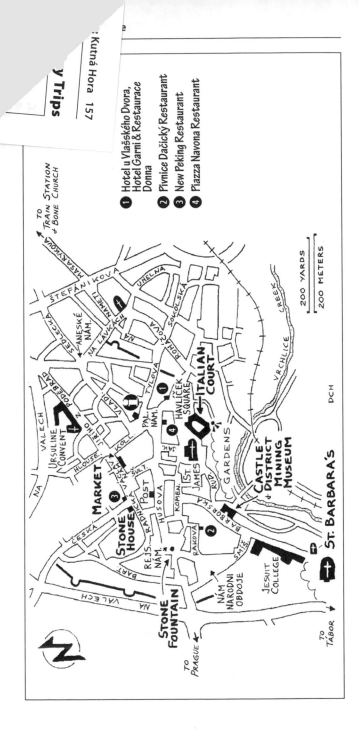

TO TRAIN STATION & BONE CHURCH

MASARYKOVA

ŠTEFÁNIKOVA

SEDLECKA

ANESKÉ NÁM.

NA LAVKÁCH

NA MARKET

UNELNA

POD BRAD

VLADI.

JIŘÍHO

HLOUSE

NA VALECH

URSULINE CONVENT

MARKET

STONE HOUSE

ČESKÁ

BART.

NA VALECH

TO PRAGUE

REJS. NÁM.

RADNICKA

Post

HUSOVA

KOMEN.

RAKOVA

STONE FOUNTAIN

NÁM. NÁRODNÍ OBROJE

JESUIT COLLEGE

TO TABOR

ST. BARBARA'S

CASTLE DISTRICT MINING MUSEUM

GARDENS

ST. JAMES

RUD.

BARBORSKA

SMIS.

VRCHLICE CREEK

DCH

ITALIAN COURT

HAVLÍČEK SQUARE

SOKOLSKÁ

ROHA

TYLOVA

PAL. NÁM.

JACK.

SULT.

KOLL.

➊ Hotel u Vlašského Dvora,
   Hotel Garni & Restaurace
   Donna
➋ Pivnice Dačický Restaurant
➌ New Peking Restaurant
➍ Plazza Navona Restaurant

200 YARDS
200 METERS

ORIENTATION

Tourist Information

The main TI is on Palackého Náměstí (Mon–Fri 9:00–18:00, Sat–Sun 10:00–16:00, tel. 327-512-378, www.kutnahora.cz) and a TI kiosk is in front of the cathedral.

Helpful Hints

Local Guide: You can arrange a local guide at the TI kiosk at the cathedral; it's smart to reserve ahead (500 Kč/hr Tue–Sun, no tours Mon, tel. 327-516-710, mobile 736-485-408, infocentrum@kh.cz).

Car Rental: If you need a car for your Czech travels, you'll pay more to rent in Prague. Instead, consider renting a Škoda (a proudly Czech type of car) from Autopůjčovna Morava here in Kutná Hora (840–1,250 Kč/day depending on size of car, includes unlimited mileage and insurance, Masarykova street, tel. 327-512-715, mobile 777-013-020, auta.morava@quick.cz).

SIGHTS

In Kutná Hora

St. Barbara's Cathedral (Chrám Sv. Barbory)—The cathedral was founded in 1388 by miners, who dedicated it to their patron. The dazzling interior celebrates the town's sources of wealth with frescoes featuring mining and minting. Even the Renaissance vault—a stunning feat of the two Gothic geniuses of Prague, Matyáš Rejsek and Benedict Ried—is decorated with miners' coats of arms. The artistic highlight is the Smíšek Chapel to the right of the altar. The late-Gothic frescoes—*The Arrival of the Queen of Sheba*, *The Trial of Trajan*, and especially the fresco under the chapel's window depicting two men with candles—are the only work of a Dutch-trained master in Gothic Bohemia (30 Kč, daily 9:00–18:00 in season, shorter hours off-season).

As you exit the cathedral, you'll see the Baroque Jesuit college on your left. Jesuits arrived here in 1626 with a mission: to make the Protestant population Catholic again. The statues of saints on the artificial terrace in front of the college were inspired by the statues on Charles Bridge.

Hrádek and the Czech Museum of Silver—At this museum, located in Kutná Hora's 15th-century castle, you'll see an exhibit on mining and an intriguing horse-powered winch that hoisted 2,000 pounds of rock at a time out of the mine. Then you'll don a miner's coat and helmet and climb deep into the mine for a wet, dark, and claustrophobic 45-minute tour of the medieval shafts that honeycomb the land under the town (April–Oct Tue–Sun

10:00–18:00, closed Mon and Nov–March, tours generally every half hour, tel. 327-512-159). When you arrive in Kutná Hora, find out when the next English tour will run and reserve a spot; ask for Mr. Matuška, a charming retired miner.

Stone Fountain (Kamenná Kašna)—Because of the intensive mining under the town, Kutná Hora always struggled with the problem of obtaining drinking water. Water was brought to town by a sophisticated system of water pipes and stored in large tanks. At the end of the 15th century, the architect Rejsek built a 12-sided, richly decorated Gothic structure over one of these tanks. While no longer functioning, the fountain survives unchanged, the only structure of its kind in Bohemia (on the square called Rejskovo Náměstí).

Stone House (Kamenný Dům)—Notice the meticulous detail in the wine leaves, branches, and animals on the facade and up in the gable. Talented Polish craftsmen delicately carved the brittle stone into what was considered a marvel of its time. Skip the boring museum of local arts and crafts inside (40 Kč, daily 10:00–17:00, Radnická 183).

Italian Court (Vlašský Dvůr)—This palace building, located on the site where the first real Czech currency was made, became Europe's most important mint and the main residence of Czech kings in the 1400s. Today it hosts a museum on minting and local history. The 70-Kč entry gets you into the main Gothic hall (now a wedding chamber) and the Art Nouveau–decorated St. Wenceslas Chapel (daily 9:00–18:00, less Oct–March, Havlíčkovo Náměstí). But neither the museum nor the building itself—largely a 19th-century imitation of the former palace—is particularly interesting. The flower-filled square in front of it, on the other hand, is worth a look...

Havlíček Square (Havlíčkovo Náměstí)—The monuments on this square are a *Who's Who* of important Czech patriots.

The statue in the middle of the square (and the square's namesake) is **Karel Havlíček** (1821–1856), the founder of Czech political journalism. From Kutná Hora, Havlíček ran an influential magazine highly critical of the Hapsburg government. In 1851, he was forced into exile and detained for five years in the Tirolean Alps under police surveillance. His integrity is illustrated with the inscription on the statue: "You can try to bribe me with favors, you can threaten me, you can torture me, yet I will never turn a traitor." His motto became an inspiration for generations of Czech intellectuals, most of whom faced a similar combination of threats and temptations. Havlíček (whose name means "little Havel") was much revered in the 1970s and 1980s, when the *other* Havel (Václav) was similarly imprisoned for his dissent.

The bronze statue in front of the Italian Court commemorates the founder of Czechoslovakia, **Tomáš Garrigue Masaryk**

Czechs After Communism

Czech survivors of communist prisons feel a great sense of injustice. Following World War II, many of the Czechs who collaborated with the Nazis were brought to justice. But in contrast, after communism fell in 1989, supporters of that regime never faced retribution. In fact, when the country's industrial infrastructure was privatized in the early 1990s, these former Communist Party big-shots used their connections to take control of some of the country's new capitalist enterprises. Many of the old Party leaders morphed into the bosses of the new Czech economy.

The Communist Party was never outlawed, so no one was ever charged. The Velvet Revolutionaries believed that, with time, communism would disappear naturally. But it didn't. Because the Czechs must form coalition governments, non-communist parties find that they have to make deals with the reds to gain political leverage. Today the Communist Party of Bohemia and Moravia (with its Stalinist roots) draws a steady 20 percent of the electorate (in 2002 national and 2004 European elections) and is a substantial force in Czech politics.

(1850–1937; see sidebar on page 110). The brief inscription on the back of the pedestal illustrates the country's troubled 20th-century history: erected by Kutná Hora townsmen on October 27, 1938 (the eve of the 20th anniversary of Czech independence); torn down in 1942 (by occupying Nazis, who disliked Masaryk as a symbol of Czech independence); erected again on October 27, 1948 (by freedom-loving locals, a few months after the communist coup); torn down again in 1957 (by the communists, who considered Masaryk an enemy of the working class); and erected once again on October 27, 1991. But notice that the Czechs, ever realistic, have left a blank space below the last entry....

On the wall to the left of the gate, you'll find the small, bronze tablet covered with barbed wire. This is an unassuming little **memorial** to the victims of communist misrule and torture.

Walk down the steps into a little park, and then turn right to reach a great viewpoint. It overlooks the tent-shaped roof of the cathedral and the scenic valley below. Nearby benches under the shade of linden trees invite you to sit back and think about those to whom the memorial is dedicated.

Market (Tržiště)—This double row of stalls selling fake Nike shoes and cheap jeans is as integral a part of today's Czech town as farmers markets were in the past. The bazaars are run by Vietnamese immigrants, the largest minority in the Czech Republic. Many came in the 1970s as part of a communist solidarity program that sent Vietnamese workers to Czech textile factories. They learned the language, adapted to the environment, and, after 1989, set off on a road to entrepreneurial success that allowed them to bring over friends and relatives.

Czechs love these markets. Get an Adidas shirt—it's a more truly authentic Czech souvenir than anything you can buy in Prague's Old Town (Mon–Fri 7:30–16:45, shorter hours Sat, closed Sun, near Stone House and New Peking Restaurant).

Near Kutná Hora

Sedlec Bone Church (Kostnice u Sedlci)—Located a mile away from the center of town, in Sedlec, this little church looks normal on the outside. Inside, the bones of 40,000 people decorate the walls and ceilings. Fourteenth-century plagues and 15th-century wars provided all the raw material necessary for the creepily creative monks who made these designs. Those who first placed these bones 400 years ago wanted viewers to remember that the earthly church is a community of both the living and the dead, a countless multitude that will one day stand before God. Later bone-stackers were more interested in design than theology...as evidenced by the chandelier that includes every bone in the human body (30 Kč, July–Aug daily 8:00–  18:00, April–June and Sept–Oct daily 9:00–17:00, Nov–March Tue–Sun 9:00–16:00, closed Mon). To get to the Bone Church, you can walk, catch a taxi (less than 100 Kč), or ride the city bus (leaves from Masarykova street, buy ticket at a newsstand).

SLEEPING

Although one day is enough for Kutná Hora, staying overnight saves you money (hotels are much cheaper here than in Prague) and allows you to better savor the atmosphere of a small Czech town.

Hotel u Vlašského Dvora and **Hotel Garni** are two newly renovated townhouses run by the same management. Furnished in a mix of 1930s and modern style, the hotels come with access to a fitness center and sauna. Hotel Garni is slightly nicer (Db-1,350 Kč, a few steps off main square at Havlíčkovo Náměstí 513, tel. 327-515-773, www.hotel.cz/garni-na-havlicku).

EATING

Pivnice Dačický is the best restaurant in town, with local beer on tap and excellent game and fish. Solid wooden tables rest under perky illustrations of medieval town life. Don't miss the vanilla ice cream with hot pears, egg liqueur, and whipped cream (daily 11:00–23:00, Rakova 8, tel. 327-512-248, mobile 603-434-367).

Restaurace Donna features the fastest and tastiest ready-to-serve Czech dishes in town. If the weather's nice, sit in the courtyard behind the restaurant, shaded by chestnut trees (daily, lunch specials until 15:00, at Havlíčkovo Náměstí, right above Hotel Garni).

Cuisines evolve. Today, the chicken roasted in paprika at the **New Peking** restaurant (next to the Stone House) and the spaghetti swimming in a sea of Czech ketchup and *klobasa* at **Piazza Navona** (daily, on the main square) are as Czech as the typical pork and sauerkraut.

TRANSPORTATION CONNECTIONS

Getting to Kutná Hora: The town is 40 miles east of Prague. Trains from Prague's Main Station (7/day, 60 min) stop near Kutná Hora, two miles from the town center. From there, local trains shuttle visitors to the central Kutná Hora Město station.

Terezín Concentration Camp

Terezín (TEH-reh-zeen), an hour by bus from Prague, was a fortified town named after Maria Theresa (it's called "Theresienstadt" in German). It was built in the 1780s with state-of-the-art walls designed to keep out the Prussians. In 1941, the Nazis removed its 7,000 inhabitants and brought in 60,000 Jews, creating Terezín Concentration Camp. The town's medieval walls, originally meant to keep Germans out, were now used by German conquerors to keep the Jews in.

This was the Nazis' model "Jewish town," a concentration camp dolled up for propaganda purposes. Here in this "self-governed Jewish settlement area," Jewish culture seemed to thrive, as "citizens" put on plays and concerts, published a magazine, and raised their families in ways impressive to Red Cross inspectors. But virtually all of Terezín's Jews (155,000 over the course of war) ultimately ended up dying either here (35,000) or at the extermination camps farther east. (The art of the children of Terezín survives as a striking testimony to the cruel horror of the Holocaust. It's well-displayed and described in English in Prague's Pinkas Synagogue—see page 69.)

Today Terezín is an unforgettable day trip from Prague for those interested in touring a concentration camp memorial and museum. Allow three hours to see the entire camp thoroughly (although some visitors recommend that 5 hours is more realistic). With more time, consider a visit to the nearby town of Litoměřice (see below) for lunch before returning to Prague.

Cost, Hours, Information: The 180-Kč combo-ticket gets you into all parts of the camp, including the Museum of the Ghetto and the Small Fortress (daily April–Oct 9:00–18:00, Nov–March 9:00–16:00). Tel. 416-782-225, mobile 606-632-914, www.pamatnik-terezin.cz.

Touring the Camp: Start with the **Museum of the Ghetto** and the Magdeburg barracks, where you buy the Terezín combo-ticket (also pick up a map, note show times for movies, and ask when the next English tour of the fortress will be). You'll find two floors of exhibits about the camp and a theater showing two excellent 10-minute films: a slice-of-camp-life video and a propaganda video produced by the Nazis and used to fool the Red Cross about conditions here for the Jewish inmates (the same movies also play in the Small Fortress).

Then walk through the **walled town,** following the numbered map that explains the various sights. After you finish, leave the fortified city and cross the river. Walk about 300 yards around the vast cemetery to the **Small Fortress**—you'll see its black-and-white-striped gate. Inside the gate, at the ticket checkpoint, wait for the obligatory guided tour (English tours leave about every 30 min). This Gestapo police prison—opened in 1942—was filled not with Jews, but with other enemies of the Third Reich (who fill the graveyard you passed to get here). The powerful 45-minute tour shows the demonic modus operandi used by the SS: torture followed by execution. On the second floor of the building, on the right from the gate, is an exposition of paintings with themes of ghetto life and the Spanish Civil War from three prominent Czech artists.

As you explore the camp, ponder the message of all such memorials: Never again.

TRANSPORTATION CONNECTIONS

Getting to Terezín: The camp is about 40 miles northwest of Prague. Buses leave nearly hourly from Prague's Florenc station and arrive in Terezín about one hour later at the public bus stop, which is on the marketplace in the town center facing the museum.

The most convenient daily bus leaves Prague at 9:30; several other buses run weekdays or weekends only (for schedules, see www .vlak-bus.cz; you want "Terezín LT"). For the return trip to Prague, note bus departure times when you arrive.

Near Terezín: Litoměřice

With a bustling, beautifully restored Renaissance square, Litoměřice (lee-TOH-myer-zheet-seh, pop. 26,000)—located three miles north of Terezín—is a perfect lunch spot to lift your spirits after the bleakness of the camp. During the communist era,

Litoměřice had the only seminary in the country. Today, there are still two huge Baroque churches here. Linger on the main square, Mírové Náměstí, and experience the life of this friendly, untouristy Czech town.

If arriving by bus from Terezín, get off at the first stop after the bridge; from here it's a two-minute walk (slightly uphill) to the main square. From the square, several small streets filled with bakeries and convenience shops radiate outwards. The onion-shaped tower is south, and the higher part of the square is due west. Stroll around and get lunch on the square (see "Eating," below). After lunch, climb up the onion-shaped tower of the **Town Hall** (the guide in the tower loves to talk), but skip the uninteresting museum on the square.

The short street next to the Town Hall leads onto the city walls, with good views. The statue at the viewpoint depicts the Romantic poet **Karel Hynek Mácha** (1810–1836), who wrote the most famous Czech poem, "Máj." He died in Litoměřice. In 1939, his body was ceremonially exhumed and transferred to the Slavín cemetery atop Prague's Vyšehrad hill. Mácha became a symbol of the irrepressible Czech spirit, stirring Czech nationalism during the occupations of first the Nazis, then the communists. In November 1989, demonstrating students who were headed for the grave of Mácha suddenly decided they were tired of the communists...and started the Velvet Revolution.

KAREL HYNEK MÁCHA

EATING

The most convenient spot is the Czech fast-food joint **Joka,** which serves standard ready-to-eat meals and good soups daily (at the top, or northwest, corner of the square). You can get a sandwich and sit on the benches under trees by the fountain, enjoying the view of the Renaissance-era townhouses. **Salva Guarda** is a bit stuffy and service is slow, but it's a decent sit-down option (daily 11:00–23:00, under the arches at the bottom, or southeast, corner of the square).

TRANSPORTATION CONNECTIONS

Between Terezín and Litoměřice: Buses from Prague to Terezín continue three miles to Litoměřice; buses returning to Prague stop first in Litoměřice, then Terezín. Easier yet, it's a five-minute **taxi** trip between the camp and Litoměřice (about 150 Kč). The museum's ticket office will be happy to call a cabbie for you (such as Mr. Poláček, based in Terezín, tel. 606-833-480).

Returning to Prague: To reach Litoměřice's bus station, walk east on main street (Dlouhá) down from the square to an intersection, cross it, and continue in the same direction along Na Kocandě street (an easy 10-min walk). The train station is nearby (though trains to Prague are a lesser option than buses because they require a transfer).

Konopiště Castle

Konopiště (KOH-noh-peesh-tyeh), the huge, neo-Gothic residence of the Archduke Franz Ferdinand d'Este, is 30 miles south of Prague.

Construction of the castle began in the 14th century, but today's exterior and furnishings date from about 1900, when the heir of the Hapsburg throne, Franz Ferdinand, renovated his new home. As one of the first castles in Europe to have an elevator, a WC, and running water, Konopiště shows "modern" living at the turn of the 20th century. Touring the castle gives you a good sense of who this powerful Hapsburg was, as well as a glimpse at one of the best medieval arms collections in the world (and lots of hunting trophies).

While the stretch between the parking lot and the castle entrance is overrun by tour groups, the **gardens** and the **park** are surprisingly empty. In the summer, the flowers and goldfish in the rose garden are a big hit with visitors. The peaceful 30-minute walk through the woods around the lake (wooden bridge at the far end) offers gorgeous castle views.

Archduke Franz Ferdinand
(1863–1914)

Archduke Franz Ferdinand was the nephew of the Hapsburg Emperor Franz Josef, who ruled from 1848–1916 (longer than Queen Victoria). Ferdinand was the impatient successor to the Austro-Hungarian throne. Local legend says that Franz Ferdinand even built a chapel at Konopiště for the sole purpose of praying that his old, hated uncle might soon die...but the emperor went on to outlive the young archduke.

Franz Ferdinand fell out of his uncle's favor when he married a beautiful Czech countess (Žofie Chotková) from too low a background for the other Hapsburgs to accept—she was "only" aristocratic, not royal. To get out of sight of his relatives, Franz Ferdinand bought Konopiště and moved here.

Obsessed with hunting, Franz Ferdinand traveled around the world twice, shooting at anything in sight: deer, bears, tigers, elephants, and crocodiles. He eventually killed 300,000 animals. Nearly 100,000 hunting trophies stare morbidly at you from the walls in Konopiště.

In the Kaiser's Pavilion on the grounds of Konopiště, Franz Ferdinand and the German Emperor Wilhelm plotted a war against Russia that would work to their mutual benefit: Germans wanted colonies, and Austria—crippled by aspirations of its many nationalities—hoped war would turn attention from its domestic problems.

Soon after, Franz Ferdinand went to Sarajevo, in the Hapsburg-annexed territories of Bosnia and Herzegovina. On that trip, the Serbian student Gavrilo Princip shot the Hapsburg archduke who so loved shooting. The assassination of Franz Ferdinand finally gave the Austrians (and their allies, the Germans) a pretense for starting the war against Serbia (and their ally, Russia). A Great War soon broke out, which was both planned by Franz Ferdinand and sparked by his death.

Tucked away in the bushes behind the pond is a simple pavilion coated with tree bark, a perfect picnic spot. This simple structure is nicknamed the **Kaiser's Pavilion.** Allegedly, the German Emperor Wilhelm and Franz Ferdinand met here to plot a war with Russia shortly before the archduke's assassination (see sidebar).

Cost and Tours: Entrance to the castle is by one-hour guided tour only. There are three different routes: I (145 Kč), II (145 Kč), and III (250 Kč).

Hours and Information: Castle open May–Aug Tue–Sun 9:00–12:30 & 13:00–17:00, closed Mon; April and Oct Tue–Fri 9:00–15:00 Sat–Sun 9:00–16:00; Sept Tue–Fri 9:00–16:00,

Sat–Sun 9:00–17:00; closed Mon and Nov–March. Tel. 317-721-366, www.zamek-konopiste.cz.

EATING

There are three touristy restaurants under the castle, but I'd bring picnic supplies from Prague (or buy them at the grocery store by the Benešov train station). While the crowds wait to pay too much for lousy food in the restaurants, you'll enjoy the peace and thought-provoking ambience of a picnic in the shaded Kaiser's Pavilion. Or eat cheaply with locals on Benešov's main square (try U Zlaté Hvězdy—"The Golden Star").

TRANSPORTATION CONNECTIONS

Getting to Konopiště: Trains from Prague's main station (Hlavní Nádraží) drop you in Benešov (hrly, 60 min). From the Benešov train station, the yellow-marked trail goes directly to the castle (1.25 miles), bypassing the enormous parking lot clogged with souvenir shops and bus fumes.

Karlštejn Castle

One of the Czech Republic's top attractions, Karlštejn Castle (KARL-shtayn) was built by Charles IV in about 1350 to house the crown jewels of the Holy Roman Empire. While a striking, fairytale castle from a distance, it's not much inside. The highlight of the castle's interior—the much venerated and sumptuous

 Chapel of the Holy Cross (built to house the crown jewels)—can be seen only with an advance reservation.

Cost and Tours: The Chapel of the Holy Cross—basically the only thing inside Karlštejn worth seeing—is part of tour route II (300 Kč). You can only visit this route with a group (12 people per group, 1 group per hour), and reservations are required (25-Kč reservation fee per person, tel. 274-008-154 or 274-008-155, rezervace@stc.npu.cz). Route I is nowhere near as interesting (200 Kč, no reservation required, bigger groups, shorter tour).

Hours and Information: May–Sept Tue–Sun 9:00–12:00 & 13:00–18:00, closed Mon; Oct and April Tue–Sun 9:00–12:00 &

13:00–15:00, closed Mon; closed Nov–March; tel. 274-008-154, www.hradkarlstejn.cz.

From Karlstejn Castle, an easy one-hour **hike** along the red-marked trail leads away from the tourists through a quiet forest to Srbsko. There, you'll find two good Czech **restaurants** and a **train station** (the Karlštejn–Prague train stops in Srbsko).

TRANSPORTATION CONNECTIONS

Getting to Karlštejn: The castle, 20 miles southwest of Prague, is accessible by train (hrly, 40 min, then a 20-min walk; depart from Prague's Smíchov Station) or by car (30 min, direction Plzeň).

Křivoklát Castle

Křivoklát (KREE-vohk-laht), an original 14th-century castle, is beautiful for its simplicity and setting, amid hills and deep woods near the lovely Berounka River valley. Originally a hunting residence of Czech kings, it was later transformed into a royal prison that "entertained" a number of distinguished guests, among them the most notorious alchemist of the 1500s, the Englishman Edward Kelly.

In summer, Křivoklát comes alive with craftspeople—woodcarvers, blacksmiths, and basket-weavers—who work as if it were the 15th century. The absence of tacky souvenir shops, the plain Gothic appearance, and the background noise of hammers and wood chisels give Křivoklát an engaging character.

The tour of the interior lasts a sensible half hour. The highlight is the king's audience hall, with its delicately arched ceiling.

Cost, Hours, Information: 160 Kč, includes English audioguide; 80 Kč if you go with a Czech group (pick up an explanation sheet in English, and you'll be fine with the Czechs). Open June–Aug Tue–Sun 9:00–12:00 & 13:00–17:00, closed Mon; May and Sept Tue–Sun 9:00–16:00, closed Mon; April and Oct Tue–Sun 9:00–15:00, closed Mon; March and Nov–Dec Sat–Sun 9:00–15:00, closed Mon–Fri; closed Jan–Feb. Tel. 313-558-440, www.krivoklat.cz.

SLEEPING

Hotel Sykora, below the castle near the train station, has been a favorite among Czech hikers since the 1930s. If you want to stay for an evening concert in the castle courtyard or for a hike in the nearby woods, sleep in one of the hotel's 11 beautifully renovated rooms (Db-600 Kč, tel. 313-558-114).

TRANSPORTATION CONNECTIONS

Getting to Křivoklát: Trains, which run through the delightful valley of the dreamy Berounka River, leave Prague's Smíchov station for Beroun every half hour (40 min trip). In Beroun, transfer to the cute little motor train to Křivoklát (dubbed by Czech hikers the *Berounka Pacific*; allow 90 min total for trip from Prague). From Křivoklát's train station, it's a 10-minute walk uphill to the castle. At the train station, confirm the schedule back—one train leaves just before noon, and three others depart during the afternoon.

Near Křivoklát: Lány

The village of Lány, about 15 miles from Krivoklat Castle, is close to patriotic Czech hearts. The castle in Lány served as the Czech "Camp David" for both Tomáš Masaryk (the WWI-era first president of Czechoslovakia) and Václav Havel (the contemporary "father of the Czech Republic" and first post-communist president of the nation).

Masaryk and his family are buried in Lány's simple village cemetery. Masaryk's humble grave on a hill in the middle of the fields is a pilgrimage place for freedom-loving Czechs. The communists, wanting to erase Masaryk from the nation's memory, destroyed all of Masaryk's statues and barely mentioned his name in history textbooks. During the communist era, Czechs risked their careers by coming here on the Czech Independence Day to put candles on Masaryk's grave. Imagine: Every year on October 28, the police sealed off all roads to the village of Lány, and anyone who wanted access had to show an ID card. When you arrived at work the next morning, the boss would be waiting at the door, asking, "Where were you yesterday—and why?"

After 1989, Václav Havel—the symbol of the new Czech freedom—strove to restore dignity to the presidency. He went back to the tradition of the first Czech president, making Lány his home away from home. Havel's weekend sojourns here symbolized a return to Czech self-governance.

Hike to Křivoklát Castle: Consider making the 15-mile hike to Křivoklát Castle from Lány. From the cemetery, it's a five-minute walk to the trailhead on the main square where you will also find two grocery stores to replenish your supplies. There are no restaurants or stores until Křivoklát. Follow the red-marked trail through woods and meadows with the help of a good map. This is one of the most beautiful hikes in the whole country as it takes you through all the varieties of woods extent in Central Europe (beech, birch, poplar, oak, pine, spruce, fir), a hidden 1950s dam, and some stunning vistas. The *Praha–Západ* or *Křivoklátsko* hiking maps are excellent (sold in most Prague bookstores).

TRANSPORTATION CONNECTIONS

Getting to Lány: The bus leaves Prague Hradčanská Metro station at 7:10 on weekdays for Lány (direction Rakovník, 40 min). The bus first stops on the main square of the town, then at the cemetery. There is no public transportation between Křivoklát Castle and Lány.

ČESKÝ KRUMLOV

Lassoed by its river and dominated by its castle, this enchanting town feels lost in a time warp. While Český Krumlov is the Czech Republic's answer to Germany's Rothenburg, it has yet to be turned into a medieval theme park. When you see its awe-inspiring castle, delightful Old Town of shops and cobbled lanes, characteristic little restaurants, and easy canoeing options, you'll understand why having fun is a slam dunk here.

Český Krumlov (CHESS-key KROOM-loff) means, roughly, "Czech Bend in the River." Calling it "Český" for short sounds silly to Czech-speakers (since dozens of Czech town names begin with "Český"). "Krumlov" for short is okay.

Since Krumlov is the second-most-visited town (1.5 million visits annually) in the Czech Republic, there's enough tourism to make things colorful and easy—but not so much that it tramples the place's charm. This town of 15,000 attracts a young, bohemian crowd, drawn here for its simple beauty and cheap living.

Planning Your Time

Because the castle and theater can be visited only with a guide (and English tours are offered just a few times a day), serious sightseers should call the castle to reserve these tours first thing, and then build their day around these times. (Those who hate planning ahead on vacation can join a Czech tour anytime with an English information sheet.)

A paddle down the river to Zlatá Koruna is a highlight (4 hrs, see "Canoeing and Rafting the Vltava," page 181), and a hike up to the mountain Kleť takes you into the heart of Czech woods (5 hrs round-trip, see "Hiking," page 183). Other sights are quick visits and worthwhile only if you have a particular interest (Egon Schiele, puppets, torture, and so on).

The town itself is the major attraction. Evenings are for atmospheric dining and drinking. Sights are generally open 10:00–17:00 and closed on Monday.

ORIENTATION

Český Krumlov is extremely easy to navigate. The twisty Vltava River, which makes a perfect S through the town, ropes the Old Town into a tight peninsula. Above the Old Town is the Castle Town. Český Krumlov's one main street starts at the isthmus and heads through the peninsula. It winds through town and continues across a bridge before snaking through the Castle Town, the castle complex (a long series of courtyards), and the castle gardens high above. The main square, Náměstí Svornosti—with the TI, ATMs, banks (close at 17:00), and taxis—dominates the Old Town and marks the center of the peninsula. All recommended restaurants and hotels are within a few minutes' walk of this square. No sight in town is more than a five-minute stroll away.

Tourist Information

The eager-to-please TI on the main square recently won an award as the best TI in the Czech Republic (daily July–Aug 9:00–20:00, June and Sept 9:00–19:00, March–May and Oct 9:00–18:00, Nov–Feb 9:00–17:00, tel. 380-704-622, www.ckrumlov.cz). Pick up the free city map. The 129-Kč *City Guide* book explains everything in town and includes a fine town and castle map in the back. The TI can check train, bus, and flight schedules, and will change traveler's checks (fair rate). Ask about concerts, city walking tours in English, car rentals, and canoe trips on the river. The TI can book rooms, but it'll take a 10 percent deposit (actually a commission) that will be "deducted" from your (inflated) hotel bill. Save your host money by going direct.

Arrival in Český Krumlov

Taxis are cheap; don't hesitate to take one into the center from the train station (about 100 Kč) or bus station (around 60 Kč).

By Train: The train station is a 15-minute walk from town (turn right out of the station, then walk downhill onto a steep cobbled path leading to an overpass into the town center).

By Bus: The bus station is just three blocks away from the Old Town (from the bus station lot, drop down to main road and turn left, then turn right at Potraviny grocery store to reach the center).

Helpful Hints

Internet Access: Fine Internet cafés are all over town and in many of the accommodations. The TI on the main square has several fast, cheap, stand-up stations good for a quick visit.

Laundry: Pension Lobo runs a self-service launderette under the castle (100 Kč/load, daily, Latrán 73).

Festivals: Locals drink oceans of beer and celebrate their medieval roots at big events such as the Celebration of the Rose (Slavnosti Růže), where blacksmiths mint ancient coins, jugglers swallow fire, mead flows generously, and pigs are roasted on open fires (mid-June). The summer also brings a top-notch jazz and alternative music festival to town, performed in pubs, cafés, and the castle gardens (mid-Aug). During the St. Wenceslas celebrations, the square becomes a medieval market and the streets come alive with theater and music (late Sept). Reserve a hotel well in advance if you'll be in town for these events.

TOURS

Walking Tours—The TI offers worthwhile guided 90-minute historic town **walking tours** in English (225 Kč, July–Sept daily at 10:00 and 12:00, meet in front of TI on main square—just show up and buy ticket from guide, minimum 2 people). Or you can do a tour yourself with an **audioguide** (rent at TI for 60 Kč/hr). Also consider the one-hour **brewing history tour,** which takes you into the Eggenberg brewery (150 Kč, July–Sept daily at 12:00, meet in front of the TI).

Private Guides—Jiří (George) Václavíček is a local teacher who enjoys showing visitors around during his off-hours (afternoons, evenings, and weekends). Jiří—a gentle and caring man who seems to fit mellow Český Krumlov perfectly—is a joy to share this town with. He's happy to work for as little as an hour (€10/hr, tel. 380-726-813, mobile 603-927-995, jiri.vaclavicek@seznam.cz). Jiří also runs a small pension in the Old Town (see page 185). Another guide service provides private tours for 250 Kč per hour (you name the place and time, mobile 723-069-561).

SIGHTS

Old Town

These sights are listed in the order you'll reach them as you wander along the main street through the Old Town.

Museum of Regional History—This small museum gives you a quick look at regional costumes, tools, and traditions. Ask for the simple English translation that also includes a lengthy history of Krumlov. Start on the second floor, where you'll see old paintings, a glimpse of noble life, and a ceramic model of Český Krumlov in 1800. The first floor comes with fine folk costumes and domestic

Český Krumlov

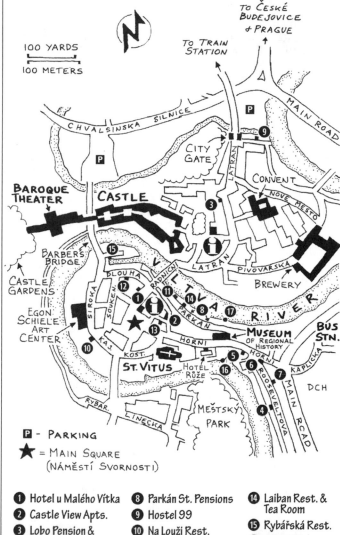

100 YARDS
100 METERS

TO ČESKÉ
BUDEJOVICE
& PRAGUE

TO TRAIN
STATION

CHVALSINSKA SILNICE

MAIN ROAD

P

CITY
GATE

LATRAN

CONVENT

NOVE MESTO

BAROQUE
THEATER

CASTLE

P

BARBERS
BRIDGE

CASTLE
GARDENS

EGON
SCHIELE
ART
CENTER

VLTAVA

DLOUHA

RADNICNI

LATRAN

PIVOVARSKA

BREWERY

RIVER

SIROKA

SOUKEN.

KAJ.

KOST.

HORNI

MUSEUM
OF REGIONAL
HISTORY

BUS
STN.

ST. VITUS

HOTEL
RŮŽE

HORNI

KAPLICKA

ROOSEVELTOVA

DCH

RYBAR.

LINECKA

MEŠTSKÝ
PARK

MAIN ROAD

P – PARKING

★ = MAIN SQUARE
(NÁMĚSTÍ SVORNOSTI)

1. Hotel u Malého Vítka
2. Castle View Apts.
3. Lobo Pension & Pension Danny
4. Little Pension Teddy
5. Pension Myší Díra
6. Pension Anna
7. Pension Landauer
8. Parkán St. Pensions
9. Hostel 99
10. Na Louži Rest.
11. Krčma u Dwau Maryi Tavern
12. Cikánská Jizba Tavern
13. Krčma v Šatlavské Restaurant
14. Laiban Rest. & Tea Room
15. Rybářská Rest.
16. Start Short River Float
17. End Short River Float

Český Krumlov History

With the natural moat provided by the sharp bend in the Vltava, it's no wonder this has been a choice spot for eons. Celtic tribes first settled here a century before Christ. Then came German tribes. The Slavic tribes arrived in the ninth century. The Rožmberks—Bohemia's top noble family—ran the city from 1302 to 1602. In many ways, the 16th century was the town's Golden Age, when Český Krumlov hosted an important Jesuit college. The Hapsburgs bought the region in 1602, ushering in a more Germanic period.

The rich mix of Gothic, Renaissance, and Baroque buildings is easy to under-appreciate. As you wander, look up... notice the surviving details in the stonework. Step into shops, snoop into back lanes and tiny squares. Gothic buildings curve with the winding streets. Many precious Gothic and Renaissance frescoes were whitewashed in Baroque times (when the colorful trimmings of earlier times were way out of style). Today these precious frescoes are being rediscovered and restored.

With its rich German heritage, it was easy for Hitler to claim that this region—the Sudetenland—was rightfully part of Germany. In 1938, the infamous Munich Agreement made it his. After the war, in a kind of Potsdam Treaty–approved ethnic cleansing, three million Germans in Czech lands were sent west to Germany. Emptied of its German citizenry, Český Krumlov turned into a ghost town inhabited mostly by thieves and Roma (Gypsies). Picture Roma squatters with their fires in the stately noble homes that line the town's main square.

In 1945, Americans liberated the town. But, in the post-WWII world as planned by Stalin and FDR, the border of the Soviet and American spheres of influence fell about here. While the communist government established order, the period from 1945 to 1989 was a smelly time capsule. The town was infamously polluted. Its now-pristine river was foamy from the paper mill just upstream. The hills around the town were marred with blocks of prefabricated concrete. The people who moved in never fully identified with the town—in Europe, a place without ancestors is without life-giving roots. The bleak years of communism here paradoxically provided a cocoon to preserve the town. There was no money, so little changed, apart from a build-up of grime.

Today, with its new prosperity, Krumlov is emerging as a fairy-tale town. In fact, movie producers consider it ideal for films. *The Adventures of Pinocchio,* starring Jonathan Taylor Thomas, was filmed right here in 1995.

art and a Bronze Age exhibit. The postcards in the hallway offer a fun look at Český Krumlov in the old days. Inside you'll also find the census from 1850, when 75 percent of the town's inhabitants were German. In 1945, the percentage was about the same... until most were expelled (50 Kč, daily 10:00–18:00, Horní 152).

Hotel Růže—Located across the street from the Museum of Regional History, this former Jesuit college hides a beautiful Renaissance courtyard. Pop inside to see a couple of bronze busts. The one on the right, dedicated by the Czech freedom fighters, commemorates the first Czechoslovak president, Tomáš Garrigue Masaryk (in office 1918–1934; see sidebar on page 110). The bust on the left recalls Masaryk's successor, Edvard Beneš (in office 1934–1948; see sidebar on page 180).

Church of St. Vitus—Český Krumlov's main church was built as a bastion of Catholicism in the 15th century, when the Roman Catholic Church was fighting the Hussites. The 17th-century Baroque high altar, showing St. Vitus and the Virgin Mary, is capped with St. Wenceslas. He's the patron saint of the Czech people, long considered their ambassador in heaven. The canopy now in the back—featuring a Rožmberk atop a horse—was once at the high altar. Too egotistical for Jesuits, it was moved to the rear of the nave (daily 10:00–19:00, Sunday Mass at 9:30).

Main Square (Náměstí Svornosti)—Lined by Renaissance and Baroque homes of burghers, the main square has a grand charm. There's continuity here. Lékárna, with the fine, red, Baroque facade on the lower corner of the square, is still a pharmacy, as it has been since 1620. McDonald's tried three times to get a spot here but was turned away. The Town Hall flies the Czech flag and the town flag, which shows the rose symbol of the Rožmberk family, who ruled the town for 300 years.

Imagine the history this square has seen: In the 1620s, the rising tide of Lutheran Protestantism threatened Catholic Europe. As Krumlov was a seat of Jesuit power and learning, the intellectuals of the Roman church burned 5,000 books on this square. Later, when there was a bad harvest, locals blamed witches—and burned them, too. Every so often, terrible plagues rolled through the countryside. In a village nearby, all but two residents were killed by a plague.

But the plague stopped before devastating the people of Český Krumlov, and in 1715—as a thanks to God—they built the plague monument that marks the center of the square today. Much later, in 1938, Hitler stood right here before a backdrop of long Nazi banners to celebrate the annexation of the Sudetenland. And in 1968, Russian tanks spun their angry treads on these same cobblestones to intimidate locals who were demanding freedom. Today, thankfully, this square is part of an unprecedented peace and prosperity for the Czech people.

Torture Museum—This is just a lame haunted house: dark, with sound effects, cheap modern models, and prints showing off the cruel and unusual punishments of medieval times (80 Kč, daily 9:00–20:00, English descriptions, facing the main square).

Egon Schiele Art Center—This classy contemporary art gallery has top-notch temporary exhibits, generally featuring 20th-century Czech artists. The top-floor permanent collection celebrates the Viennese artist Egon Schiele (pronounced "Sheila," like the woman's name), who once spent a few weeks here during a secret love affair. A friend of Gustav Klimt and an important figure in the Secessionist movement in Vienna, Schiele lived a short life, from 1890–1918. His cutting-edge lifestyle and harsh and graphic nudes didn't always fit the conservative, small-town style of Český Krumlov, but townsfolk are happy enough to charge you to see some of his edgy art today (180 Kč, daily 10:00–18:00, Široká 70, tel. 380-704-011).

Barber's Bridge (Lazebnicky Most)—This wooden bridge, decorated with 19th-century statues, connects the Old Town and the Castle Town. In the center stands a statue of St. John of Nepomuk, who's also depicted in a prominent statue on Prague's Charles Bridge (see page 80). Among other responsibilities, he's the protector against floods. In the great floods of August 2002, the angry river submerged the bridge and swept away the banisters...but the bridge survived.

Krumlov Castle (Krumlovský Zámek)

No Czech town is complete without a castle—and now that the

nobles are gone, their mansions are open to us common folk. The Krumlov Castle complex, worth ▲▲, includes bear pits, the castle itself, a rare Baroque theater, and groomed gardens.

Round Tower (Zámecká Věž)—The strikingly colorful round tower marks the location of the first castle, built here to guard the medieval river crossing. With its 16th-century Renaissance paint job colorfully restored, it looks exotic, featuring fancy astrological decor, terra-cotta symbols of the zodiac, and a fine arcade. Climb its 162 steps for a great view (30 Kč, daily 9:00–18:00, last entry 17:30).

Bear Pits—At the site of the castle drawbridge, the bear pits hold a family of European brown bears, as it has since the Rožmberks started this tradition in the 16th century. Bears implied a long and noble family lineage.

Castle—The immense castle is a series of courtyards with shops, contemporary art galleries, and tourist services. You'll get a glimpse of the places where the Rožmberks, Eggenbergs, and Schwarzenbergs dined, studied, worked, prayed, entertained, and slept. Imagine being an aristocratic guest here, riding the dukes' assembly line of fine living: You'd promenade through a long series of elegant spaces and dine in the sumptuous dining hall before enjoying a concert in the Hall of Mirrors, which leads directly to the theater (described below). After the play, you'd go out into the château garden for a fireworks finale.

Hours: June–Aug Tue–Sun 9:00–12:00 & 13:00–18:00, spring and fall until 17:00, closed Mon and Nov–March.

Visiting the Castle: To see the inside, you have to choose between two different one-hour tours: Tour I (160 Kč, Gothic and Renaissance objects—of most general interest) and Tour II (140 Kč,

19th-century castle life, Baroque art, and tapestries). Most tours are in Czech, and English tours come with an extra cost and a longer wait. (Visit the richly decorated Renaissance court-yard—the 3rd one—while you're killing time). The information on the English tour, mostly given by students working a summer job, comes straight from an English information sheet you can pick up yourself at the ticket office. If you're pressed for time or would rather go at your own pace, ask for the sheet and join a Czech-language tour. If you decide to take the English tour, chat up the guides as you go to divert them from their typical spiel. No pictures are allowed in the castle. Tel. 380-704-721.

▲▲Baroque Theater (Zámecké Divadlo)—Europe once had several hundred fine Baroque theaters. Using candles for light and fireworks for special effects, most burned down. Today only two survive in good shape and are open to tourists: one at Stockholm's Drottningholm Palace, and one here, at this castle. Along with a look at the precious theater itself and a video of it in action, you'll see lots of surviving theater gear: a dozen or so painted sets, hundreds of costumes, and original special effects and sound-making

Edvard Beneš and the German Question

Czechoslovakia was created in 1918, when the vast, multi-ethnic Hapsburg Empire broke into smaller nations after losing World War I. The principle that gave countries such as Poland, Czechoslovakia, and Romania independence was called "self-determination": Each nation had the right to its own state within the area where its people were in the majority. But the peoples of Eastern Europe had mixed over the centuries, making it impossible to create functioning states based purely on ethnicity. In the case of Czechoslovakia, the borders were drawn along historical rather than ethnic boundaries. While the country was predominantly Slavic, there were also areas with overwhelmingly German and Hungarian majorities. One of these areas—a fringe around the western part of the country, mostly populated by Germans—was known as the Sudetenland.

At first, the coexistence of Slavs and Germans in the new republic worked fine. German parties were important power brokers and participated in almost every coalition government. Hitler's rise to power, however, led to the growth of German nationalism even outside Germany. Soon 70 percent of Germans in Czechoslovakia voted for the Nazis. In September 1938, the Munich Agreement ceded the Sudetenland to Germany—and the Czech minority had to leave (for more on the Munich Agreement, see "The Never-Used Fortifications," page 204).

Czechoslovak President Edvard Beneš (in office 1934–1948) led the Czechoslovak exile government in London during the war. Like most Czechs and Slovaks, Beneš believed that after the hard feelings produced by the Munich Agreement, peaceful coexistence of Slavs and Germans in a single state was impossible. His postwar solution: move the Sudeten Germans to Germany, much as the Czechs had been forced out of the Sudetenland before. Through skillful diplomacy, Beneš got the Allies to sign on to this idea.

machinery. Scenes could be changed in 10 seconds. (Fireworks blinded the audience, and when the smoke cleared it was a new scene.) Unfortunately, the number of visitors is strictly regulated, and there are only three English tours a day—often sold out in advance. Call 380-704-721 to establish English-language tour times and reserve a space; getting a ticket can be a frustrating experience (180 Kč, 45-min tours daily May–Oct only, departures at 10:00, 11:00, 13:00, 14:00, 15:00, and 16:00).

Castle Gardens—This 2,300-foot-long garden crowns the castle complex. It was laid out in the 17th century, when the noble family would light it with 22,000 oil lamps, torches, and candles for special occasions. The lower part is geometrical and symmetrical—French-style. The upper is rougher—English-style (free,

Shortly after the end of the war, three million people of German ancestry were forced to leave their homes. Millions of Germanic people in Poland, Romania, Ukraine, and elsewhere met with a similar fate. Many of these families had been living in these areas for centuries. The methods employed to expel them included murder, rape, and plunder.

In 1945, Český Krumlov lost 75 percent of its population, and Czechs moved into vacated German homes. Having easily acquired the property, the new residents never took much care of the houses. Within a few years, the once-prosperous Sudetenland was reduced to shabby towns and uncultivated fields—a decaying, godforsaken country. After 1989, displaced Sudeten Germans—the majority of whom live in Bavaria—demanded that the Czechoslovak government apologize for the violent way in which the expulsion was carried out. Some challenged the legality of the decrees, and for a time the issue threatened otherwise good Czech-German relations.

Although no longer such a hot-button diplomatic issue, the so-called Beneš Decrees remain divisive in Czech politics. While liberals consider the laws unjust, many others—especially the older generations—see them as fair revenge for the behavior of the Sudeten Germans prior to the war. In the former Sudetenland, where Czech landowners worry that the Germans will try to claim back their property, Beneš is a hugely popular figure. His bust in Český Krumlov's Hotel Růže is one of the first memorials to Beneš in the country. The bridge behind the Old Town has been named for Beneš since the 1990s. The main square—the center of a thriving German community 70 years ago—is now ironically called "National Unity Square."

May–Sept daily 8:00–19:00, April and Oct daily 8:00–17:00, closed Nov–March).

The Church of the Annunciation of St. Mary—In 1350, the town began building this church and its attached convent. Today, you can walk under the Gothic vaults and peek into Baroque chapels where monks once meditated (30 Kč).

ACTIVITIES

▲▲▲**Canoeing and Rafting the Vltava**—Český Krumlov lies in the middle of a popular boating valley. Make time to paddle around the town or through Bohemian forests and villages of the nearby countryside.

Český Krumlov: A Town in Transition

By the 1980s, Český Krumlov was a haunted, dead town. It came briefly alive only in the summer, when Czechs paddling down the river hopped out of their canoes for a quick Eggenberg beer in one of the town's two pubs. The castle was closed, as the collapsing roof made it unsafe. The overpriced Hotel Růže was the only hotel in town. Few dared to spend the night anyway. The town had dark streets filled with unscrupulous characters and debris from falling roofs; a reeking, polluted river; and steep hills  squeezing it claustrophobically on all sides. The bizarre tower was on the verge of crashing. You could literally smell history here—it breathed at you from the mildew-covered, disintegrating houses.

In 1992, Český Krumlov was placed on the UNESCO World Heritage list. Tourists began to discover the place, and their money saved the buildings from ruin. Color returned to the facades, and the square took on a cheerful air. The town woke up from a nightmare. Český Krumlov returned to the time of the noble Rožmberks: Waiters were dressed in coarse linen shirts, medieval artisans filled the square, and hotel rooms had rustic wooden beds and were connected by crooked, narrow corridors. The town was a spirited tourist's dream come true.

But as the 1990s wore on, tour groups gradually outnumbered adventurous explorers. The main drag was flooded with tacky souvenir shops, Soukenická street turned into a nightclub row, and many hotels replaced creaking wooden floors with thick synthetic carpets.

As Český Krumlov becomes more and more like Germany's Rothenburg, as its shops resemble those found in many other similar towns in Europe, and as locals continue to move away, some Czechs feel nostalgic for the Český Krumlov of the 1980s: a gloomy town that nevertheless had the power to bewitch. Today, although much care is put into preserving the town's old buildings, little goes into saving its spirit.

Since World War II, Český Krumlov has essentially been a stage prop. The question is not whether real life will ever return to the streets, but rather whose tastes will shape its new character.

The easiest half-hour experience is to float around the city's peninsula, starting and ending at opposite sides of the tiny isthmus. (Heck, you can do it twice.) Longer trips involve a minibus transfer. If you're starting upriver from Krumlov (direction: Rožmberk), you'll go faster

with more whitewater, but the river parallels a road so it's a little less idyllic. Going downstream from Krumlov (direction: České Budějovice), you'll have more pastoral scenery and less excitement. You can choose among destinations that take one to eight hours of floating and paddling (lots of work involved, even though you're going downstream). At a set time and place, the minibus will meet you. You'll encounter plenty of inviting pubs and cafés for breaks along the way. Plan on getting wet. There's a little whitewater, but the river is so shallow that if you tip, you simply stand up and climb back in. (When that happens, pull the canoe out to the bank to empty it, since you'll never manage to pour the water out while still in the river.)

Choose from a kayak, a canoe (fastest, less work, more likely to tip), or an inflatable raft (harder rowing, slower, but very stable). Rates vary from 300 Kč for the 30-minute canoe or raft trip around the town; to 700 Kč for a three-hour, 15-km (9-mile) float; to 1,000 Kč for a 35-km (22-mile), all-day trip. Prices are per boat (2–6 people) and include a map and transportation to or from the start and end points. Several companies offer this lively activity. Perhaps the handiest are Půjčovna Lodí Maleček Boat Rental (open long hours daily April–Oct, closed Nov–March; they also run the recommended Pension Myší Díra—see "Sleeping," below, Rooseveltova 28, tel. 337-712-508, lode@malecek.cz) and the slightly less expensive Cestovní Agentura Vltava (April–Oct daily 9:00–18:00, closed Nov–March, in the Pension Vltava at Kájovská 62, tel. 380-711-988, www.ckvltava.cz). Vltava also rents mountain bikes for 320 Kč per day.

Slupenec Horseback Riding Club—Head about a mile out of town for horseback rides and lessons (Tue–Sun 10:00–18:00, closed Mon, 1 hour outdoors or in the ring-250 Kč, all-day ride-1,800 Kč, helmets provided, Slupenec 1, tel. 380-711-052, www.jk-slupenec .cz, René Srncová).

Hiking—Start at the trailhead by the bear pits below the castle. Red-and-white trail markers will take you on an easy six-mile hike around the neighboring slopes and villages. The green and yellow stripes mark a five-mile hiking trail up the Kleť mountain—with

The Šumava Mountains

The Šumava Mountains (SHOO-mah-vah)—literally, the "Whispering Mountains"—are geologically Europe's oldest range. Separating Bohemia from Bavaria, this long ridge was the physical embodiment of the Iron Curtain for 40 years: The first 15 miles or so within the Czech border were a forbidden no-man's-land, where hundreds of Czechs were shot as they tried to run across to Germany. In 1989, the barbed wire was taken down, and the entire area—over 60 miles long—was declared the Šumava-Bayerische Wald National Park. No development is permitted within the park, and visitors can't camp outside of designated areas. Since there's little industry nearby, these mountains preserve some of the most pristine woods, creeks, and meadows in Europe.

The most popular gateways into the Šumava Mountains are the trailhead villages of Nová Pec, Stožec, Borová Lada, and Modrava. The best destinations for hiking, biking, and cross-country skiing are the slopes of the tallest mountain on the Czech side of the border, Plechý; the source of the Vltava River; and the Vydra rapids, where Smetana (see page 148) composed some of his greatest works. The red-marked trail that follows the border from Plechý to Železná Ruda is a highlight of any hiker's trip to the Czech Republic.

an 1,800-foot altitude gain. At the top, you'll find the oldest observation tower in the country (now a leading center for discovering new planets). On clear days, you can see the Alps (observatory tours July–Aug, Tue–Sun every hour 10:30–15:30, 30 Kč, www .hvezdarna.klet.cz).

SLEEPING

Krumlov is filled with small, good, family-run pensions offering doubles with baths from 1,000–1,500 Kč and hostel beds for 300 Kč. Summer weekends and festivals are busiest and most expensive (see page 250); reserve ahead when possible. Hotels speak some English and accept credit cards; pensions rarely do either. While you can find a room upon arrival here, it's better to book at least a few days ahead if you want to stay in the heart of town.

In the Old Town

$$$ **Hotel u Malého Vítka**, right in the old center, consists of a tangle of Gothic vaults and staircases connecting comfy, woodsy rooms. As some standard doubles are much bigger than others and all are the same price, it's worth requesting a larger standard room.

Sleep Code

(25 Kč = about $1, country code: 420)
S = Single, **D** = Double/Twin, **T** = Triple, **Q** = Quad, **b** = bathroom, **s** = shower only. Unless otherwise noted, credit cards are accepted and prices include breakfast.

To help you sort easily through these listings, I've divided the rooms into three categories based on the price for a standard double room with bath:

$$$ **Higher Priced**—Most rooms 1,300 Kč or more.
$$ **Moderately Priced**—Most rooms between
      1,000–1,300 Kč.
$ **Lower Priced**—Most rooms 1,000 Kč or less.

The deluxe rooms—unless you're dying for a whirlpool tub—aren't worth the higher cost (standard Db-1,600 Kč, bigger deluxe Db-2,400 Kč, Radnični 27, tel. & fax 380-711-925, www.vitekhotel.cz, vitekhotel@email.cz).

$$$ **Castle View Apartments,** run by local guide Jiří Václavíček (see "Tours," page 174), offers seven apartments, all with kitchenettes and many with views (apartments 1,500–5,400 Kč depending on size, view, and season; 140 Šatlavská street, tel. 380-726-813, www.castleview.cz, info@castleview.cz).

At the Base of the Castle

A quiet, cobbled pedestrian street (Latrán) runs below the castle just over the bridge from the Old Town. It's a 10-minute walk downhill from the train station. Lined with characteristic shops, the street has a couple of fine little family-run, eight-room pensions.

$ **Lobo Pension** fills a modern, efficient, concrete building with fresh, spacious rooms (Sb-700 Kč, Db-1,000 Kč, Tb-1,400 Kč, includes parking, Latrán 73, tel. & fax 380-713-153, www.pensionlobo.cz).

$ **Pension Danny** is a little funkier, with homier rooms and a tangled floor plan above a restaurant (Db-890 Kč, apartment Db-1,190 Kč, breakfast in room, Latrán 72, tel. 380-712-710, www.pensiondanny.cz).

Between the Bus Station and the Old Town

Pensions on Rooseveltova

Rooseveltova street, midway between the bus station and the Old Town (a 4-minute walk from either), is lined with fine little eight-room places, each with easy free parking.

$$$Little Pension Teddy has several riverview rooms sharing a common balcony (Db-1,500 Kč, Tb-1,950 Kč, cash only, Rooseveltova 38, tel. 380-711-595, www.teddy.cz, info@teddy.cz).

$$ Pension Myší Díra (literally, "Mouse Hole") hides eight sleek, spacious, bright, and woody Bohemian contemporary rooms overlooking the Vltava River just outside the Old Town. The reception, which closes at 20:00, also runs a tourist service and rents river boats (Db-1,000–1,690 Kč, bigger deluxe riverview Db-1,200–1,990 Kč, prices depend on day and season, Fri–Sat most expensive, breakfast in your room, 28 Rooseveltova, tel. 380-712-853, fax 380-711-900, www.malecek.cz).

$$ Pension Anna is well-run, with cozy rooms and a restful little garden (Db-1,250 Kč, 1,550-Kč apartment Db is a great deal, Rooseveltova 41, tel. & fax 380-711-692, pension.anna@quick.cz).

$$Pension Landauer, with small and simple but comfortable rooms, is a fair value (Sb-700 Kč, Db-1,200 Kč, cash only, Rooseveltova 32, tel. & fax 380-711-790).

Cheap Pensions on Parkán

Parkán street, which runs along the river below the square, has a row of pensions with one or two rooms each. These places have a family feel and are cheap (all rated **$**), charging around 1,000 Kč for two people: **U Vltavy** (Parkán 107, tel. 380-716-396, mobile 603-338-008), **Miroslava Janotová** (Parkán 115, tel. 380-714-805), and **Sladová Hana** (Parkán 125, tel. 602-363-049). For more rooms, visit www.ckrumlov.cz.

Hostel

$ Hostel 99, one of several hostels in the Old Town, is closest to the train station and has a pleasant, mellow feel. Its fine picnic-table terrace looks out on the Old Town, and the gentle sound of the river gurgles outside your window. It caters to its guests, offering free inner tubes for river floats, rental bikes, and a free keg of beer each Wednesday. The adjacent Hospoda 99 restaurant serves good, cheap soups, salads, and meals (55 beds in 6- to 10-bed rooms-300 Kč, D-700 Kč, T-900 Kč, use the lockers, no curfew or lockout, a 10-min downhill walk from train station or two bus stops to Spicak, Vezni 99, tel. & fax 380-712-812, www.hostel99.com, hostel99@hotmail.com).

EATING

Na Louži seems to be everyone's favorite little Czech bistro, with 40 seats in one 1930s-style room decorated with funky old advertisements. They serve inexpensive, tasty Czech cuisine and the hometown Eggenberg beer. If you've always wanted to play the piano for an appreciative Czech crowd in a colorful little tavern... do it here (daily, Kájovská 66, tel. 337-711-280).

Krčma u Dwau Maryi (literally, "Tavern of the Two Marys") is a characteristic old place with idyllic riverside picnic tables, serving traditional Czech cuisine and drinks (daily 11:00–23:00, Parkán 104, tel. 337-717-228). The fascinating menu explains the history of the house and makes a good case that the food of the poor medieval Bohemians was tasty and varied. Buck up for buckwheat, millet, greasy meat, or the poor-man's porridge.

Cikánská Jizba is a Roma (Gypsy) tavern filling one den-like, barrel-vaulted room. Krumlov has a big Roma history, and even today 1,000 Roma people live on the edge of town. While this little 40-seat restaurant won't win any cuisine awards, the typical Roma food is served under a mystic-feeling Gothic vault, and you never know what festive and musical activities will erupt (daily, 2 blocks toward castle from main square at Dlouhá 31, tel. 380-717-585).

Krčma v Šatlavské is an old prison gone cozy, with an open fire, big wooden tables under a rustic old medieval vault, and tables outdoors on the pedestrian lane. It's great for a late drink or game cooked on an open spit. *Medovina* is the hot honey wine (daily 12:00–24:00, on Šatlavská, follow lane leading uphill from TI on main square, tel. 608-973-797).

Laiban is the modern vegetarian answer to the carnivorous Middle Ages. Sit back in comfy straw chairs or head out onto the river terrace, and lighten up your pork-loaded diet with soy goulash or Mútábúr soup (daily 11:00–23:00, Parkán 105). The Krumlov Buddha dwells in the attached tea room (Tajemná Čajovna).

Rybářská Restaurace (literally, "Fisherman's Restaurant") doesn't look particularly inviting from outside, but don't get discouraged. This is *the* place in town to taste freshwater fish you've never heard of (and never will again). Try eel, perch, shad, carp, trout, and more (daily 11:00–22:00, on the island by the mill wheel).

TRANSPORTATION CONNECTIONS

Virtually all train rides to and from Český Krumlov require a transfer in the city of České Budějovice, a transit hub just to the north. České Budějovice's bus and train stations are next to each other.

From Český Krumlov by Train to: České Budějovice (6/day, 1 hr), **Prague** (7/day, change usually required, 4 hrs—bus is faster, cheaper, and easier), **Vienna** (4/day, 6 hrs), **Budapest** (4/day with at least one change, 11 hrs).

From Český Krumlov by Bus to: Prague (140 Kč, 7/day, 3.5 hrs; 2 departures a day—11:35 and 16:45—can be reserved and paid for at TI, or simply buy tickets from driver), **Vienna** (the Travellers' Hostel offers a direct bus service to Vienna 3 times weekly in summer: Mon, Wed, and Fri at 14:00; 900 Kč, 4 hrs, tel. 380-711-345, www .travellers.cz). The Český Krumlov bus station, a five-minute walk out of town, is just a big parking lot with numbered stalls for various buses.

From České Budějovice to Třeboň, Telč, and Třebíč: An express bus goes from České Budějovice (the big city near Český Krumlov—see above) to the Moravian city of Brno (5/day Mon–Fri, 2/day Sat–Sun). Along the way, it stops at Třeboň (30 min from České Budějovice), Telč (2 hrs from České Budějovice), and Třebíč (3.25 hrs from České Budějovice).

By Private Car: If money is no object, hiring a private car can be efficient, especially to Budapest (the TI has referrals).

TŘEBOŇ, TELČ, AND TŘEBÍČ

Many travelers to South Bohemia visit only Český Krumlov. While it's delightful, three nearby towns are less packaged, more authentic, and—for most—equally worthwhile.

If you draw a line between České Budějovice (the capital of South Bohemia) and Brno (the capital of Moravia), you'll go right through the "Three Ts": Třeboň is an inviting medieval town famous for its peat spas, network of manmade lakes, and fish specialties. Telč, telčnically in Moravia, boasts the Czech Republic's most impressive main square. And Třebíč is home to the country's most intact historic Jewish quarter.

Getting Around the "Three Ts"

An express bus line between the big cities of České Budějovice and Brno stops in Třeboň, Telč, and Třebíč (5/day Mon–Fri, 2/day Sat–Sun; České Budějovice to Třeboň—30 min, to Telč—2 hrs, to Třebíč—3.25 hrs, to Brno—4.5 hrs). You can reach České Budějovice easily by direct train from Prague (almost hrly, 2.5 hrs) or from Český Krumlov (6/day, 1 hr). In České Budějovice, the bus and train stations are next to each other.

Direct buses also connect these towns to Prague and other destinations; see "Transportation Connections" for each destination.

Třeboň

Třeboň (TREH-bohn, pop. 18,000), a well-preserved medieval town centered around a gorgeous Renaissance square, is a charming place to explore a unique biosphere of artificial lakes dating back to the 14th century.

Over the centuries, people have transformed what was a flooding marshland into a seductive combination of lakes, oak-lined dikes, wild meadows, Baroque villages, peat bogs, and pine woods. Rather than useless wet fields, the nobles wanted ponds swarming with fish—and today Třeboň remains the fish-raising capital of the Czech Republic. But 16th-century landscape architects managed to strike an amazing balance between civilization and nature, which today is a protected ecosystem (about 15 percent covered by water) with the biggest diversity of bird species in Eastern Europe. Nature enthusiasts come here to bird-watch, bike along dikes held together by roots of centuries-old oaks, and devour the best fish specialties in the country.

While Třeboň enjoys plenty of tourism, its fish industry makes its relative affluence feel a little less touristy than other popular towns. Its peat spas have attracted patients from all over the world for decades—but since the facilities are small, Třeboň is never as overrun as more famous spa towns.

Planning Your Time

With a full day in Třeboň, spend the morning enjoying the square, climbing up the Town Hall Tower, touring the Dean Church, and visiting the "Man and the Landscape" exhibition in the castle. (The castle itself and the brewery are less interesting.) After trying fish soup and trout for lunch, rent a bike and follow the educational trail along the ancient dikes. If it's hot, bring a bathing suit.

Soaking yourself in the peat of the spas is unforgettable; unfortunately, since the spa treatments are overbooked, it's difficult to get a spot. If you get in, build your day around it (see page 195).

If you're here in October and November, lend a hand in the fascinating ritual of clearing the fish ponds, warming yourself with shots of potato rum as you wade through the mud.

ORIENTATION

The old town—separated from newer construction by city walls, Renaissance gates, a water channel, and a castle garden—encircles the main square, Masaryk Square (Masarykovo Náměstí). Sights, hotels, restaurants, and ATMs are all within a couple blocks of Masaryk Square. From the train station, enter the square through the east gate. Standing in the middle of the square and facing west (with the station and gate at your back), the street to the left leads to the brewery and to Svět lake. The castle is at the far (west) end of the square.

Tourist Information: The TI is next to the Town Hall on Masaryk Square (Mon–Fri 9:00–12:00 & 13:00–18:00, Sat–Sun

Třeboň, Telč, and Třebíč

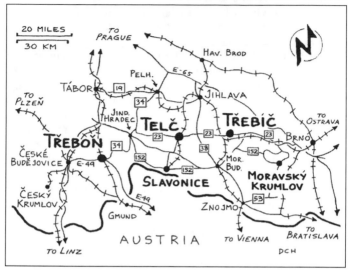

9:00–12:00 & 13:00–19:00, tel. 384-721-169, www.trebon-mesto
.cz). They hand out an exhaustive, glittering brochure called *The
Region of Třeboň*, which includes a town map.

Arrival in Třeboň

The train station and the local bus stop are within easy walking
distance from Masaryk Square.

By Train: Get off at the Třeboň-Lázně station, *not* the
Třeboň-Město station. From Třeboň-Lázně, walk along the road
directly in front of the station and you'll reach Masaryk Square in
five minutes.

By Bus: The bus from Prague leaves you at the main bus station, a 20-minute walk (or 100-Kč taxi ride, tel. 384-722-200) west
of the old town. Most buses arriving from České Budějovice continue from the main station to the Sokolská stop, which is a short
walk through the castle park to Masaryk Square.

Helpful Hints

Internet Access: Lázně Berta is just outside the east gate (daily
6:00–22:00). The more user-friendly **Town Library** (Mon–Fri
8:00–17:00, closed Sat–Sun) and **Café Bar-Computer Center
Roháč** (daily 18:00–2:00 in the morning) are in the same
building by the castle park, at Na Sadech 349.

Bike Rental: Hotel Zlatá Hvězda, located on the main square,
rents 10 mountain and trekking bikes (daily 24 hrs, 40 Kč/hr,
100 Kč/half-day, 200 Kč/day, tel. 384-757-200). For a much

bigger selection of bikes, walk 15 minutes from the center to **František Víta** at Komenského 870 (in front of large Aurora Spas, daily 8:00–22:00, 15 Kč/hour, 130 Kč/day, tel. 384-722-700, mobile 721-545-155).

Private Guides: Your visits to the Dean Church, "Man and the Landscape" exhibition, and castle interiors will tell you most everything about the town and its environs. While hiring a guide probably isn't necessary, it does offer you the chance to see the town through the eyes of a friendly local. From July through September, arrange a time with **Květa**—she's a young, bright guide from the Dean Church (mobile 728-670-197). **Lenka,** the knowledgeable young manager of Legner Hotel, is happy to show people around in her free time (see "Sleeping," below). Neither has set rates, but offering €10 per hour is fair.

SIGHTS

Masaryk Square (Masarykovo Náměstí)—Třeboň's fine main square artfully blends Renaissance and Baroque building styles. It was built by the town's 17th-century burghers, whose wealth came

from the booming fish industry. Neither big nor small, the rectangular market plaza—with a humble plague column and fountain in the middle—creates a feeling of unusual harmony. Grab a seat at one of the outdoor cafés, and watch local life circulate with the serenity of ducks on a lake.

The dominating **Town Hall Tower,** whose moderate height of 100 feet just fits with the size of the square, is worth the climb (15 Kč, June–Aug daily 10:00–18:00, unpredictable hours rest of year). Surveying the view from its top, you feel you can reach out and touch the circular old town. Beyond that, the lakes glimmer against the green backdrop of stately oaks.

Across from the Town Hall, the impossible-to-miss, rampart-like white gable marks the famous 16th-century **Inn at the White Horse** (U Bílého Koníčka—look for the small horse on the facade).

At the other end of the square, notice the only modern building here, a **Spar supermarket.** Some 30 years ago, when the square was veiled in the shabby gray of communism, the regime decided to give it a facelift and "brighten it up" with a modern building that fit the ancient space like a UFO. After 1989, locals carefully added a facade and a new roof to the concrete box, effectively blending the former eyesore into the 16-century townscape.

Castle (Zámek)—The castle is covered with rectangular sgraffiti, a characteristic decoration of the late 1500s. As with other South Bohemian towns, all this sgraffiti is a reminder that the 16th century was Třeboň's heyday. Třeboň belonged to the Český Krumlov–based Rožmberk family. In 1600, Petr Vok—the last of the Rožmberks—moved here permanently after selling Český Krumlov to the emperor. He brought along his archive, still considered the most valuable collection of medieval documents in the Czech Republic. Your best basic castle visit is Route A, which includes Petr Vok's Renaissance rooms and the 19th-century apartments, kitchens, and stables of the later, equally distinguished Schwarzenbergs (60 Kč, April–Oct Tue–Sun 9:00–11:45 & 12:45–17:00, closed Mon and Nov–March, tel. 384-721-193).

The great **"Man and the Landscape"** exhibition (enter from castle garden) covers the history of lake-making, the balance between natural and human ecosystems, 16th-century economics, traditional and modern fish farming, and so on. At each display, you can select from short and engaging video clips (available in English). This little museum is focused, educational, and entertaining—as long as you skip the last section of stuffed animals. An hour here is time well-invested (50 Kč, Tue–Sun 9:00–17:00, closed Mon).

Dean Church and Augustine Monastery (Děkanský Kostel a Augustiánský Klášter)—A highlight of this modest Gothic church is its delicately curved Madonna statue by the central column. The church once showcased marvelous Gothic sculptures and altars, but these were deemed too valuable, so they were zipped off to the Museum of Medieval Art in Bohemia and Central Europe, located within the Convent of St. Agnes in Prague (see sight listing on page 73). The well-preserved frescoes on the vaults of the monastery courtyard show the Augustinian monks in action. Notice the focus on public service and on book preservation. Augustinians were some of the most ardent medieval copyists in the time before Gutenberg's moveable type revolutionized printing. Through the efforts of monks in this monastery, Třeboň became a center of medieval learning for Czechs and Austrians alike (30 Kč, June–early Sept daily 9:00–11:30 & 13:30–17:00 or pop in just before the nearly nightly 18:30 Mass, closed mid-Sept–May, Husova 142, tel. 384-722-390, in the summer ask for the young guide, Květa, who has a knack for making those Augustinians come alive).

Regent Brewery—This place offers basically the same standard tour you'll take at most other Czech breweries, but it's a bit more interesting than the norm, since you'll see the original 16th-century spaces in which the beer is brewed. Call Markéta Stasková to arrange a visit (50 Kč per person, or 500 Kč per group, 90 min, mobile 602-302-622).

The Lakes

The medieval lake-builders of Třeboň created an ingenious landscape of regulated channels, marshes turned into lakes, and fields changed into marshes. Birds otherwise unseen in the region began to nest here. Many other new animal species appeared. Peat provided a rich soil for pines and blueberry bushes.

The good lake-builders knew that small is beautiful... but, of course, not all of them were good. The most famous of Třeboň lake-builders was Jakub Krčín, the architect of the largest lakes, Svět and Rožmberk. Krčín was a man driven more by his ego than by practical considerations. Much of the water in his huge, deep lakes is dead, lacking enough oxygen to support large fish colonies. His predecessor, Štěpánek Netolický—while less celebrated—was more of a fishing expert. He built small, and his lakes were successful. His Golden Channel, which connects dozens of lakes, is the region's biggest marvel.

The Třeboň lakes were built for flood control as well as fishing. The marshy area around the town used to be regularly flooded by the Lužnice River. The artificial lakes were designed to absorb the floods. In 2002, the largest floods in Czech history tested the work of those medieval lake-builders. While the 20th-century dams built on the Vltava River to protect Prague failed, these 16th-century dams held, and the people of Třeboň emerged with dry feet.

ACTIVITIES

Boating and Swimming—A motorboat sets sail from the small wharf behind the brewery once an hour for a 30-minute (60 Kč) or 45-minute (90 Kč) cruise over the second-largest of Třeboň's lakes, Svět (daily 10:00–19:00, mobile 723-929-640). The nearest sandy beach is a 10-minute walk, to the right from the wharf along the dike.

Biking—The area is flat, so biking is a fun and convenient way to get around. A bike trip along the dirt trails on the ancient dikes is a fine way to experience the land and water. Either buy a cycling map from the TI, or follow the clearly marked 24-mile educational trail that snakes along channels and through traditional villages.

Hiking—The best hiking is in the area of Nová Reka (New River), directly east of town. Or catch a bus (or drive) to Chlum u Třeboně, and hike in the blueberry-filled pine woods along the Austrian border.

Peat Spa (Bertiny Lázně)—Třeboň is an important peat spa. Patients from all over the world arrive here for weeklong stays to get buried in the black, smelly sludge that's thought to cure aching joints and spines. Well, it doesn't hurt to try.

The complete peat bath *(slatinná koupel celková)* combined with a hand massage *(ruční masáž část)* will give you the best opportunity to judge the power of peat (500 Kč total). While treatments in the spas are booked months ahead, you can get a spot if someone cancels. Have your hotel clerk call Bertiny Lázně the night before or in the morning to check availability (tel. 384-754-413; the spa is through the east gate and just off to the left).

SLEEPING

Although there are many pensions in Třeboň, most only take spa guests who stay for a couple of weeks. But these two hotels usually allow one- or two-night stays on short notice.

$$$ Legner Hotel, run by a friendly young couple, has 10 recently renovated rooms, each furnished and painted differently. The colorful pictures in the breakfast room and reception are on sale, with proceeds that benefit charity. Lenka, the manager-receptionist, will be happy to tell you about her experience running Dutch and Czech charities, as well as share the history of the house, town, and region. Notice the slightly buried storage room by the reception hall—since Třeboň stands on floating sands, no house in town has a basement (Sb-1,900 Kč, Db-2,200 Kč, 300 Kč less off-season, extra bed-400 Kč, Rožmberská 35, tel. 384-721-754, mobile 737-770-537).

$ Hotel Bílý Koníček, on the main square, is a pale shadow of what once was a Renaissance inn famous throughout the country.

Sleep Code

(25 Kč = about $1, country code: 420)
S = Single, **D** = Double/Twin, **T** = Triple, **Q** = Quad, **b** = bathroom, **s** = shower only. Unless otherwise noted, credit cards are accepted and prices include breakfast.

To help you sort easily through these listings, I've divided the rooms into three categories based on the price for a standard double room with bath:

$$$ **Higher Priced**—Most rooms 1,500 Kč or more.
$$ **Moderately Priced**—Most rooms between 1,000–1,500 Kč.
$ **Lower Priced**—Most rooms 1,000 Kč or less.

At 1,000 Kč per double, the rooms are a great value. Out of the 23 rooms, half were recently renovated (the higher room numbers). Since rooms cost the same whether new or old, request a new room when reserving (tel. 384-721-213). Breakfast is not included—but that's probably a good thing, since the dingy ground-floor restaurant should be avoided by all means. Instead, walk around the corner by the Town Hall to a little bakery that serves a large selection of fine pastries and good coffee from 7:00.

EATING

Since the 1200s, Třeboň has lived on a steady diet of fish. The variety of fish raised here is amazing...as are the chefs. Austrians and Czechs alike drive for hours just to dine here. While you can find trout and carp throughout the country, the perch and pike from the lakes are unique. The pine woods south of the lakes are filled with blueberries—and, when it's the season, the blueberry dumplings are another must.

Na Rožmberské Baště is a little eatery with warm wooden walls and nets and fishing rods hanging from the ceiling (you can borrow one and bring in your own catch to be cooked). They serve tasty and cheap meals made from everything that swims in the surrounding lakes (Mon–Sat 10:30–24:00, Sun 10:30–22:30, on Rožmberská).

Šupina and Šupinka Restaurant is run by the local fishers' union, which makes sure the meals is cooked just right. The dishes are top-notch, but the modern, sterile interior detracts from the experience (daily 10:30–24:00, Novohradská Brána, tel. 384-721-149).

Schwarzenberská Pivnice is the large and colorful brewery/pub serving every variety of local Regent beer, including the fresh yeast kind you won't find in regular pubs. This is a drinking place—the only snacks available are Czech munchies, such as pickled sausage (*utopenec*) and pickled brie (*nakládaný hermelín*; Mon–Fri 11:00–22:00, Sat–Sun 12:00–23:00, in Regent Brewery).

TRANSPORTATION CONNECTIONS

While buses between Třeboň and Prague are about as fast as the train (2.5 hrs), bus departures are less frequent, and the bus station is far from the center of Třeboň.

From Třeboň by Train to: Prague (7/day, 2.5 hrs, transfer at Veselí nad Lužnicí). Remember, get off at Třeboň-Lázně, not Třeboň-Město.

By Bus to: Prague (2/day, 2.5 hrs), **Český Krumlov** (10/day to České Budějovice, 30 min, then transfer to Český Krumlov—see page 187), **Telč** (5/day Mon–Fri, 2/day Sat–Sun, 90 min), **Třebíč** (5/day Mon–Fri, 2/day Sat–Sun, 2.75 hrs), **Brno** (5/day Mon–Fri, 2/day Sat–Sun, 4 hrs).

Telč

Telč (telch, pop. 6,000) is famous for its castle and its glorious square—the country's best. The old town, surrounded by a sophisticated system of protective ponds and defense walls, has retained the same street plan since the 1300s. After 1800, all new construction took place outside the core of the town. Today, Telč remains an unspoiled, sleepy Czech town where neighbors chat in pastry shops and Vietnamese traders sell dirt-cheap textiles to the country folk in the medieval arcade stalls.

There are basically no attractions aside from the square and the castle. Telč is made to order as a lunch stop on the way to or from Slavonice (see next chapter), Třeboň, and Třebíč, or on the longer haul between Prague, Brno, and Vienna.

ORIENTATION

Everything you'll need—including ATMs, exchange offices, shops, hotels, and restaurants—is on the main square (Náměstí Zachariáše z Hradce), easily reachable on foot from the bus station. For a taxi, call mobile 603-255-048.

Tourist Information: The TI has information on activities in the area, train and bus schedules, and Internet access (Mon–Fri 8:00–18:00, Sat–Sun 10:00–17:00, tel. 567-112-407, www.telc-etc .cz). They can also help you find a room (see "Sleeping," below).

Helpful Hints

Festivals: Every year during the first two weeks of July, young musicians pour into Telč from all over Europe for the French-Czech Music Academy, which hosts workshops on classical music interpretation. The young virtuosos show off their skills in a number of concerts and recitals.

The "Telč Vacations" (Prázdniny v Telči) festival, held during the first two weeks of August, makes the squares, gardens, and castle chambers come alive with folk music, open-air theater, and exhibitions.

Internet Access: The Internet spot next to the TI is open only on weekdays.

Bike Rental: You can rent bikes at the shop next to the TI (40 Kč/ hour, 200 Kč/day, daily 9:00–18:00, tel. 567-243-562). Locals enjoy the half-day bike trip to the castle ruin of Roštejn and back (10 miles round-trip).

SIGHTS

Main Square (Náměstí Zachariáše z Hradce)—Telč's spacious square, lined by fairytale gables resting on the characteristic vaulted arcades that still cover local shops and bakeries, is the most impressive in the Czech Republic. The uniqueness of the square lies in its enormous size, unexpected proportions in such a small town, and the purity of its style—of the 40 houses lining the square, there isn't a single one younger than 300 years.

Telč Castle—In its early years, this castle belonged to the clan of the Five Roses (symbolized by a golden rose on a blue field). In the 1500s, the nobleman Zachariáš z Hradce imported a team of Italian artists who turned the earlier Gothic palace into a lavish Renaissance residence. (Their work also influenced most of the burgher houses in the square.)

You have two options for touring the castle (both with live guides). Tour A, the best basic castle tour, takes you through some stately Renaissance chambers. Marvel at a dissected elephant ear and a 16th-century water-pipe system. Tour B goes through the 19th-century apartments of the Lichtenstein family, who lived here until 1945. You can wait for an English tour (inquire as you enter), or you can borrow an English-language handout and go with a Czech tour (140 Kč per tour, May–Aug Tue–Sun 9:00–12:00 & 13:00–17:00, closed Mon; April and Sept–Oct Tue–Sun 9:00–12:00 & 13:00–16:00, closed Mon; closed Nov–March; last tour 1 hr before closing, can't miss the castle at end of main square).

Gallery of Jan Zrzavý—Tucked away in the garden to the right of the castle entrance, this small gallery is worth a peek to learn about pointillism. Zrzavý, one of the most prolific Czech painters, had a style similar to earlier Impressionists, but used dots (or points) instead of lines to construct images. Paintings in the five-room gallery span themes from mining to religion. Don't try to make much sense of it—just enjoy looking at steelworks and villages dissolved into points (30 Kč, April–Oct Tue–Sun 9:00–12:00 & 13:00–17:00, closed Mon; Nov–March Tue–Sun 9:00–12:00 & 13:00–16:00, closed Mon).

Gustav Mahler and Jihlava

Gustav Mahler (1860–1911) was the most important composer in Vienna at the turn of the 20th century. Mahler composed some of the last of the classical symphonies and was the first to venture into the musical never-never-land of atonality (while his contemporary Arnold Schönberg, also Jewish, took up residence there). The age of harmony ended—by 1910 there was nothing to hold the world together, and art preceded the shots of World War I.

Mahler, born in the nearby village of Kaliště, spent the first 15 years of his life in Jihlava, at a house at Znojemská 4 that now functions as a vibrant cultural center and the composer's museum (tel. 567-306-239, www.dum-gustava-mahlera.cz). This is a worthwhile stop for music buffs en route from Prague to Telč.

SLEEPING

The TI can arrange a room at a private pension (about 300 Kč per person) without taking a commission. There's generally no need to reserve ahead unless you want to stay at one of the following hotels.

$$$ Hotel Telč, under the church tower across the square from the castle, has 10 memorably furnished rooms and a warm family atmosphere (Sb-1,200 Kč, Db-1,510–1,820 Kč, extra bed-200 Kč, cheaper off-season, reserve well ahead in summer, tel. 567-243-109, www.hotelsprague.cz/telc/telc).

$$$ Hotel Celerin, another recently renovated townhouse, is slightly bigger than Hotel Telč, so it's more likely to have space on short notice. Some of its comfy rooms have traditional burgher furniture (Sb-900–1,100 Kč, Db-1,400–1,600 Kč, 200 Kč less Nov–April; rooms #4, #5, #9, and #10 face the square and are more expensive; tel. 567-243-477, fax 567-213-581, www.hotelcelerin.cz).

EATING

Osvěžovna u Marušky, behind the Church of the Holy Spirit and across the street from Hotel Telč, is not just the best eatery in town—but also a local cultural institution. The walls are decorated by local artists and vacationing out-of-towners, and jazz and classical concerts take place here twice a month. Young locals congregate to chat and eat. Use the Czech food explanations on page 31 to navigate the lunch menu (Sun–Thu 11:00–22:00, Fri–Sat 11:00–24:00, mobile 603-398-128).

TRANSPORTATION CONNECTIONS

From Telč to: Třeboň (5 buses/day Mon–Fri, 2/day Sat–Sun, 90 min), **Třebíč** (5 buses/day Mon–Fri, 2/day Sat–Sun, 45 min), **Brno** (5 buses/day Mon–Fri, 2/day Sat–Sun, 2.5 hrs), **Slavonice** (2 trains in morning, 3 in afternoon, 1 hr), **Prague** (3/day, 4–5 hrs, requires 2 changes—bus is better; 5 buses/day Mon–Fri, 3/day Sat–Sun, 2–3 hrs, more with a transfer in Jihlava—3 hrs total). Note that some buses to Prague may arrive at the Roztyly station (on the red Metro line), not the main bus station, Florenc.

Třebíč

A few miles east of Telč is the big, busy town of Třebíč (TREH-beech, pop. 40,000), with the largest intact Jewish ghetto in the country. While Prague's Jewish Quarter is packed with tourists, in Třebíč you'll have an entire Jewish town to yourself. Though Třebíč's Jewish settlement was relatively small, what remains is amazingly authentic.

ORIENTATION

Three hours in Třebíč is sufficient. To walk to the ghetto from the station, follow the *Židovské Město* signs (marked with Stars of David). The two main streets that run parallel to the river (which separates the ghetto from the Christian town) are connected by a maze of narrow passages, courtyards, and tunnels.

Tourist Information: The TI is in the ghetto's Rear Synagogue (described below, daily 10:00–12:00 & 13:00–17:00, Subakova 1, tel. 568-823-005, www.kviztrebic.cz).

Helpful Hints

Festival: Třebíč's annual Šamajim festival of Jewish music and film brings Jews and their culture back into the old ghetto for one week a year in early August (details at TI).

Local Guide: If you want to look deeper into the life of Moravian Jews, call the knowledgeable local guide **Alena Gottliebová** (450 Kč/hr, mobile 777-197-835, www.trebicenzi.cz).

SIGHTS

Jewish Ghetto (Židovské Město)—Time has stopped here entirely: The houses are essentially as the Jews left them 60 years ago. Many of the houses were resettled by Roma (Gypsies), who have done little to change the look and feel of the place. Lines

of drying clothes and kids kicking around a soccer ball on the cobblestones make today's ghetto come alive.

Walk along one of the winding streets through the ghetto to the **Rear Synagogue** (Zadní Synagoga), which displays artifacts of the once-thriving local Jewish community (30 Kč, daily 10:00–12:00 & 13:00–17:00), hosts temporary exhibits, serves as a concert venue, and is home to the TI (see above).

Jewish Cemetery—A 20-minute walk above the ghetto, this evocative memorial is covered with spreading ivy and bushes of wild strawberries. With 11,000 gravestones (the oldest dating to 1625), it's about three times the size of the one in Prague. Notice how the tombstones follow the assimilation of the Jews, from simple markers to fancy 19th-century headstones that look exactly like those of the rich burghers in Christian cemeteries (daily May–Sept 8:00–20:00, March–April and Oct 8:00–18:00, Nov–Feb 8:00–16:00, confirm hours at synagogue before ascending the hill; for a guided visit, contact Mr. Malášek at tel. 568-827-111).

St. Procopius Basilica—This enormous church, looming on the hill a five-minute walk above the ghetto, is worth a look. In a region of Baroque churches, this rich fusion of late Romanesque and early Gothic styles is like a silver dollar in a pile of copper pennies (30 Kč, visits with a guide only, tours take 45 min and start every hour; May–Sept Tue–Fri 9:00–12:00 & 13:00–17:00, Sat–Mon 13:00–17:00; closed Oct–April, tel. 568-824-692).

SLEEPING

$ Penzion u Synagogy, next door to the TI and Rear Synagogue, is right in the old Jewish ghetto (Db-650 Kč, extra bed-150 Kč, Subakova 43, check in at TI, tel. 568-823-005, www.mkstrebic .cz—click on "Eng" and then "Boarding house").

TRANSPORTATION CONNECTIONS

From Třebíč to: Telč (5 buses/day Mon–Fri, 2/day Sat–Sun, 45 min), **Třeboň** (5 buses/day Mon–Fri, 2/day Sat–Sun, 2.75 hrs), **Brno** (5 buses/day Mon–Fri, 2/day Sat–Sun, 75 min; also 10 trains/day, 75 min), **Prague** (nearly hrly, 4–5 hrs, transfer in Brno—bus is better; 7 buses/day, 2.5 hrs). Note that some buses to Prague may arrive at the Roztyly station (on the red Metro line), not the main bus station, Florenc.

SLAVONICE

Slavonice (SLAH-voh-neet-seh)—a charming little town of 2,000 people, with two elegant Renaissance squares separated by a Gothic church and Town Hall—is a perfect base for venturing into the most romantic of Czech landscapes. Enormous castle ruins top rugged hills, deep woods surround wild meadows, and WWII bunkers covered with sprawling blueberry bushes evoke the dark shadow of the past.

Centuries ago, this thinly populated borderland between Bohemia, Moravia, and Austria was filled with thieves and thugs—and therefore, nearly impossible to tax. The town was founded in the 1200s—and named "Zlabings"—by German settlers invited to colonize and civilize the region.

During the 14th century, when the main trading route between Prague and Vienna passed through here, Zlabings boomed. Most of the exquisite architecture dates from this period. But after the Thirty Years' War (1618–1648), the town declined, and few new buildings broke the medieval harmony.

In 1945, after the war, Zlabings' German residents—90 percent of the population—were forced out by vengeful Czechs. The town became fully Czech (and was officially renamed "Slavonice"), and a curtain of barbed wire sealed it from the West on three sides. This region—always sparsely populated, and even more so after its predominantly German population was removed—grew wilder throughout the Cold War, when it earned the nickname "Czech Canada" (Česká Kanada).

In 1989, the deep woods of the military zone were opened up to hikers and cyclists, the border a mile south of Slavonice was reopened, and Austrians began flocking here for cheap lunch and shopping—stoking business and polishing Slavonice into a jewel of a town.

ORIENTATION

Everything of interest is on Slavonice's main square, Náměstí Míru. The train and bus stations are each within a few minutes' walking distance of the center (head for the church tower, which overlooks the square).

Tourist Information

The TI is on the main square (daily 9:00–12:00 & 13:00–18:00, Náměstí Míru, tel. 384-493-320, www.slavonice-mesto.cz). They hand out useful tourist maps of the Slavonicko region and sell the detailed *Česká Kanada* hiking map.

The little-frequented roads in the area are ideal for **biking;** you can borrow bikes from Dům u Růže if you're staying there (see "Sleeping," below).

SIGHTS

The city tower and the simple town museum are nothing special and probably not worth your time (both open daily June–Aug, weekends only May and Sept, closed Oct–April). Instead, consider the following attractions.

Underground Passages—The medieval cellars under the town, connected by an intricate network of underground passages, are fun to explore. Starting from the entrance (on the main square, next to the TI), you can choose from the easy, shorter route (20 min, 40 Kč) or the strenuous, longer route, which goes through some very narrow corridors (1 hr, 70 Kč). If you ask for a bucket and offer to carry it out full of mud, you could get in for free (July–Aug daily 9:00–18:00, arrange a visit during the rest of the year by calling tel. 384-493-805 or mobile 605-906-333).

Landštejn Castle (Hrad Landštejn)—The region is dominated by the spectacular ruins of the Gothic castle that once guarded the border (May–Aug Tue–Sat 9:00–17:00, closed Mon; Sept Tue–Sat 9:00–16:00, closed Mon; April and Oct Sat–Sun 9:00–16:00, closed Mon–Fri; closed Nov–March; tel. 384-498-580, www.hradlandstejn.cz). On summer weekends, the castle serves as a venue for open-air folk and rock concerts.

Landštejn Castle is seven miles west of Slavonice, on the road to Nová Bystřice. Hardy travelers can reach the castle on foot (follow red-marked trail, see below) or by bike (follow the road or get

The Never-Used Fortifications

As soon as Adolf Hitler came to power in Germany in 1933, Czechoslovakia grew nervous about invasion. The area around Slavonice was part of the so-called Sudetenland: It belonged to Czechoslovakia, but was predominantly inhabited by ethnic Germans (see sidebar on page 180). Czechoslovakia began constructing a ring of fortifications along its borders. Iron-enforced concrete bunkers were connected by underground tunnels.

By September 1938, when Hitler met with the French and the British in Munich to claim the Sudetenland, these fortifications were filled with 1.5 million mobilized Czechs and Slovaks. Morale was high, and nobody doubted that the French and British would honor treaties with Czechoslovakia and help the young democracy. But instead, British Prime Minister Neville Chamberlain proclaimed to the British public, "Why should we care about the fate of a quarreling people about whom we know nothing?"—and signed off on the Munich Agreement, ceding the German areas of Czechoslovakia to Hitler without even inviting Czech representatives to the negotiations. (Chamberlain won a Nobel Prize for this appeasement policy.) Alone, the Czechoslovak army—outnumbered by the Germans three to one—stood no chance. The frustrated soldiers were ordered home, and Czechs were forced out of the Sudetenland. Half a year later, Hitler occupied the rest of the territory.

Today the never-used bunkers along the hiking trails around Landštejn stand witness to the futility of appeasement policies and to the Czechs' bitter sense of betrayal. At the close of the war, this feeling led to the Czechs' siding with the Soviet Union, rather than with the unreliable French and British allies. Ironically, the Munich Agreement probably saved Czechoslovakia from the fate of Poland, which was reduced to rubble during the war. Nevertheless, it took until 1989 for the Czechs to get over the frustration of the Munich Agreement in 1938, the communist take-over in 1948, and the failed "Prague Spring" uprising in 1968—moments when instead of being able to fight for freedom, Czechs had to give up without firing a single shot.

map at TI to go through the countryside). You can also reach the summit by bus (Slavonice–Nová Bystřice line, 3/day, weekdays only, 15 min, ask to be let off at Landštejn) or car (drive towards Nová Bystřice).

Suggested Day Hike: Follow the red-marked trail from Slavonice to Landštejn, visit the castle, then descend along the blue-marked trail in the direction of Nová Bystřice for less than a mile to reach the WWII fortifications (see sidebar). Come back along the same blue-marked trail, then follow the yellow-marked trail in the direction of Dačice to Velký Troubný lake, a perfect swimming spot. From there, return to Slavonice along the red-and-white-marked nature trail.

Sleeping and Eating at Landštejn Castle: Thriving with life during the day, the castle area becomes deserted in the evenings. To spend the night, consider **$ Hotel Restaurant Landštejnský Dvůr** (Db-1,000 Kč, tel. 384-498-727 or 384-498-726, Mr. Peřina). Three rough, atmospheric pubs by the castle offer well-cooled beer and a variety of medieval, Indian, Hungarian, and Slovak cuisine, plus meats grilled over an open fire.

SLEEPING

$$ Dům u Růže, on Slavonice's main square, has 12 rooms in a restored late-19th-century house. Each room has its own bath and kitchen; the sauna, pool, and bikes are free for hotel guests to use (Db-1,400 Kč, Náměstí Míru 452, tel. 384-493-987, mobile 603-493-879, www.dumuruze.cz, hotel@dumuruze.cz).

$ Hotel Arkáda, also on the main square, is more spartan and seems designed for hikers. They're happy to get you back into town from wherever your legs run out of steam—prearrange a pickup spot or borrow a fellow hiker's mobile phone and call them to come

---

Sleep Code

(25 Kč = about $1, country code: 420)
S = Single, **D** = Double/Twin, **T** = Triple, **Q** = Quad, **b** = bathroom, **s** = shower only. Unless otherwise noted, credit cards are accepted and prices include breakfast.

To help you sort easily through these listings, I've divided the rooms into two categories based on the price for a standard double room with bath:

$$ **Moderately Priced**—Most rooms between 1,000–1,500 Kč.

$ **Lower Priced**—Most rooms 1,000 Kč or less.

to your rescue (Sb-690 Kč, Db-880 Kč, no breakfast, Náměstí Míru 466, tel. 384-408-408, fax 384-408-401, www.hotelarkada .cz, info@hotelarkada.cz).

EATING

Restaurant Besídka, between the two parts of the square separated by the church, is a welcoming place with modern, artsy decor, a solid Czech menu, excellent pizzas, and divine blueberry dumplings (daily 11:00–22:00, tel. 384-493-293).

TRANSPORTATION CONNECTIONS

The only way in and out of Slavonice is by train from **Telč** (2 trains in morning, 3 in afternoon, 1 hr; see Telč's "Transportation Connections," page 200).

OLOMOUC

Olomouc (OH-loh-moats), the historical capital of Moravia, is a showcase of Baroque city planning. Today it's the Czech Republic's fourth-largest city (pop. 100,000) and harbors Moravia's most prestigious university. Students rule the town. With its wealth of cafés, clubs, and restaurants, Olomouc is the place to taste vibrant local culture—without the hassles and scams of Prague.

Although Olomouc's suburbs sprawl with 1960s apartment complexes and factories, its historic core was spared Stalin's experiments in urban design. It's not lost in a time warp like the old-town areas of Český Krumlov, Telč, and Slavonice. Trams clatter through the streets, fancy boutiques sell stylish Versace fashions, and locals pack the busy pubs. Few tourists come here, so the town lives on its own booming economy.

In the mornings, proud farmers dig out their leeks and carrots and descend upon the colorful open-air market. Haná, the region that immediately surrounds Olomouc, is the most fertile in the Czech Republic. The big landowners here have never had trouble converting their meat, milk, and bread into gold and power. The most distinguished landowner of all has always been the Church. Archbishops have ruled from here for a thousand years, filling the town with churches and monasteries. In 1946, these buildings were turned into faculties of Palacký University.

Being a student town, Olomouc feels young and alive (though quiet during summer weekends and school vacations, when the students clear out). Olomouc has managed to blend the old and the new better than any other town in the country. The McDonald's on the Baroque main square is not an intruder, but simply a contented acknowledgment of modern times. Olomouc is a fine place to just kick back for a day or two in a beautiful Baroque town with its gaze fixed on the future.

Olomouc

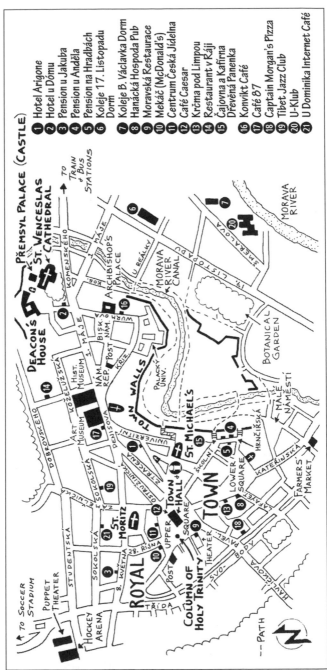

1. Hotel Arigone
2. Hotel u Dómu
3. Pension u Jakuba
4. Pension u Anděla
5. Pension na Hradbách
6. Koleje 17. Listopadu Dorm
7. Koleje B. Václavka Dorm
8. Hanácká Hospoda Pub
9. Moravská Restaurace
10. Mekáč (McDonald's)
11. Centrum Česká Jídelna
12. Café Caesar
13. Krčma pod Limpou
14. Restaurant v Ráji
15. Čajovna a Kafírna Dřevěná Panenka
16. Konvikt Café
17. Café 87
18. Captain Morgan's Pizza
19. Tibet Jazz Club
20. U-Klub
21. U Dominika Internet Café

Planning Your Time

Olomouc is a delightful mix of Baroque space and 21st-century life. Don't approach the city as a sightseer; Olomouc is to be experienced and enjoyed. The only must-see "sights"—the two squares and plague column—can be covered in an hour. You could happily spend additional time in the city's restaurants, bars, and clubs.

If you're passing through, consider hopping off the train for a three-hour lunch stop on the main square. Better yet, stay the night to relax and sample the rich nightlife. On a more leisurely visit, consider the worthwhile day trips to Kroměříž (with a sumptuous château—see below) and the Wallachia region (see next chapter).

ORIENTATION

Olomouc's historic core is small, compact, and just five tram stops from the train station (see "Arrival in Olomouc," below). The core has two parts: the original settlement around the former royal palace and cathedral (north of the castle) and the royal town (west of the castle). The royal town is concentrated around two connected squares: Upper Square (Horní Náměstí), with the Town Hall and plague column; and Lower Square (Dolní Náměstí), with many restaurants.

Tourist Information

While most visitors use the information offices at the train station (see below), the disinterested main TI is in the Town Hall on the Upper Square (daily 9:00–19:00, tel. 585-513-385, www.olomouc.com). Pick up the free map and a handful of unusually well-written fliers describing monuments. The TI sells tickets to concerts, can set you up with a local guide (500 Kč/hr, reserve 10 days ahead), and might be able to help you find a room.

Arrival in Olomouc

Olomouc's circa-1950s train station is downright cute: Bright and happy workers and peasants still greet you with their hammers and sickles.

As you exit through the main station hall, you'll see three information offices on the left. First is the railway center, with 24-hour help on train connections (tel. 585-785-620). Next is a simple TI that offers basic help—such as directions to hotels—and will sell a good town map (Mon–Fri 5:00–19:00, Sat 7:00–13:00, closed Sun). And third is a city transit office, with information about trams and tickets.

Take the **tram** into the center. Buy a 6-Kč tram ticket in the city transit office. Tram #1 stops in front of the train station and goes past the cathedral (U Dómu, 3rd stop), then continues

Olomouc's History

The fortune and misfortune of Olomouc has always come from its strategic location at the intersection of Eastern Europe's main east–west and south–north routes: Merchants, pilgrims, kings, and armies had to pass through the city.

Until the 1640s, Olomouc was the second-largest city in the Czech lands. The king's younger brother governed Moravian politics from here, while the archbishop kept the spirits (and the lands) of Moravians in God's hands—that is, his own.

Olomouc was trashed by passing armies during the Thirty Years' War (1618–1648). More than 70 percent of the town's population died in battles or from plagues, and the Moravian capital was moved to Brno. In 1709, Olomouc burned to the ground...only to emerge from the ashes with a Baroque flair. The new Olomouc—filled with churches, colleges, statues, and fountains—became the largest Baroque town in the country. But its prosperity again came to an abrupt end, as Prussia (occupying what is now western Poland and eastern Germany) threatened to invade Vienna—and Olomouc was right in the way. The Hapsburgs had Olomouc's students and monks leave and replaced them with soldiers to defend the city. They surrounded Olomouc with tall, thick walls, and what once was a cultural center became an immense fortress. The Prussians besieged the city but never managed to take it. The ring of walls and moats that protected the town also ended up protecting the historic center from the encroachment of modern-day architecture.

Olomouc eventually began to thrive again, but it remains overshadowed by Brno. Today it still comes in second as the economic powerhouse of Moravia. But ever since Palacký University was founded here in 1946—on the grounds of the centuries-old theological university—Olomouc has become Moravia's intellectual center.

to Koruna (5th stop) right by the main square.

Taxis are inexpensive (figure on 100 Kč to the center). Call Citytaxi (toll-free tel. 800-223-030) or Eurotaxi (toll-free tel. 800-113-030).

Helpful Hints

Pharmacy: A 24-hour pharmacy is on Aksamitova street.

Open-Air Market: At Olomouc's open-air market, Moravian farmers sell produce and Vietnamese traders hawk knock-off jeans (Mon–Fri 7:00–17:00, closed Sat–Sun, just off the Lower Square in the opposite direction from the Upper Square).

Festivals: During the summer (July–Sept), the town organizes a cultural festival. Top Czech artists perform weekly under the open sky in the Town Hall courtyard or in one of the numerous churches and student clubs around town (www.okl.info). The Jesuit Konvikt (former monastery) simultaneously hosts a Baroque music festival. Outside of festival time, when school is in session (Sept–June), Olomouc is lively with good independent movie theaters (www.olomouckakina.cz) and live music in bars (see "Cafés and Clubs," below).

Internet Access: U Dominika has a mellow decor and comfy chairs (Mon–Fri 9:00–21:00, Sat–Sun 10:00–21:00, across the street from Dominican monastery on Sokolská).

SIGHTS

In the Royal Town, West of the Castle

These sights cluster around the Upper Square (Horní Náměstí) in the royal town.

▲**Town Hall**—Olomouc's grand Town Hall is a testimonial to the city's 600 years of prominence in Moravia. The three wings around a rectangular courtyard once served as both council chambers and market halls. In the late 1400s, part of the building was converted into an armory, guards' house, and jail. On the outside, notice the beautiful Mannerist loggia, used for the entry into the council chambers and for ceremonial purposes (such as the mayor's declarations to the public).

You can visit the Town Hall's interior with a guided tour. You'll see the largest Gothic room in Moravia, used continuously since the 1400s for city council meetings. You'll also get to the top of the tower and into the Renaissance courtyard (60-min tours daily at 11:00 and 15:00, book and depart from the TI located within the Town Hall).

▲**Astronomical Clock**—The huge clock on the Town Hall was once far more complex than even the one in Prague. Originally, it depicted the medieval universe divided into three spheres, but it was periodically rebuilt to correspond with new advances in knowledge. In 1898, purists tried to restore it to its pristine state—stripping it of the layers of additions that had made it more interesting. The 1940s dealt a fatal blow: Like Prague's clock, it was intentionally destroyed by the Germans. Today's version, rebuilt by the communists, is a far cry from the original.

▲▲▲**Column of the Holy Trinity (Sousoší Nejsvětější Trojice)**—This is the artistic pride of Olomouc and the tallest plague column in Europe. Squares throughout Eastern Europe are dotted with similar structures, erected by locals to give thanks for

The Baroque Fountains of Olomouc

Sprinkled around Olomouc's old town is a series of seven allegorical fountains with statues. Since pagan times, Olomouc—whose wealth has always been based on agriculture—has had a close relationship to water. Most of the fountains were inspired by classical mythology. The seventh (and biggest) depicts Julius Caesar, who, according to local legend, founded Olomouc.

See if you can find all seven fountains. One features a statue of **Neptune,** the god of water. **Hercules** is depicted as the guardian of Olomouc, holding the Moravian checkered eagle in his left hand and a mace in his right. **Jupiter,** the overlord of the gods, replaced an earlier sculpture of the only Christian saint who appeared on the fountains: St. Florian, protector from fires and floods. The **Tritons** fountain—closely based on the one at Rome's Piazza Barberini—has the most developed composition: a pair of water spirits and a dolphin carrying a conch, with a fragile boy leading two dogs. The culmination of the cycle is the equestrian statue of **Caesar,** who looks proudly towards Michael Hill (where he supposedly founded Olomouc). The water gods Morava and Danubius carry the coats of arms of Moravia and Lower Austria, and the dog represents Olomouc's fidelity to the Austrian emperor. The **Mercury** statue is artistically the most successful. Mercury fulfilled the same role in classical mythology as the archangel Michael in the Old Testament: He was the guide through the land of the dead and the messenger of gods.

The town began planning the construction of the **Arion** statue in the 18th century, but it was only actually created in the last decade. According to legend, Arion was a Greek singer who earned a fortune performing in Rome. On his way home, Arion was robbed and thrown into the sea. His singing attracted a dolphin, who saved him. Arion symbolized the atonement of injustice and salvation from destruction—ideas that weighed heavy on the minds of Olomouc townspeople during the time when their town was turned from the Moravian capital into a border fortress.

The placement of the fountains and statues at the intersections of roads and squares—reminiscent of stage props in Baroque theater—imitates the spectacular cycle of Bernini's fountains in Rome. Since the second half of the 18th century, every view down any main street in Olomouc ends with a sculpture. Look for these as you sightsee and you'll better appreciate the town as theater.

surviving the plague. This one was started in 1716 by a local man named Render, who announced—with a confidence characteristic of the Haná region—that he would create a work that in "its height and ornamentation would not have a peer in terms of excellence." He donated his entire fortune, employing many great artists for decades to build the monument. Sadly, he died before its consecration, which occurred in the presence of Hapsburg Empress Maria Theresa.

The Holy Trinity group on the highest point of the column features God the Father making a blessing, Christ with a cross sitting on a globe, and the dove in gold (representing the Holy Spirit) crowning everything. In the lower half, the archangel Michael—with his fiery sword and shield—reminds us that the Church is in a constant struggle with evil. A third of the way down from the top of the column, we see Mary—the mediator between heavenly and earthly spheres—carried off by angels (the Assumption).

The bottom third features three reliefs with allegories of the Christian virtues (Faith, Hope, and Charity), surrounded by six saints. Four of the saints are closely connected with the life of Jesus (Saints Joachim and Anne—the parents of St. Mary—as well as St. Joseph and St. John the Baptist) and the other two are the patron saints of Olomouc (Saints Jerome and Lawrence). This particular arrangement of saints shows that universal faith is often combined with a distinctly local myth and belief.

Churches—Olomouc has been the seat of bishops from its origin. The great number of churches—concentrated in such a small area—shows the strong presence of the Church here. Of the many churches in town, two are worth a mention (each one is a block off the Upper Square).

St. Michael's Church (Sv. Michál), located at the highest point in town, dominates Olomouc's skyline. It's a fine, single-nave Baroque church full of illusory paintings and fake armor.

St. Moritz Church (Sv. Mořic) is a must-see for its pair of asymmetrical towers, which look more like fortresses. The church has an original Gothic vault and a narrow spiraling staircase between the towers.

Near the Cathedral, North of the Castle
St. Wenceslas Cathedral (Dóm Sv. Václava)—This has supposedly been the resident church of Olomouc's bishops ever since the

Christian missionaries Cyril and Methodius visited in the 9th century. The present church, begun in the 1200s and rebuilt many times, is now 19th-century pseudo-Gothic, with rich Art Nouveau frescoes. The crypt houses a collection of liturgical ornaments—the second-largest in the country, after Loreta Church in Prague (see page 106).

Přemysl Palace (Přemyslovský Palác)—Once the king's principal Moravian residence, this palace later became home to Olomouc's archbishop. The exterior is a humble mix of Romanesque and Gothic elements. The Romanesque interior features an exhibition on the architecture and history of the palace and the Church in Olomouc (15 Kč, April–Sept Tue–Sun 10:00–18:00, closed Mon and Oct–March, entrance to the left of cathedral).

Deacon's House—Across the square from the cathedral is the deaconry, well-known to every Czech schoolchild as the site of the most famous Czech assassination. In 1306, the 17-year-old King Václav III—who was the last surviving member of the Přemysl dynasty—was killed here on his way to Kraków, Poland, where he was to be crowned the Polish king. Though the murder remains a mystery, many researchers (who seem more like Czech Agatha Christies than real historians) have reconstructed the detective story. All we know for sure is that the assassin hid in Václav III's toilet, then shot the king when he sat upon his throne. If you've always wanted to start a revolution, the "toilet assassination"—along with "defenestration" (throwing someone out a window) and "wrapping in velvet"—are uniquely Czech methods for getting rid of opponents.

Archbishop's Palace (Arcibiskupský Palác)—The space between the castle hill and the royal town is dominated by this 17th-century palace. On the slopes below the palace are Jesuit colleges (now university classrooms) and a Clarist convent, now a museum.

SLEEPING

$$$ Hotel Arigone is in a tastefully renovated townhouse with a garden restaurant. Its 12 fancy rooms have 17th-century wooden ceilings, 19th-century-style furniture, and 21st-century cable TV (Sb-1,700 Kč, Db-2,000 Kč, Univerzitní 20, tel. 585-232-350 or 585-232-351, fax 585-232-350, www.arigone.web.tiscali.cz, arigone .olomouc@tiscali.cz).

$$$ Hotel u Dómu, a little six-room place on a quiet street next to the cathedral, is run with a personal touch by Marie and Josef Jiříček (Sb-1,200 Kč, Db-1,800 Kč, Tb-2,000 Kč, free parking, Dómská 4, tel. 585-220-502, fax 585-220-501, www .udomu.360-panorama.net, hoteludomu@email.cz).

Sleep Code

(25 Kč = about $1, country code: 420)
S = Single, **D** = Double/Twin, **T** = Triple, **Q** = Quad, **b** = bathroom, **s** = shower only. Unless otherwise noted, credit cards are accepted and prices include breakfast.

To help you sort easily through these listings, I've divided the rooms into three categories based on the price for a standard double room with bath:

$$$ **Higher Priced**—Most rooms 1,000 Kč or more.
$$ **Moderately Priced**—Most rooms between
500–1,000 Kč.
$ **Lower Priced**—Most rooms 500 Kč or less.

$$ Pension u Jakuba rents six self-contained apartments in a recently renovated 400-year-old house in the center. The rooms are large and modern, each with its own Ikea-style kitchen and bathroom. The penthouse has two bedrooms, a living room, and a huge bathroom. The cleaning lady, who has a sense of humor, folds the clean towels to look like elephants (Db-990 Kč, Tb-1,300 Kč, Qb-1,700 Kč, 8. Května #9—watch for house number since the sign is hard to see, tel. 585-209-995, mobile 777-747-688, www.ujakuba.euweb.cz, ujakuba@iol.cz).

$$ Pension u Anděla ("By the Angel") fits right into Hrnčířská ("Potter's Street"), a quiet row of two-story village houses with brightly painted facades and window-boxes full of geraniums. A couple of the four homey apartments overlook the bastion and park (Db-700 Kč, no breakfast, Hrnčířská 10, tel. 585-228-755, mobile 602-512-763, www.uandela.cz).

$$ Pension na Hradbách, directly across the street, rents six modern rooms (Db-800 Kč, no breakfast, Hrnčířská 3, tel. 585-233-243, mobile 602-755-848, nahradbach@quick.cz).

$ Dorms and Hostels: During school vacations (late June–Oct), the university dorms function as hostels. The simple rooms are clean and a great value. There's always room—walk in any time of day or night, pay at the reception, and you'll get a small towel and a room key. Checkout is at 9:00. **Koleje 17 Listopadu** (dorm building A), on the street called 17 Listopadu, is a five-minute walk from the cathedral. Its three-bedded student rooms share recently renovated showers (180 Kč per person; they won't make you take a room with anyone outside your party). For a room with a private bathroom in a modern building, walk along the path to the right of building A to the tallest building in sight, the **Koleje B. Václavka** (dorm building C). Double rooms with showers here start at 300

Kč (30 percent discount with ISIC student card, central university accommodation office tel. 585-226-057, mobile 777-000-202).

EATING

Try the sour, foul-smelling, yet beloved specialty of the Haná region, Olomouc cheese sticks *(olomoucké syrečky)*. The milk goes through a process of natural maturation under chunks of meat. Czechs figure there are two types of people in the world: *syrečky*-lovers and sane people. The *syrečky* are so much part of the Haná and Czech identity that when the European Union tried to forbid the product, the Czech government negotiated for special permission to continue to rot their milk. Zip a few of these stinkers in a baggie and you can always get a train compartment to yourself.

Hanácká Hospoda, on the Lower Square, is a simple and hearty village pub that serves regional specialties to visitors and locals alike (Mon–Sat 10:00–24:00, Sun 10:00–20:00, Dolní Náměstí, tel. 585-237-186).

Moravská Restaurace (literally, "Moravian Restaurant"), on the Upper Square, is the one touristy place in town. If you're feeling homesick, step in here, and you'll see happy tourists attracted by ads all over town, "authentic" Moravian folk costumes of the waiters, walls decorated with Moravian painted ceramics...and prices that will make you feel like you're back at home (essentially the same menu as Hanácká Hospoda for triple the price, daily 11:30–23:00, reservations recommended, Horní Náměstí, tel. 585-222-868).

Mekáč (McDonald's), on the Upper Square, is the favorite of local children. They demand French fries and vanilla ice cream for birthdays, and eat with gusto while the whole family sits around and watches. It's a great place to hang out with the folks from the countryside who proudly come here dressed in their Sunday best for a "Bikmek" taste of the world.

Centrum Česká Jídelna (literally, "Czech Eatery") is ideal if you're short on time and want some local-style fast food. They offer a world of traditional Czech dishes, ready and warmed, for you to claim by pointing your finger (sometimes closed Sat–Sun, next to McDonald's on the Upper Square).

Café Caesar, filling the Gothic vaults in the Town Hall, is a popular pizza place (daily 11:00–24:00, tel. 585-229-287). The fine little gallery next door, run by the café, promotes local artists.

Krčma pod Limpou, on the Lower Square next to Hanácká Hospoda (see above), mixes stone-and-brick ceilings of dark medieval cellars with the music of Pink Floyd. Since it's hugely popular with locals, evenings here get lively, but a bit stuffy. Come for well-prepared meats rather than typical local food. The menu explains why Mr. Bernard does not pasteurize his beer...and why

Mr. Anheuser-Busch should follow suit (daily 16:00–24:00, Dolní Náměstí, tel. 585-221-500).

Restaurant v Ráji (literally, "In the Paradise"), tucked in the gateway of a newly constructed apartment house, serves a range of fine game dishes amid artsy, modern decor (Mon–Thu 11:00–22:00, Fri–Sat 11:00–23:00, Sun 11:00–20:00, Hanáckého Pluku 10, tel. 585-221-689).

EXPERIENCES
Cafés and Clubs

Olomouc is the Moravian university town, and every aspect of student life (except sleeping) happens right in the old center. During the summer, Czech students are replaced by foreign ones learning about Czech language, music, and history.

Čajovna a Kafírna Dřevěná Panenka (literally, "Wooden Maiden Tea and Coffee House") consists of five small rooms and a little terrace above the city walls. Slim wooden sculptures give this place its name. Meditate and converse over a cup of China's and Arabia's greatest gift to the world (Mon–Fri 11:00–23:00, Sat–Sun 15:00-23:00, Hrnčířská 12).

Konvikt is a hip café right next to classrooms in a historic courtyard of the former Jesuit college. During the summer, it's a popular hangout for foreign students (Mon–Sat 14:00–24:00, closed Sun).

Café 87 has the longest list of espresso drinks, iced coffees, frappes, and decadent desserts in town (daily 10:00–19:00, next to Arts Museum on Náměstí Republiky).

Captain Morgan's Pizza fills three large, red-brick, 18th-century barrack rooms. It offers atmospheric dining during the day and becomes a thriving disco after 22:00 (open daily from 10:00 until very late, on Mlýnská).

Tibet Jazz Club has nothing to do with Tibet, but does have good food, plus live jazz twice a week in a modern, pub-like setting (Mon–Fri 10:00–24:00, Sat 12:00–24:00, closed Sun and in Aug, Sokolská 48, tel. 585-230-399).

U-Klub, a 10-minute walk out of the center in the dorms, is the university's own concert hall. Bands play folk, jazz, rock, punk...you name it (Šmeralova 12, tel. 585-638-117).

TRANSPORATION CONNECTIONS

Olomouc is on several major rail lines, making it an easy stop when traveling to or from Kraków, Vienna, or Budapest.

From Olomouc by Train to: Kroměříž (hrly, 1–1.5 hrs, transfer in Hulín, see page 220), **Vsetín** (with connections to

Wallachia—see next chapter; 4/day, 1 hr), **Prague** (hrly, 3.5 hrs direct), **Brno** (buses and trains at least hrly, 1.5 hrs), **Kraków** (2/day, 4.5 hrs, transfer in Přerov, Czech Republic, or in Katowice, Poland), **Vienna** (6/day, 3.5 hrs, transfer in Brno, Břeclav, or Přerov), **Budapest** (3/day, 5.5–6 hrs, transfer in Brno or Přerov).

To Třeboň, Telč, and Třebíč: Take the bus or train to **Brno** (at least hrly, 1.5 hrs—see above), then take the bus in the direction of **České Budějovice** (5/day Mon–Fri, 2/day Sat–Sun—see page 188).

Kroměříž

While Olomouc was the official seat of the Moravian archbishops, Kroměříž (KROH-myehr-eezh) was the site of their lavish summer château. In 1948, this castle and its enormous gardens were nationalized and opened to the public. Kroměříž—showing off the richness of this corner of the Czech Republic—is the most lavish and best-renovated rococo castle in the country. The 19th-century English-style park, with lakes, woods, and Chinese pavilions, is good for a walk or picnic.

While there are no other worthwhile sights in town, the pleasant square, streets filled with little bakeries, and a chance to experience a small Moravian town offers a perfect complement to the grandeur of the archbishop's estate. The town and château of Kroměříž combine for a perfect half-day excursion from Olomouc to enjoy the genteel art and gentle life of Moravia.

ORIENTATION

Tourist Information: The humble TI on the main square hands out a useful map with brief descriptions of all major sights, as well as a list of events (Mon–Fri 8:30–18:00, Sat–Sun 9:00–13:00, Velké Náměstí, tel. 573-331-473, www.mesto-kromeriz.cz).

Arrival in Kroměříž: Turn right out of the train station, then take the first left over the bridge. The main square (Velké Náměstí) and the entrance to the château are an easy 10-minute walk away.

Helpful Hints

Music: Throughout the summer, the city government joins forces with art schools and conservatories to enliven the historical spaces by holding weekly concerts. The quality of the performers and the unique setting—in the château halls and gardens—make a visit worthwhile (ticket booking and purchase at Velké Náměstí 50, tel. 573-331-473, www.hudba-kromeriz.cz). The Kroměříž Music Summer Festival is held in September (tel. 573-341-400).

Internet Access: Internet Café u Maxe is on the main square, right below the town museum.

SIGHTS

Archbishop's Château (Arcibiskupský Zámek)—Dominating the main square and the whole town, this château was rebuilt in Baroque style by archbishop Karel Lichtenstein (dubbed the

"Moravian Richelieu") after an earlier castle was severely damaged in a Swedish siege during the Thirty Years' War. The furniture and decorations are in the rococo style (from the second half of the 18th century). The breathtaking chandeliers are made of Czech crystal.

The château is famous for one historic event: The Austrian parliament moved here from unstable Vienna during the tumultuous year of 1848, when a wave of revolutions spread across the Hapsburg lands. The parliament drafted the first Austrian constitution in the château's main hall.

Hours: May–Sept Tue–Sun 9:00–17:00, closed Mon; April and Oct Sat–Sun only 9:00–17:00, closed Mon–Fri; closed Nov–March. Tel. 573-502-011, www.azz.cz.

Tours: You can see the art gallery (see below) and climb the tower (40 Kč) on your own, but you can tour the château interior only with a guide (80 Kč with a Czech group). Try asking for an English tour—you'll pay double, but you might be the only one in the group. Tours run about every hour and last 70 minutes, with the time about evenly split between the first floor (8 rooms) and second floor (has a beautifully painted ceiling depicting the history of the bishopric and overlooks a stunning library interior with 80,000 books).

Art Gallery: Art-lovers should consider visiting the bishop's art gallery. Sure, it's not the Louvre—but it's the best Moravian collection of European paintings from 1400—1800, with works by Titian, Cranach, Dürer, and Veronese (60 Kč, same hours as château).

Castle Garden (Podzámecká Zahrada)—This green space, filled with little ponds, exotic trees, and Chinese pavilions, offers a peaceful refuge. It's in the English style—wilder and more natural than the geometrically designed French gardens (July–Aug daily 5:30–20:30; May–June and Sept Tue–Sun 9:00–17:00, closed Mon; April and Oct Sat–Sun only, closed Mon–Fri).

SLEEPING

Kroměříž works best as a day trip from Olomouc, but if you want to see a concert and stay the night, try **$$$ Hotel Bouček.** This well-renovated traditional townhouse on the main square rents 11 decent rooms (Db-1,600 Kč, Velké Náměstí 108, tel. 573-342-777).

EATING

All of these eateries are on or just off the main square (Velké Náměstí).

Bistro u Zámku is a popular place to sip a frappe or iced coffee (daily, on the corner of main square next to château).

Zámecká Myslivna (literally, "Château Hunting Lodge") specializes in game. Your venison might have been shot by the archbishop, who still comes here during the summer—ask your waiter (Sun–Thu 11:00–22:00, Fri–Sat 11:00–24:00, just off main square, Sněmovní Náměstí 41, tel. 573-340-498).

Radniční Kavárna is perfect if you want to eat on cushioned chairs outside—because it's a bit stuffy inside (daily 9:00–22:00, at top of main square across street from Town Hall).

Bistro Avion, a blue-collar, self-service cafeteria on the main square, is good for a basic, filling meal (Mon–Fri 6:00–18:00, Sat 8:00–15:00, Sun 7:00–14:00). The place has no menus—just point to what looks good, and wash it down with Slovakia's best beer, Zlatý Bažant ("Golden Pheasant").

TRANSPORTATION CONNECTIONS

Day-trip from Olomouc to Kroměříž: From Olomouc, take one of the frequent trains in the direction of Přerov and Břeclav (hrly, 7:46 train is convenient). Get off at Hulín (second stop after Přerov on fast trains, 35 min), walk through the train station to the other side of the building, and hop on the small motor train to Kroměříž (departure scheduled to coincide with the arrival of Břeclav-bound trains, 8 min). On the way back, most trains from Kroměříž to Hulín connect with an Olomouc-bound train.

WALLACHIA

The mountainous region of Wallachia (vah-LAH-chee-ah)—where Slovakia and Poland meet the eastern edge of the Czech Republic—is ideal for an escape into nature, where you can enjoy both the ruggedness of the mountains and the easy tourist facilities of an accessible recreational area.

Wallachia (Valašsko) is made up of three east–west ridges separating three long valleys. The Beskydy Mountains—the westernmost part of the Carpathian mountain range—make an impressive backdrop.

Wallachia has a sparse but proud population, the Wallachians (Valaši). They were originally Romanian shepherds who, following their sheep, drifted west along the pristine meadows and rugged canyons of the hauntingly beautiful Carpathians. In exchange for guarding the border, these shepherds received many privileges—most importantly, exemption from taxes.

Today the Wallachians have their own tongue-in-cheek, tax-free "kingdom." In local restaurants and hotels, you can buy Wallachian "passports," which come with a brochure explaining in English why you should emigrate. The 90 Kč is a small price to pay for a passport when you consider that it frees you from the far-reaching clutches of the IRS.

Getting Around Wallachia

This region is best with a car. It's a headache, though doable, by public transportation. **Olomouc** is the nearest big city (see Olomouc's "Transportation Connections," page 217). From Olomouc, direct buses take you to **Rožnov** (3/day, 90 min). By train from Olomouc, you can get to Frenštát pod Radhoštěm (near **Trojanovice** and **Pustevny,** 8/day, transfer in Valašské Meziříčí, most require additional transfer in Hranice na Moravě, allow

2.5 hrs total) and Velké Karlovice (8/day, transfer in Vsetín, may require additional transfer in Hranice na Moravě, figure on 3 hrs total). For specifics on getting up to the mountaintop at Pustevny, see below.

Rožnov

Industrial Rožnov, the largest town in the region, may not be worth an overnight stay, but it certainly merits a visit for its Wallachian Open-Air Folk Museum (Valašské Muzeum v Přírodě). The museum, which re-creates a traditional Wallachian village, is divided into three parts. Touring the "Little Wooden Town" is sufficient to give you a good sense of Eastern European mountain architecture, which blends here with elements of Moravian house-building.
The museum is also the resting place for the most distinguished Wallachians, among them the incredible runner Emil Zátopek, who won three gold medals at the Helsinki Olympics in 1952.

Cost, Hours, Location: 50 Kč, May–Aug daily 8:00–18:00; Jan–March and Oct Tue–Sun 9:00–16:00, closed Mon; April Tue–Sun 9:00–17:00, closed Mon (www.vmp.cz). On Rožnov's main square, you'll find direction markers for the museum (it's a 10-min walk).

Tours: Although you can visit the complex on your own, you can more fully appreciate the site if you call ahead to reserve an English-speaking guide (400 Kč extra for an hour-long tour, reserve at tel. 571-757-111, prohlidka@vmp.cz).

TRANSPORTATION CONNECTIONS

From Rožnov by Bus to: Olomouc (3/day, 90 min), **Frenštát pod Radhoštěm** (near Trojanovice; 6/day, 20 min), **Velké Karlovice** (6/day, 45 min).

Pustevny

Pustevny (POO-stehv-nee, "Hermitage") is a small, pleasant resort atop the Beskydy (BEH-skih-dee) Mountains' most sacred ridge, in a spot where a legendary hermit once lived. The style of the mountain huts here is an imaginative combination of Art

Nouveau and wooden village architecture. Peak season here is June through August for hiking, and from Christmas through Easter for skiing. Restaurants are open only on weekends during other months.

The 30-minute **hike** from Pustevny along the red-marked trail on the ridge toward the west will take you to a statue of Radegast, the old Slavic god of sun, friendship, and harvest. (Eerily, the area around the

statue is the only place in the Czech Republic without mobile phone coverage.) If you hike farther along the ridge for two miles, you'll reach the top of the sacred Radhošť mountain and statues of the Slavic missionaries, Cyril and Methodius. They hold a page of the beginning of the Gospel According to John, which they translated for the Slavic people over 1,100 years ago. A wooden church dedicated to these two patrons of all Slavs stands behind the statue.

At the base of the mountain below Pustevny is the crossroads village of **Trojanovice** (TROH-yah-noh-veet-seh). Basically a wide spot in the road, it offers nothing of interest besides a nice hotel (u Kociána—see below) and convenient chairlift access up to Pustevny (see below).

Getting to Pustevny

To get to Trojanovice and Pustevny by **public transportation,** take the train to the town of Frenštát pod Radhoštěm (2 miles away). Arrange a pickup with the Hotel u Kociána or take a taxi (less than 100 Kč). A 15-minute walk up the road from Trojanovice's Hotel U Kociána takes you to a chairlift that runs up to Pustevny (40 Kč, hourly, takes about 30 min, daily in summer 9:00–18:00, daily in winter 9:00–16:00, confirm hours with hotel off-season). On arriving in Pustevny, be sure to check the schedule for the last chairlift back down to Trojanovice.

If **driving,** follow signs from Frenštát to Trojanovice; the Hotel u Kociána will be on the left. The easiest way up to Pustevny is to simply park at the hotel and walk to the chairlift (described above). If you want to drive all the way to Pustevny, you'll have to take the long (45-min), poorly marked route around the back of the mountain. The advantage of driving is that the route takes you through Rožnov, so you can stop on the way to tour the Wallachian Open-Air Folk Museum (see above).

Sleep Code

(25 Kč = about $1, country code: 420)
S = Single, **D** = Double/Twin, **T** = Triple, **Q** = Quad, **b** = bathroom, **s** = shower only. Unless otherwise noted, credit cards are accepted, English is spoken, and breakfast is included.

To help you sort easily through these listings, I've divided the rooms into three categories based on the price for a standard double room with bath:

$$$ **Higher Priced**—Most rooms 1,000 Kč or more.
$$ **Moderately Priced**—Most rooms between 500–1,000 Kč.
$ **Lower Priced**—Most rooms 500 Kč or less.

SLEEPING AND EATING

At Pustevny

$$$ **Hotel Tanečnica,** large and modern, is the best option for sleeping on top of the mountain (Db-1,000 Kč, 20 percent less off-season, tel. 556-835-341, www.tanecnica.cz).

The nearby **Koliba u Záryša** restaurant, with a shepherd's-hut setting, is run by big-hearted Mrs. Veřmířovská, who serves great Wallachian food: garlic soup and hearty dishes of pork, potatoes, kraut, and cabbage.

Below Pustevny, in Trojanovice

$$$ **Hotel u Kociána,** a popular local hangout run by a can-do family, is a delightful alternative to the comparatively impersonal Hotel Tanečnica (Db-800–1,200 Kč, tel. 556-835-206, mobile 604-858-967, www.hotelukociana.cz).

TRANSPORTATION CONNECTIONS

From Frenštát pod Radhoštěm (near Trojanovice) by Train to: Olomouc (8/day, transfer in Valašské Meziříčí, most require additional transfer in Hranice na Moravě, allow 2.5 hrs total).

Velké Karlovice

Velké Karlovice is a large Wallachian village combining the best of the Old and the New Worlds in a picturesque mountain valley amidst the Carpathian ridges. The most beautiful hike in the region is along the border ridge from Velký Javorník to Horní Liběř. The Czech side of the border features plenty of convenient tourist amenities while preserving its authenticity; the Slovak side is made up entirely of little villages with no tourists at all.

There are two train stops in Velké Karlovice. Right by the first one is the oldest wooden church in the country, a folk museum, and local favorite restaurant/pub. Continue to the second (final) stop three miles up the road to approach the Leskové recreational area (www.valachy.cz).

SLEEPING

In Leskové
Consider **$$$ Hotel Lanterna** (Db-800–1,200 Kč, tel. 571-454-310, lanterna@valachy.cz) or **$$Hotel Galik** (Db-650–900 Kč, tel. 571-454-294, galik@valachy.cz).

TRANSPORTATION CONNECTIONS

From Velké Karlovice by Train to: Olomouc (8/day, transfer in Vsetín, may require additional transfer in Hranice na Moravě, allow 3 hrs total). Arrange with hotels in Leskové to pick you up at the station.

MIKULOV WINE REGION

The Mikulov region produces the Czech Republic's most famous wine. The village of Pavlov, with its beautiful rural architecture and wine cellars filled with singing Moravians, is the ideal place to experience Moravia's wine culture. The surrounding Pálava Hills and water sports make days here as enjoyable as the nights. The historic town of Mikulov—the center of the region—is a pleasant lunch stop between Pavlov and Lednice. And the large Lednice-Valtice complex of castles and 19th-century English-style parks is a unique feat of environment-friendly landscaping.

Getting Around the Mikulov Wine Region

The main railway junction of Břeclav is the gateway to the Mikulov wine region.

From Břeclav to: Mikulov (10 trains/day, 30 min, goes through Valtice), **Valtice** (10 trains/day, 15 min), **Lednice** (8 buses/day Mon–Fri, 4/day Sat–Sun, 20 min; on summer weekends, a cute historical train runs between Břeclav and Lednice: 4/day, 20 min), **Prague** (trains every 2 hrs, 3.5 hrs direct, most departing from Prague's Holešovice station), **Olomouc** (hrly trains, 1.5–2.5 hrs, sometimes with transfer in Brno). For **Pavlov,** you'll first take the train to Mikulov (see above), then a bus to Pavlov (4/day Mon–Fri, 1/day Sat–Sun, 30 min).

By Car: Although it's possible to connect all these destinations by public transportation, renting a car in Břeclav or elsewhere can save lots of time (see Mikulov's "Helpful Hints" on page 232).

Mikulov Wine Region

Pavlov and the Pálava Hills

The traditional village of Pavlov, stretching from the banks of the Nové Mlýny dam up toward the dramatic hilltop ruin of Dívčí Hrady ("Girls' Castle"), has everything you need for a fun one- or two-day wine adventure. In deep brick cellars, you can taste local wines and spicy Hungarian salami while hearing the dreamy tunes of Moravian songs. You'll see Moravian village architecture; choose from a wealth of neat, family-run pensions; take nature walks along the wooded slopes of the white Pálava Hills; and tackle an expanse of water however you like, from swimming to wind-surfing.

The only drawback is communication: While German works well, few locals speak more than broken English. But fear not—the genuine hospitality of the locals makes struggling with the language barrier both fun and rewarding. So be brave, and pull your hands and phrase books out of those pockets.

ACTIVITIES

Wandering the Town—Česká street, stretching from Restaurace u Venuše to the parking lot above the church, is lined with traditional vintners' houses. The owners live on the first floor, wine is pressed on the ground floor, and extensive cellars run deep into the mountain. The farmsteads along the park by the church are some of the finest examples of Moravian Baroque village architecture.

Wine Cellars—Ask your host whether any dulcimer bands are playing in any of the wine cellars. Locals often bring their guitars along. September is a wild month here—the whole country converges on the region, and everyone drinks the hugely popular young wine *(burčák)*.

Floating on the River—During the day, the Yacht Club at the bottom of the village rents a variety of floatables, including paddleboats, canoes, and windsurfing boards. The shallow water is warm for most of the summer and the beaches seem endless.

Three successive dams, planned for decades as part of an immense irrigation project intended to water most of southern Moravia, were completed in the early 1990s. By then, the collectivized fields and vineyards had been returned to individual owners. For these small producers, building channels or pumping water from the dams turned out to be too expensive. So in the end, the costly project boosted the local economy only indirectly—by drawing in thousands of fishing and sailing enthusiasts.

Hiking in the Pálava Hills—For a perfect half-day hike, follow the green-marked trail from the church past Pension Florián, then up through the beech woods to the ruined castle (1.5 miles, 45 min). Continue along the red-marked trail on the ridge to the highest point of the hills, Děvín (1 hr). Descend on the other side of the mountain to Klentnice. From here, you can return to Pavlov either along the blue-marked trail through the woods on the western slopes of the Pálava Hills, or along the educational wine-making route (marked by white signs with diagonal green stripes) through the vineyards east of the hills.

SLEEPING

During hot summer months and in September, getting a room on short notice can be difficult—book ahead. While the small pensions often require a minimum one-week stay, larger places (and those listed here) are happy to take you for a night or two.

Sleep Code

(25 Kč = about $1, country code: 420)
S = Single, **D** = Double/Twin, **T** = Triple, **Q** = Quad, **b** = bathroom, **s** = shower only. Unless otherwise noted, credit cards are accepted, English is spoken, and breakfast is included.

To help you sort easily through these listings, I've divided the rooms into three categories based on the price for a standard double room with bath:

$$$ **Higher Priced**—Most rooms 1,000 Kč or more.
$$ **Moderately Priced**—Most rooms between 500–1,000 Kč.
$ **Lower Priced**—Most rooms 500 Kč or less.

$$$ Hotel Iris, part of a Czech chain, is the only real hotel in the village. Its 22 rooms are expensive, but a suitable fallback if the pensions (below) are full. The standardized experience comes with TV, a sauna, and a fitness center. The ease of communication in English might make up for the lack of village ambience (Db-1,200 Kč, tel. 519-515-310, www.orea.cz, hotel.iris@iol.cz).

$$ Pension a Restaurace Florián, with six homey rooms, is run by an energetic woman who speaks no English—though her daughter worked in England, and is by far the best English-speaker in the village. Both would like to see more Americans come to Pavlov, so even if they're full, ask for help arranging a room elsewhere. They make you feel like part of the family—home-cooking is available all day. In the evenings, they run a wine cellar–restaurant behind the pension (Db-700 Kč, 5 percent discount for readers of this book in 2006, Podhradní 195, tel. & fax 519-515-323, mobile 723-633-022, www.pensionflorian.cz, info@pensionflorian.cz).

$$ Pension u Bednařů rents 27 rooms scattered through three houses—two traditional, one hotelesque. Although this place is less personal than Pension Florián (above), you're more likely to get a room here. The owners also run their own wine cellar–restaurant (Db-750 Kč, avoid windowless rooms #110–113, tel. 519-515-110, fax 519-515-341, mobile 607-108-450, penziony@breclavske.cz).

EATING

Your host can recommend a music performance or a wine tasting in one of the many small wine cellars in the village. In addition to the Restaurace u Venuše (below), both of the pensions listed above run large, traditional wine cellar–restaurants (daily 17:00–23:00).

Restaurace u Venuše is the most atmospheric of the wine cellar–restaurants. The owner, Antonín Brenko, has been making and

Mikulov Wines

"The Czech Republic is beer country—forget about the wine," one weathered wise man told me. Sure, the local reds cannot compare to French or Italian wines, but the whites are surprisingly good. Czech wine is more than just a drink—it's a way of life. Although the Moravians might not have captured the sweetness of the Portuguese varieties, they did manage to ferment the taste of grapes into their own authentic culture. Without experiencing the wine tradition of southern Moravia, you will have missed a good part of the country's spirit.

Wine has been made in the Mikulov region since Roman times. Because no Roman soldier would fight without his daily two-liter ration of wine, and since it was difficult to transport the unpasteurized wine over large distances, the 10th legion of Marcus Aurelius planted its own vines on this region's limestone hills (which reminded them of their homes in Tuscany). The Slavs and the Germans found the vines long after the Romans were gone, and continued the tradition. In the 16th century, Anabaptist refugees from Switzerland brought new energy to the wine-making process. Today the warm climate and calcium-rich soil make the Mikulov region one of the best wine-producing areas in Eastern Europe.

The most commonly used grapes are Ryzlink, Veltlínské Zelené, Rulandské Bílé, Chardonay, and Sauvignon for whites, and Svatovavřinecké, Frankovka, and Cabernet Sauvignon for reds. The locally bred grapes are Pálava and Aurelius. The variety of grape is only one factor that contributes to each wine's distinct

serving wine here for 38 seasons. A good host, he is keen on finding a wine to suit the tastes of each of his guests. He's a treasure trove of hospitality and wine knowledge, but speaks only Czech and German. Ask about his daughter, a former "Miss Body of Moravia" who now works as a model in New York City. Antonin can also help you arrange a home stay in some of the neighboring villages (closed Sun–Mon, tel. 519-415-742 or 519-515-230, www .sklepymoravy.cz).

Mikulov

An important border town on the amber road from the Baltic Sea to the Adriatic, Mikulov (MEE-kuh-lohv, think "Mikulov, not war") was briefly the capital of Moravia. When the Austrian kings expelled the Jews from Austria in the early 1400s, the Jews settled taste. Vintners discern wines by the type of soil in which they grow, the orientation of the slope, and—most importantly—the sugar content. The best wines are from hand-picked late vintages, with sugar content reaching 27 percent.

The quirky local specialties are straw and ice wines. The grapes for straw wines mature in barns for months spread on dry straw. Ice wines, a Moravian and German specialty, are made by storing grapes for most of the winter, then pressing them at negative 6 degrees Celsius. As these two wines are very difficult to make—much of it is practically alchemy, as even the best vintners cannot predict which grapes will turn into a good ice wine—they are also the most expensive. A tiny .3-liter bottle (about 10 oz.) costs more than 700 Kč.

The communists mismanaged wine production by using bad shoots prone to diseases. Over the last 15 years, vintners have replaced most of these old vines with young, quality ones. Moravian wines improve from year to year. Look for vintages from odd years, which have been better in the past decade than the even ones. Among older vintages, 1994 was outstanding.

One of the most prominent wine companies in the country is **Reisten,** the exclusive supplier of Prague's luxury restaurants and the president. Reisten produces its wines in Pavlov, in the cellars next door to Restaurace u Venuše. The owner will take you down for a tasting (open most of the day; coming from the church and Florán, turn left by U Venuše and then look on your right for a small *Reisten* sign; tel. 519-515-222, mobile 777-151-299).

here on the border, making up half the town's population and forming the largest Czech Jewish community outside of Prague. The railway line to Vienna bypassed Mikulov, condemning it to a stagnation that mercifully protected it from Industrial Age construction. Mikulov  was the seat of the leading Moravian rabbi until World War II.

Today all that remains of Mikulov's past glory are a synagogue, a cemetery, and a few traditional houses along Husova street below the castle. Still, it's an enjoyable and historic town that comes alive during vintage festivals. Mikulov makes a fine lunch stop if you're driving to Lednice or Vienna.

ORIENTATION

Tourist Information: The TI on the main square is a wealth of information about the entire region—giving out free maps and good biking information—and can help arrange accommodations (Mon–Fri 8:00–18:00, Sat–Sun 9:00–18:00, tel. 519-510-855 or 519-512-200, www.mikulov.cz).

Helpful Hints

Bike Rental: A popular way to explore the surrounding wine region is on bicycle (the TI hands out a free map describing trails and can direct you to a rental place).

Car Rental: If you're arriving in the Czech Republic from Vienna or Budapest and will need to return there, consider getting off in nearby Břeclav to pick up a rental car. Bors in Břeclav is handy and rents Renaults (1 day with unlimited mileage: 590 Kč for the smallest Renault Clio, 1,490 Kč for a deluxe car; Mon–Fri 8:00–17:00, Sat 8:00–11:00, closed Sun, tel. 519-323-440, www.bors.cz). To get to Bors from Břeclav's train station, either take a cab (less than 50 Kč) or walk for 10 minutes (exit into park, turn left, walk along main street past the post office, then under railway bridge to gas station and Bors Renault dealership).

SIGHTS

Of the scant sights in town, only the **synagogue museum,** which chronicles the history of local Jews, is worth a visit (July–Aug daily 10:00–17:00, May–June and Sept 13:00–17:00, closed Oct–April, on Husova street). You can skip the large castle complex in the middle of the town; the castles in nearby Lednice and Valtice are far more interesting (see below).

SLEEPING

$$$ Hotel Rohatý Krokodýl ("The Horned Crocodile") is a beguiling Baroque townhouse, formerly the home of one of Mikulov's richest Jewish families. When you step in the atmospheric interior, you're transported back to the 1930s (Db-900–1,300 Kč depending on season, across from synagogue at Husova 8, tel. 519-510-692, fax 519-511-695, www.rohatykrokodyl.cz, rohaty .krokodyl@worldonline.cz).

EATING

Restaurace Alfa, the best restaurant in town, is on the main square in the white Renaissance house with sgraffiti decorations. Their fresh daily specials, available from 11:00, land on your table before the foam settles on your beer (daily 11:00–23:00, Náměstí 27, tel. 519-510-877).

At **Le Patio Café,** in a graceful Renaissance courtyard complete with balconies and a gallery, you can peacefully sip a Turkish coffee and munch sweet Moravian crêpes under the blue sky (daily, enter from left side of same house as Restaurace Alfa and walk through the passageway).

TRANSPORTATION CONNECTIONS

From Mikulov to: Pavlov (4 buses/day Mon–Fri, 1/day Sat–Sun, 30 min), **Valtice** (10 trains/day, 15 min), **Lednice** (2 buses Mon–Fri afternoons only, 20 min), **Moravský Krumlov** (4 trains/day, 1.5 hrs, transfer in Hrušovany).

Lednice and Valtice

The twin towns of Lednice and Valtice—connected by a lush, walkable green belt—each boast a proud castle. Located along the Austrian border southeast of Mikulov, they make up one of the Czech Republic's most visit-worthy castle regions.

Since the 1200s, Lednice and Valtice have been part of the Mikulov-based Lichtenstein family. The Lichtensteins were to South Moravia what the Rožmberks were to South Bohemia: either caring benefactors who turned marshes and beech woods into the promised land, or despotic aristocrats who mercilessly impoverished their serfs...depending on whom you ask. While the Rožmberks died out in the early 1600s, the Lichtensteins thrived during the Thirty Years' War (they wisely stayed loyal to the victo-

rious Hapsburgs) and continued to enrich the region until the 1940s. While Valtice was their winter residence, they summered at Lednice (even though Lednice means "fridge," so named because this stretch of the Dyje River is known for frequent frosts). Of the two castles, Lednice is more interesting to tour.

Even more interesting than the castles, and a more compelling reason to make the short side-trip from Mikulov or Břeclav, is the spectacular 19th-century English park extending for miles between the Lednice and Valtice castles. Native oaks and exotic cedars span their gnarled branches over wild meadows and green lakes, Mogul minarets and Romantic castles rise in the middle of woods like apparitions, and rare birds silently glide through the sky.

ORIENTATION

The "Lednice-Valtice Area" (Lednicko-Valtický Areál) is made up of two small towns, about four miles apart: Lednice (LEHD-neet-seh, pop. 2,400) and Valtice (VAHLT-eet-seh, pop. 3,600).

Tourist Information: Lednice's TI, by the main parking lot in front of the entrance to the Lednice Castle, has free Internet access and sells an inexpensive info brochure and maps of the garden complex (daily May–Sept, April and Oct weekends only, closed off-season; tel. 519-340-986, www.lednice.cz). For information on Valtice, see www.radnice-valtice.cz.

SIGHTS

In Lednice
Lednice Castle (Zámek Lednice)—This castle is the Moravian answer to Windsor, an immense structure built in English neo-Gothic style. Today the castle houses the university for wine-makers, and anyone is welcome to sign up for a short summer course.

To tour the palace, choose between two routes: Route A goes through the halls, and Route B through the apartments (110 Kč for either route, May–Aug Tue–Sun 9:00–12:00 & 13:00–17:15, closed Mon; Sept Tue–Sun 9:00–12:00 & 13:00–16:15, closed Mon; April and Oct Sat–Sun only 9:00–12:00 & 13:00–15:15, closed Mon–Fri, tel. 519-340-128).

Castle Parks—From Lednice Castle, parks extend both north and south. The 19th-century nobles loved everything Romantic, peppering these woods with a quirky architectural hodgepodge: a neo-Roman aqueduct, a neo-Gothic castle ruin, a neo-Greek temple, a victory column, a rendezvous pavilion, and so on. Navigate between these perfect dating spots with the help of the map from the TI (see "Orientation," above). Here are some highlights:

The **Palm Greenhouse** near the castle entrance takes you from Moravia to the tropics (40 Kč, same hours as castle). Notice the construction above you, one of the oldest examples of a cast-iron roof in Europe. Created in England in the 1830s, this innovation was one of the great technical marvels of the 19th century, gradually spreading to create spacious train stations and market halls throughout Europe. From the greenhouse, it's a five-minute walk to the predator bird show; en route you'll see a small archery stand.

If you've ever dreamed of being William Tell, stop by the **archery stand** and try your skill on the medieval and modern crossbows. No need to bring an apple or a son—they provide the target discs and instruction (60 Kč for 5 shots, daily in summer, weekends only in spring and fall).

The 45-minute show of live **predator birds** features more than 20 kinds of birds from all over the world. The falcons, mer-

lins, marsh harriers, buzzards, and goshawks demonstrate their hunting skills on simulated rabbits and quails. Some are breathtakingly fast, others comically slow (you can leave whenever you want—it's 20 Kč for short visit, 60 Kč for whole show, pick up English brochure in ticket tent that describes every bird; July–Aug daily at 11:30, 14:15, and 16:30; May, June, and Sept weekends at 12:00 and 15:00, plus occasional shows during the week; call mobile 608-100-440 for details).

My favorite part of the park stretches north, from the castle to the minaret. The **minaret** is an impressive bit of Romantic garden planning. Those climbing its 302 winding steps (60 Kč) are rewarded with a grand view.

Locals say that Count Alois Josef I intended to build a new church for the village of Lednice, but no plan seemed quite right to the villagers. Their pickiness finally irritated the count so much that he decided to build a mosque with a minaret instead of a church. The mosque never materialized, but the minaret did (completed in 1804). Since the ground around the Dyje River is made up of moving sands, the 200-foot-tall tower had to be anchored almost as deep underground, on beech and oak pilings. The minaret's architect, Josef Hardmuth, was a versatile genius. The most successful of his patents was the idea of mixing graphite and mud, and coating it with wood. The pencil factory he founded (and which bears his name) is still one of the largest in Europe.

Other scholars date the minaret a few centuries back, to the late 1500s. For a short period, the great Mogul emperor Aurangzeb subdued even the mighty Turks and expanded his empire from Sri Lanka to southern Moravia. The minaret, which marks the northernmost point of his exploits, was purportedly built by the Delhi "World Conquerer" to give thanks to Allah.

The four Arabic inscriptions on the sides of the minaret roughly translate: "There is no God except God, and Mohammed is his prophet. The world betrayed its people. Do not forsake your worldly possessions. There is no difference between wealth and renunciation. True happiness can be reached only in the world beyond. Only through industry and hard work can you reach well-being in this world. When fate stands against you, all plans lose meaning; indeed, without the help of fate, man does not reach redemption."

To reach the minaret from Lednice Castle, you can walk (1 mile), hire a horse carriage (30 min), or take a boat. Boats and carriages depart from the little dam just behind the castle; prices depend on the number of participants. Although most horse-carriage rides throughout Europe are tourist traps, here it feels appropriate to ride through the alleys like the nobles once did—even the school groups do it. The best plan is to ride to the minaret and walk back.

TRANSPORTATION CONNECTIONS

Consider taking the bus to Lednice, walking through the gardens to Valtice (a level, 4-mile stroll), and then taking the train from there.

From Lednice by Bus to: Mikulov (2/afternoon Mon–Fri only, 20 min).

From Valtice by Train to: Mikulov (10/day, 15 min), **Prague** (hrly, 4 hrs, one transfer), **Olomouc** (3/day, 2.5–4 hrs, several transfers).

MORAVSKÝ KRUMLOV

Don't mistake the shabby industrial town of Moravský Krumlov (MOH-rahv-skee KROOM-loff) for its enchanting Bohemian counterpart, Český Krumlov. A "bend in the river" (the literal meaning of "Krumlov") is the only thing these two towns have in common.

Moravský Krumlov has only one restaurant, and every store is closed by 17:00. In the evening, steam from the nearby nuclear power plant envelops the setting sun. The clumsy ugliness of the circa-1950s main square (rebuilt after the town was bombed out by Russians in 1945) feels weirdly exotic after the picture-perfect villages you've seen elsewhere in the country.

But despite its flaws, there's one big reason to visit Moravský Krumlov: Discovering the masterpiece of the Czech Republic's greatest painter, Alfons Mucha, tucked away in the town's decaying castle. Laying eyes on this grand work gives you the feeling of a true adventurer.

SIGHTS

Mucha's *Slavic Epic*

People come to Moravský Krumlov solely to see Alfons Mucha's epic 20-canvas masterpiece, a ▲▲▲ sight.

Cost, Hours, Location: Open April–Oct Tue–Sun 9:00–12:00 & 13:00–16:00, July–Aug until 17:00, closed Mon, closed Nov–March. The ticket office sells a few brochures and pictures. Notice how out of place Mucha's characteristic posters feel here. Allow two hours—it's hard to appreciate the work in less time.

Background: Alfons Mucha (1860–1939), born in the nearby town of Ivančice, made a hugely successful commercial career for himself in Paris and the U.S. as *the* Art Nouveau poster artist and illustrator. In Paris, Mucha conceived the idea of dedicating the second half of his life to a work that would edify his nation. Throughout history, bards in every culture have composed poems eulogizing the best moments of their tradition. Mucha would do the same for the Czechs and the Slavs, on a grand, epic scale...and on canvas.

Mucha convinced the Chicago industrialist Charles Crane to sponsor his project. Both men believed that the purpose of a truly patriotic work was to inspire human beings to understand one another better, and thereby bring humanity closer together. Mucha returned home, and by 1912, finished the first three paintings (each 25 by 20 feet). It took another 16 years before Mucha could dedicate the cycle of 20 enormous canvases to the Czech nation and the city of Prague. The response of his fellow artists was lukewarm—in the experimental age of Picasso, Mucha's slinky style and overt nationalism were out of fashion.

During the war, the patriotic work was hidden from the Nazis and became damaged in the process. After years of restoration, the paintings were unveiled in 1963 in the Moravský Krumlov castle, near Mucha's birthplace.

Appreciating the *Slavic Epic:* Mucha's huge paintings depict momentous events in Slavic history, but his work is more than a chronicle, rising above the typical shallow, overly nationalistic products of the politicized 19th century. Mucha was a brilliant craftsman and designer; his composition and sense for colors will capture your attention. Like any true artistic masterpiece, Mucha's work goes beyond the style of the time, beyond Art Nouveau, beyond Slavic.

Consider contemplating Mucha's canvases on three levels. First, with the help of the handout you'll get at the ticket office, decipher the history. The great feast is the celebration of the Slavic pagan god, the zealous preacher is Jan Hus (the revolutionary Czech priest), and the subdued old man contemplating the dark horizon is the first Czech exile, Comenius. Red is the color of war; white is the color of peace; blue is the past; and orange is the future.

When you get tired of being told what's what, step back and figure out Mucha's intention. His technique will help you. The grand-scale background—showing historic events—is executed in egg-based tempera. Against that low-resolution, foggy base stand out clear details: the terrified couple, the mother with the child, the bearded sage with the young man, the face of the lady-in-waiting. These are painted in oil. The lucid oil detail tells the experience of a single, often anonymous individual; it suggests that Mucha's epic is not about monumental depiction of a particular event, but about the fate of the individual against the backdrop of history. It is as if the entire weight of events were condensed into the expressions on the faces. In the scene showing a print shop, the young man in the foreground is Mucha's own self-portrait.

Finally, step even farther back and contemplate the painting as a work of an Impressionist or an abstract artist. The fusion of colors stands far beyond any particular meaning. Like the tones of a 19th-century symphony, Mucha's visual concert has the power to stir the deepest emotions.

EATING

The only restaurant in town, in **Hotel Epopej,** is a five-minute walk above the castle on the main square (www.epopej.hotel-cz.com). Despite its location on the ugly square, the food is surprisingly good. Of course, being in Moravský Krumlov, the dining comes with a couple of quirks. The dining room is split into two sections: One half is decorated with paper lanterns and red napkins covered by odd Chinese pictures; the other half has walls inlaid with wood and tables lavishly covered with white tablecloths and champagne glasses. The menu is an impressive list of Czech and Chinese classics. To top each section, the Vietnamese chef has added some local specialties (e.g., Krumlov roast beef) and his own "Chinese" creations. For your safety, stick to the classics, as the waiter will bring you enough surprises regardless. No matter what language you use, you might get chopsticks if you ask for bread, or fried potatoes instead of white rice. If you happen to order from both the Czech and Chinese sections of the menu, the waiter will bring you two separate bills. And if you add a beer from the tap at the bar and one of the Dutch ice-cream dishes, you'll end up with four slips of paper to take home as souvenirs of your unforgettable Mucha adventure.

TRANSPORTATION CONNECTIONS

With easy connections in and out, no hotels worth recommending, and no excuse to spend more time in Moravský Krumlov than it takes to see Mucha's masterpiece, I'd sleep elsewhere.

From Moravský Krumlov to: Mikulov (2 trains per afternoon, transfer in Hrušovany, 1.5 hrs total to Mikulov), **Brno** (10 trains/day, 45 min; bus connections mainly on weekdays). Since Brno is right on the Prague–Vienna–Budapest train lines, Moravský Krumlov is a handy stop in the middle of a long travel day. (Consider taking the **bus from Prague to Brno,** which is faster than any train: 2/hr from Prague's Florenc bus station, 2.5-hr trip.)

By Car: If driving to Moravský Krumlov, figure about 30 minutes from Třebíč or Mikulov and one hour from Telč or Slavonice.

CZECH HISTORY

The Czechs have always been at a crossroads of Europe—between the Slavic and Germanic worlds, between Catholicism and Protestantism, and between the Cold War East and West. As if having foreseen all of this, the mythical founder of Prague—the beautiful princess Libuše—named her city "Praha" (meaning "Threshold" in Czech). Despite these strong external influences, the Czechs have retained their distinct culture...and a dark, ironic sense of humor to keep them laughing through it all.

Charles IV and The Middle Ages

Prague's castle put Bohemia on the map in the ninth century. About a century later, the region was incorporated into the German Holy Roman Empire. Within a couple hundred years, Prague was one of Europe's largest and most highly cultured cities—even more important than Vienna.

The 14th century was Prague's Golden Age, when Holy Roman Emperor Charles IV ruled from here. Born to a German nobleman and a Czech princess, Charles IV was a dynamic man on the cusp of the Renaissance. He spoke five languages, counted Petrarch as a friend, imported French architects to make Prague a grand capital, founded the first university north of the Alps, and invigorated the Czech national spirit. (He popularized the legend of the good king Wenceslas to give his people a near mythical, King Arthur–type cultural standard-bearer.) Much of Prague's history and architecture (including the famous Charles Bridge and St. Vitus Cathedral) can be traced to this man's

Notable Czechs

St. Wenceslas (907–935): Bohemian duke who allied the Czechs with the Holy Roman Empire. He went on to become the Czech Republic's patron saint, and was memorialized as a "good king" in the Christmas carol. For more on Wenceslas, see page 84.

Jan Hus (c. 1370–1415): Proto-Protestant Reformer who was burned at the stake (see page 63).

Antonín Dvořák (1841–1904): Inspired by a trip to America, he composed his *New World Symphony*. For more on Czech composers, see page 149.

Jára Cimrman (c. 1853–1914): Illustrious inventor, explorer, philosopher, and all-around genius. Despite being overwhelmingly voted the "Greatest Czech of All Time" in a recent nationwide poll, he was not awarded the title; for details on the controversy, see page 98.

Alfons Mucha (1860–1939): You probably haven't heard of him, but you might recognize his turn-of-the-century Art Nouveau posters of pretty girls entwined in vines. Visit his museum in Prague (see page 87), marvel at his marvelous stained-glass window in St. Vitus Cathedral (page 110), and make a pilgrimage to see his magnum opus in the town of Moravský Krumlov (see page 237).

Franz Kafka (1883–1924): While working for a Prague insurance firm, he wrote (in German) *Metamorphosis* (man awakes as a cockroach), *The Trial,* and other psychologically haunting stories and novels.

Milan Kundera (1929—): Wrote the novel *The Unbearable Lightness of Being* (which became a film). For more on Czech authors and filmmakers, see page 12.

Václav Havel (1936—): The country's first post-Soviet president, who's also known as a playwright and philosopher.

Martina Navrátilová (1956—): Tennis star of the 1980s. For more on Czech sports, see page 151.

rule. Under Charles IV, the Czech people gained esteem among Europeans.

Jan Hus and Religious Wars

Jan Hus (c. 1370–1415) was a local preacher and professor who got in trouble with the Vatican a hundred years before Martin Luther. Like Luther, Hus preached in the people's language rather than Latin. To add insult to injury, he complained about Church corruption. Tried for heresy and burned in 1415, Hus became both a religious and a national hero. While each age has defined Hus

It's Not You, It's Me: The Velvet Divorce

In the autumn of 1989, hundreds of thousands of Czechs and Slovaks streamed into Prague to demonstrate on Wenceslas Square. Their "Velvet Revolution" succeeded, and Czechoslovakia's communist regime peacefully excused itself.

The Czechs and Slovaks were forced to redefine their roles in the post-communist world. Ever since they joined with the Czechs in 1918, the Slovaks felt like second-class citizens within their own nation. Prague was unmistakably the political, economic, and cultural capital of Czechoslovakia. And the Czechs, for their part, resented the financial burden of their poorer neighbors to the east. With their new freedoms, the Czechs found themselves with a 10 percent unemployment rate...compared to 20 or 30 percent unemployment in the Slovak lands. In this new world of flux, long-standing tensions came to a head.

The dissolution of Czechoslovakia began over a hyphen, as the Slovaks wanted to rename the country Czecho-Slovakia. Ideally, this symbolic move would come with a redistribution of powers: two capitals and two UN reps, but one national bank and a single currency. The Slovaks were also less enthusiastic about abandoning the communist society altogether, since the Soviet regime had fundamentally changed their agriculture-based economy to a heavily industrialized one that depended on a socialist element for survival.

to its liking, the way he challenged authority while staying true to himself has always inspired and rallied the Czech people. (For more on Hus, see the sidebar on page 63).

Inspired by the reformist ideas of Jan Hus, the Czechs rebelled against both the Roman Catholic Church and German political control. This burst of independent thought led to a period of religious wars, and ultimately the loss of autonomy to Vienna. Ruled by the Hapsburgs of Austria, Prague stagnated—except during the rule of King Rudolf II (1552–1612), a Holy Roman Emperor. With Rudolph living in Prague, the city again emerged as a cultural and intellectual center. Astronomers Johannes Kepler, Tycho de Brahe, and other scientists flourished, and much of the inspiration for Prague's great art can be attributed to the king's patronage.

Not long after, Prague entered one of its darkest spells. The Thirty Years' War (1618–1648) began in Prague Castle when Czech nobles wanting religious and political autonomy tossed two Catholic/Hapsburg officials out the window of the Prague Castle. The Czech Estates Uprising lasted for two years, ending in a crushing defeat of the Czech army in the Battle of White Mountain (1620), which marked the end of Czech freedom. Twenty-seven

The Czechs rebuffed the Slovaks' requests—the Slovaks were just being silly, and should just keep quiet and enjoy riding the ample coattails the Czechs were providing. The first post-communist president of Czechoslovakia, the Czech Václav Havel, made matters worse when he took a rare trip to the Slovak half of his country in 1990. In a fit of terrible judgment, Havel promised he'd close the ugly, polluting Soviet factories in Slovakia... neglecting the fact that many Slovaks still depended on these factories for survival. Havel left in disgrace and visited the Slovak lands only twice more in the next two and a half years.

In June 1992, the Slovak nationalist candidate Vladimír Mečiar fared surprisingly well in the elections—proving that the Slovaks were serious about secession. At the ballot box, the Slovaks decisively sent the message: "We want to separate!" The Czechs said, incredulously, "Really?" Then, "Okay!"

Though public opinion in both halves of the country opposed separation (the people never actually voted on the split), the politicians soon agreed on the terms. The Velvet Divorce became official on January 1, 1993, and each country ended up with its own capital, currency, and head of state. The Slovaks let loose a yelp of excitement and the Czechs emitted a sigh of relief.

leaders of the uprising were executed (today commemorated by crosses on Prague's Old Town Square—see page 61), most of the old Czech nobility was dispossessed, and Protestants had to leave the country or convert to Catholicism. Often called "the first world war" because it engulfed so many nations, the Thirty Years' War was particularly tough on Prague. During this period, its population dropped from 60,000 to 25,000. The result of this war was 300 years of Hapsburg rule from afar, as Prague became a backwater of Vienna.

Czech Nationalist Revival

The end of Prague as a "German" city came gradually. As the Industrial Revolution attracted Czech farmers into the cities, the demographics of the Czech population centers began to shift. Between 1800 and 1900, though it remained part of the Hapsburg Empire, Prague went from being an essentially German town to a predominantly Czech one. Like in the rest of Europe, the 19th century was a time of nationalism, as the age of divine kings and ruling families came to a fitful end. The Czech spirit was stirred by the completion of Prague's St. Vitus Cathedral, the symphonies of

Antonín Dvořák, and the operas of Bedřich Smetana performed in the new National Theatre.

After the Hapsburgs' Austro-Hungarian Empire suffered defeat in World War I, their vast holdings broke apart and became independent countries. Among these was a union of Bohemia, Moravia, and Slovakia, the brainchild of a clever politician named Tomáš Garrigue Masaryk (see page 110). The new nation, Czechoslovakia, was proclaimed in 1918, with Prague as its capital.

Troubled 20th Century

Independence lasted only 20 years. In the notorious Munich Agreement of September 1938—much to the dismay of the Czechs and Slovaks—Great Britain and France peacefully ceded to Hitler the so-called "Sudetenland" (a fringe around the edge of Bohemia, populated mainly by people of German descent). It wasn't long before Hitler seized the rest of Czechoslovakia...and the Holocaust began.

For centuries, Prague's cultural make-up consisted of a rich mix of Czech, German, and Jewish people—historically about evenly divided. But only 5 percent of the Jewish population survived the Holocaust. After World War II ended, the three million people of Germanic descent who lived in Czechoslovakia were pushed into Germany. This forced resettlement—which led to the deaths of untold tens of thousands of Germans—was the idea of Czechoslovak President Edvard Beneš, who had been ruling from exile in London throughout the war (see page 180). As a result of both of these policies (the Holocaust and the expulsion of Germans), today's Czech Republic is largely homogenous—about 95 percent Czechs.

Although Prague escaped the bombs of World War II, it went directly from the Nazi frying pan into the communist fire. A local uprising freed the city from the Nazis on May 8, 1945, but the Russians "liberated" them on May 9.

The communist chapter (1948–1989) was grim. The "Prague Spring" uprising—initiated by a young generation of reform-minded communists in 1968—was crushed. The charismatic leader, Alexander Dubček, was exiled (and made a forest ranger in the backwoods), and the years following the unsuccessful revolt were particularly disheartening. In the late 1980s, the communists began constructing Prague's huge TV tower (now the city's tallest structure)—not only to broadcast Czech TV transmissions, but also to jam Western signals. The Metro, built around the same time, was intended for mass transit, but first and foremost it was designed to be a giant fallout shelter for protection against capitalist bombs.

The Wisdom of Babička Míla ("Granny Míla")

Co-author Honza Vihan's grandmother, Bohumila Vihanová, was born in 1907 in the Austro-Hungarian town of Prag (today's Praha), then ruled from Vienna. In the 99 years since, she's lived under seven different governments: Hapsburgs, interwar Czechoslovakia, Nazis, communists, post-communist Czechoslovakia, the Czech Republic, and the European Union. Wise beyond even her many years, she counsels family and visitors alike as follows:

- "I liked each change, because it always brought something new."
- "You must be able to take the best from whatever comes."
- "When the communists took over, that was bad—really bad. But then, my mother used to say, 'There's no point in crying over spilled milk. There's enough water in it already.' So, I tried to get by, and somehow we managed to live through it all."
- "The main thing is to keep your inner balance."
- "You should never take yourself too seriously."
- "Let everyone do whatever they want, as long as they believe something and behave accordingly."
- "Money will always be here. We won't."
- "Parents should never mix in their children's lives."
- "Good health and happy mind!"

But the Soviet empire crumbled. Czechoslovakia regained its freedom in the student- and artist-powered 1989 "Velvet Revolution" (so called because there were no casualties). Václav Havel, a writer who had been imprisoned by the communist regime, became Czechoslovakia's first post-communist president. In 1993, the Czech and Slovak Republics agreed on the "Velvet Divorce" and became two separate countries (see sidebar).

Havel ended his second (and, constitutionally, last) five-year term in 2003. While he's still admired by Czechs as a great thinker, writer, and fearless leader of the opposition movement during the communist days, many consider him less successful as a president. Some believe that the split of Czechoslovakia was partly caused by Havel's initial insensitivity to Slovak demands. The current president, Václav Klaus, was the pragmatic author of the economic reforms in the 1990s. Klaus' election in 2003 symbolized a change from revolutionary times, when philosophers became kings, to humdrum politics, when offices are gained by bargaining with the devil (Communist votes in the Parliament were the decisive factor in Klaus' election). Another major turning point occurred on May 1, 2004, when the Czech Republic joined the European Union (see page 107).

Today, while not without its problems, the Czech Republic is enjoying a growing economy and a strong democracy, and Prague has emerged as one of the most popular tourist destinations in Europe.

APPENDIX

Let's Talk Telephones
To make international calls, you need to break the codes: the international access codes and country codes (see below). For specifics on making local, long-distance, and international calls, please see the "European Calling Chart" in this appendix. You'll find more information on telephones in the introduction on page 25.

Country Codes
After you've dialed the international access code (011 if you're calling from the U.S. or Canada; 00 if you're calling from Europe), dial the code of the country you're calling.

Austria—43	Italy—39
Belgium—32	Morocco—212
Britain—44	Netherlands—31
Canada—1	Norway—47
Croatia—385	Poland—48
Czech Rep.—420	Portugal—351
Denmark—45	Slovakia—421
Estonia—372	Slovenia—386
Finland—358	Spain—34
France—33	Sweden—46
Germany—49	Switzerland—41
Gibraltar—350	Turkey—90
Greece—30	U.S.A.—1
Ireland—353	

European Calling Chart

Just smile and dial, using this key:
AC = Area Code, LN = Local Number.

European Country	Calling long distance within ...	Calling from the U.S.A./ Canada to ...	Calling from a European country to ...
Austria	AC + LN	011 + 43 + AC (without the initial zero) + LN	00 + 43 + AC (without the initial zero) + LN
Belgium	LN	011 + 32 + LN (without initial zero)	00 + 32 + LN (without initial zero)
Britain	AC + LN	011 + 44 + AC (without initial zero) + LN	00 + 44 + AC (without initial zero) + LN
Croatia	AC + LN	011 + 385 + AC (without initial zero) + LN	00 + 385 + AC (without initial zero) + LN
Czech Republic	LN	011 + 420 + LN	00 + 420 + LN
Denmark	LN	011 + 45 + LN	00 + 45 + LN
Finland	AC + LN	011 + 358 + AC (without initial zero) + LN	00 + 358 + AC (without initial zero) + LN
France	LN	011 + 33 + LN (without initial zero)	00 + 33 + LN (without initial zero)
Germany	AC + LN	011 + 49 + AC (without initial zero) + LN	00 + 49 + AC (without initial zero) + LN
Greece	LN	011 + 30 + LN	00 + 30 + LN
Hungary	06 + AC + LN	011 + 36 + AC + LN	00 + 36 + AC + LN
Ireland	AC + LN	011 + 353 + AC (without initial zero) + LN	00 + 353 + AC (without initial zero) + LN
Italy	LN	011 + 39 + LN	00 + 39 + LN

European Country	Calling long distance within...	Calling from the U.S.A./ Canada to...	Calling from a European country to...
Netherlands	AC + LN	011 + 31 + AC (without initial zero) + LN	00 + 31 + AC (without initial zero) + LN
Norway	LN	011 + 47 + LN	00 + 47 + LN
Poland	AC + LN	011 + 48 + AC (without initial zero) + LN	00 + 48 + AC (without initial zero) + LN
Portugal	LN	011 + 351 + LN	00 + 351 + LN
Slovakia	AC + LN	011 + 421 + AC (without initial zero) + LN	00 + 421 + AC (without initial zero) + LN
Slovenia	AC + LN	011 + 386 + AC (without initial zero) + LN	00 + 386 + AC (without initial zero) + LN
Spain	LN	011 + 34 + LN	00 + 34 + LN
Sweden	AC + LN	011 + 46 + AC (without initial zero) + LN	00 + 46 + AC (without initial zero) + LN
Switzerland	LN	011 + 41 + LN (without initial zero)	00 + 41 + LN (without initial zero)
Turkey	AC (if no initial zero is included, add one) + LN	011 + 90 + AC (without initial zero) + LN	00 + 90 + AC (without initial zero) + LN

- The instructions above apply whether you're calling a fixed phone or mobile phone.
- The international access codes (the first numbers you dial when making an international call) are 011 if you're calling from the U.S.A./Canada, or 00 if you're calling from anywhere in Europe.
- To call the U.S.A. or Canada from Europe, dial 00, then 1 (the country code for the U.S.A. and Canada), then the area code and number. In short, 00 + 1 + AC + LN = Hi, Mom!

2006

JANUARY						
S	M	T	W	T	F	S
1	2	3	4	5	6	7
8	9	10	11	12	13	14
15	16	17	18	19	20	21
22	23	24	25	26	27	28
29	30	31				

FEBRUARY						
S	M	T	W	T	F	S
			1	2	3	4
5	6	7	8	9	10	11
12	13	14	15	16	17	18
19	20	21	22	23	24	25
26	27	28				

MARCH						
S	M	T	W	T	F	S
			1	2	3	4
5	6	7	8	9	10	11
12	13	14	15	16	17	18
19	20	21	22	23	24	25
26	27	28	29	30	31	

APRIL						
S	M	T	W	T	F	S
						1
2	3	4	5	6	7	8
9	10	11	12	13	14	15
16	17	18	19	20	21	22
23/30	24	25	26	27	28	29

MAY						
S	M	T	W	T	F	S
	1	2	3	4	5	6
7	8	9	10	11	12	13
14	15	16	17	18	19	20
21	22	23	24	25	26	27
28	29	30	31			

JUNE						
S	M	T	W	T	F	S
				1	2	3
4	5	6	7	8	9	10
11	12	13	14	15	16	17
18	19	20	21	22	23	24
25	26	27	28	29	30	

JULY						
S	M	T	W	T	F	S
						1
2	3	4	5	6	7	8
9	10	11	12	13	14	15
16	17	18	19	20	21	22
23/30	24/31	25	26	27	28	29

AUGUST						
S	M	T	W	T	F	S
		1	2	3	4	5
6	7	8	9	10	11	12
13	14	15	16	17	18	19
20	21	22	23	24	25	26
27	28	29	30	31		

SEPTEMBER						
S	M	T	W	T	F	S
					1	2
3	4	5	6	7	8	9
10	11	12	13	14	15	16
17	18	19	20	21	22	23
24	25	26	27	28	29	30

OCTOBER						
S	M	T	W	T	F	S
1	2	3	4	5	6	7
8	9	10	11	12	13	14
15	16	17	18	19	20	21
22	23	24	25	26	27	28
29	30	31				

NOVEMBER						
S	M	T	W	T	F	S
			1	2	3	4
5	6	7	8	9	10	11
12	13	14	15	16	17	18
19	20	21	22	23	24	25
26	27	28	29	30		

DECEMBER						
S	M	T	W	T	F	S
					1	2
3	4	5	6	7	8	9
10	11	12	13	14	15	16
17	18	19	20	21	22	23
24/31	25	26	27	28	29	30

U.S. Embassy

In Prague: Tržiště 15, tel. 257-530-663, www.usembassy.cz

Czech Holidays and Festivals in 2006

Note that this isn't a complete list; holidays strike without warning. For more information, contact the Czech tourist information office in the U.S. (see page 7), or visit www.whatsonwhen.com.

Jan 1	New Year's Day
Jan 19	Anniversary of Jan Palach's Death (flowers in Wenceslas Square)
April 16	Easter Sunday
April 17	Easter Monday
April 20-23	Prague Accordion and Harmonica Festival, Prague (www.accordion.cz)

Late April-early May	One World International Human Rights Film Festival, Prague (www.oneworld.cz)
April 30	Witches' Night (similar to Halloween, with bonfires)
May 1	Labor Day
May 8	Liberation Day
Mid-May-early June	"Prague Spring" Music Festival, Prague (www.festival.cz)
Mid-June	Celebration of the Rose, Český Krumlov (medieval festival, music, theater, dance, knights' tournament)
June	Dance Prague (modern dance festival, www.tanecpha.cz)
July 5	Sts. Cyril and Methodius Day
July 6	Jan Hus Day
First 2 weeks of July	French-Czech Music Academy Festival, Telč
Mid-July-late Aug	International Music Festival, Český Krumlov (www.czechmusicfestival.com)
July–Aug	Summer of Culture, Olomouc (www.okl.info)
1 week in early Aug	Šamajim festival, Třebíč (Jewish music and film)
First 2 weeks of Aug	"Telč Vacations" Festival (folk music, open-air theater, exhibitions), Telč
Mid-Aug	Jazz at Summer's End Festival, Český Krumlov
Mid-Sept-mid-Oct	Prague Autumn Music Festival (www.pragueautumn.cz)
Sept 28	St. Wenceslas Day (celebrates national patron saint and Czech statehood)
Oct 28	Independence Day
Late Oct–Early Nov	International Jazz Festival, Prague
Nov 17	Velvet Revolution Anniversary
Throughout Dec	Christmas markets, Prague
Dec 5	Saint Nicholas Eve, Prague
Dec 25	Christmas Day
Dec 31	St. Sylvester's Day, Prague (fireworks)

Temperature Conversion: Fahrenheit and Celsius

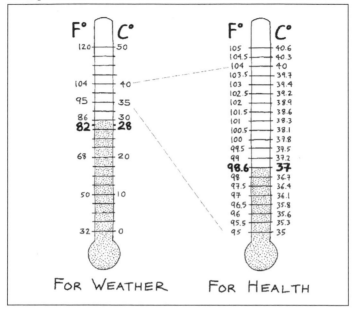

Europe takes its temperature using the Celsius scale, while we opt for Fahrenheit. For weather, remember that 28°C is 82°F—perfect. For health, 37°C is just right.

Prague's Climate

Here is a list of average temperatures (first line—average daily low; second line—average daily high; third line—days of rain). This can be helpful in planning your itinerary, but I have never found European weather to be particularly predictable, and this chart ignores humidity.

J	F	M	A	M	J	J	A	S	O	N	D
23°	24°	30°	38°	46°	52°	55°	55°	49°	41°	33°	27°
31°	34°	44°	54°	64°	70°	73°	72°	65°	53°	42°	34°
13	11	10	11	13	12	13	12	10	13	12	13

Metric Conversion (Approximate)

1 inch = 25 millimeters
1 foot = 0.3 meter
1 yard = 0.9 meter
1 mile = 1.6 kilometers
1 centimeter = 0.4 inch
1 meter = 39.4 inches
1 kilometer = 0.62 mile

32 degrees F = 0 degrees C
82 degrees F = about 28 degrees C
1 ounce = 28 grams
1 kilogram = 2.2 pounds
1 quart = 0.95 liter
1 square yard = 0.8 square meter
1 acre = 0.4 hectare

Numbers and Stumblers

- Europeans write a few of their numbers differently than we do: 1 = $\measuredangle$, 4 = φ, 7= $\mathcal{7}$. Learn the difference or miss your train.
- Europeans write dates as day/month/year (Christmas is 25/12/06).
- Commas are decimal points, and decimals are commas. A dollar and a half is 1,50. There are 5.280 feet in a mile.
- When counting with fingers, start with your thumb. If you hold up your first finger to request one item, you'll probably get two.
- What we Americans call the second floor of a building is the first floor in Europe.
- Europeans keep the left "lane" open for passing on escalators and moving sidewalks. Keep to the right.

Making Your Hotel Reservation

Most hotel managers know basic "hotel English." Faxing or e-mailing are the preferred methods for reserving a room. They're more accurate than telephoning and much faster than writing a letter. Use this handy form for your fax or find it online at www.ricksteves.com/reservation. Photocopy and fax away.

One-Page Fax

To: _____ @ _____
            hotel   *fax*

From: _____@ _____
              name   *fax*

Today's date: _____ /_____ /_____
                    day   *month*   *year*

Dear Hotel _____ ,
Please make this reservation for me:

Name: _____

Total # of people:_____ # of rooms: _____ # of nights: _____

Arriving: _____ /_____ /_____   My time of arrival (24-hr clock): _____
              day *month* *year*   (I will telephone if I will be late)

Departing: _____ /_____/_____
                day *month* *year*

Room(s): Single _____ Double ____ Twin _____ Triple ____ Quad_____

With: Toilet _____ Shower_____ Bath _____ Sink only _____

Special needs: View_____ Quiet ____ Cheapest ____ Ground Floor ____

Please fax, mail, or e-mail confirmation of my reservation, along with the type of room reserved and the price. Please also inform me of your cancellation policy. After I hear from you, I will quickly send my credit-card information as a deposit to hold the room. Thank you.

_____
Signature

_____
Name

_____
Address

_____
City   *State*   *Zip Code*   *Country*

_____
E-mail Address

INDEX

Start your trip at
www.ricksteves.com

Rick Steves' website is packed with over 3,000 pages of timely travel information. It's also your gateway to getting FREE monthly travel news from Rick—and more!

Free Monthly European Travel News

Fresh articles on Europe's most interesting destinations and happenings. Rick will even send you an e-mail every month (often direct from Europe) with his latest discoveries!

Timely Travel Tips

Rick Steves' best money-and-stress-saving tips on trip planning, packing, transportation, hotels, health, safety, finances, hurdling the language barrier...and more.

Travelers' Graffiti Wall

Candid advice and opinions from thousands of travelers on everything listed above, plus whatever topics are hot at the moment (discount flights, packing tips, scams...you name it).

Rick's Annual Guide to European Railpasses

The clearest, most comprehensive guide to the confusing array of railpass options out there, and how to choo-choose the railpass that best fits your itinerary and budget. Then you can order your railpass (and get a bunch of great freebies) online from us!

Great Gear at the Rick Steves Travel Store

Enjoy bargains on Rick's guidebooks, planning maps and TV series DVDs—and on his custom-designed carry-on bags, wheeled bags, day bags and light-packing accessories.

Rick Steves Tours

Every year more than 6,000 lucky travelers explore Europe on a Rick Steves tour. Learn more about our 30 different one-to-three-week itineraries, read uncensored feedback from our tour alums, and sign up for your dream trip online!

Rick on Radio and TV

Read the scripts and run clips from public television's "Rick Steves' Europe" and public radio's "Travel with Rick Steves."

Respect for Your Privacy

Ordering online from us is secure. When you buy something from us, join a tour, or subscribe to Rick's free monthly travel news e-mails, we promise to never share your name, information, or e-mail address with anyone else. You won't be spammed!

Have fun raising your Travel I.Q. at
www.ricksteves.com

Travel smart...carry on!

The latest generation of Rick Steves' carry-on travel bags is easily the best—benefiting from two decades of on-the-road attention to what really matters: maximum quality and strength; practical, flexible features; and no unnecessary frills. You won't find a better value anywhere!

Convertible, expandable, and carry-on-size:
Rick Steves' Back Door Bag $99

This is the same bag that Rick Steves lives out of for three months every summer. It's made of rugged water-resistant 1000 denier Cordura nylon, and best of all, it converts easily from a smart-looking suitcase to a handy backpack with comfortably-curved shoulder straps and a padded waistbelt.

This roomy, versatile 9" x 21" x 14" bag has a large 2600 cubic-inch main compartment, plus three outside pockets (small, medium and huge) that are perfect for often-used items. And the cinch-tight compression straps will keep your load compact and close to your back—not sagging like a sack of potatoes.

Wishing you had even more room to bring home souvenirs? Pull open the full-perimeter expando-zipper and its capacity jumps from 2600 to 3000 cubic inches. When you want to use it as a suitcase or check it as luggage (required when "expanded"), the straps and belt hide away in a zippered compartment in the back.

Attention travelers under 5'4" tall: This bag also comes in an inch-shorter version, for a compact-friendlier fit between the waistbelt and shoulder straps.

Convenient, expandable, and carry-on-size:
Rick Steves' Wheeled Bag $129

At 9" x 21" x 14" our sturdy Rick Steves' Wheeled Bag is rucksack-soft in front, but the rest is lined with a hard ABS-lexan shell to give maximum protection to your belongings. We've spared no expense on moving parts, splurging on an extra-long button-release handle and big, tough inline skate wheels for easy rolling on rough surfaces.

Wishing you had even more room to bring home souvenirs? Pull open the full-perimeter expando-zipper and its capacity jumps from 2600 to 3000 cubic inches.

Rick Steves' Wheeled Bag has exactly the same three-outside-pocket configuration as our Back Door Bag, plus a handy "add-a-bag" strap and full lining.

Our Back Door Bags and Wheeled Bags come in black, navy, blue spruce, evergreen and merlot.

For great deals on a wide selection of travel goodies, begin your next trip at the Rick Steves Travel Store!

Visit the Rick Steves Travel Store at
www.ricksteves.com

FREE-SPIRITED TOURS FROM
Rick Steves

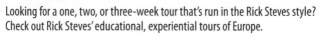

Small Groups
Great Guides
No Grumps

Best of Europe ▪ **Eastern Europe**
Italy ▪ **Village Italy** ▪ **South Italy**
France ▪ **Britain** ▪ **Ireland**
Heart of France ▪ **South of France**
Turkey ▪ **Spain/Portugal**
Germany/Austria/Switzerland
Scandinavia ▪ **London** ▪ **Paris** ▪ **Rome**
Venice ▪ **Florence…and much more!**

Looking for a one, two, or three-week tour that's run in the Rick Steves style?
Check out Rick Steves' educational, experiential tours of Europe.

Rick's tours are an excellent value compared to "mainstream" tours. Here's a taste
of what you'll get…

- **Small groups:** With just 24-28 travelers, you'll go where typical groups of
40-50 can only dream.

- **Big buses:** You'll travel in a full-size 40-50 seat bus, with plenty of empty
seats for you to spread out and be comfortable.

- **Great guides:** Our guides are hand-picked by Rick Steves for their wealth of
knowledge and giddy enthusiasm for Europe.

- **No tips or kickbacks:** To keep your guide and driver 100% focused on giving
you the best travel experience, we pay them well—and prohibit them from
accepting tips and merchant kickbacks

- **All sightseeing:** Your tour price includes all group sightseeing, with no hidden extra charges.

- **Central hotels:** You'll stay in Rick's favorite small, characteristic, locally-run
hotels in the center of each city, within walking distance of the sights you
came to see.

- **Visit www.ricksteves.com:** You'll find all our latest itineraries, dates and
prices, be able to reserve online, and request a free copy of our "Rick Steves
Tour Experience" DVD!

Rick Steves

More *Savvy*. More *Surprising*. More *Fun*.

COUNTRY GUIDES 2006

England
France
Germany & Austria
Great Britain
Ireland
Italy
Portugal
Scandinavia
Spain
Switzerland

CITY GUIDES 2006

Amsterdam, Bruges & Brussels
Florence & Tuscany
London
Paris
Prague & The Czech Republic
Provence & The French Riviera
Rome
Venice

BEST OF GUIDES

Best of Eastern Europe
Best of Europe

As the #1 authority on European travel, Rick gives you inside information on what to visit, where to stay, and how to get there—economically and hassle-free.

www.ricksteves.com

PHRASE BOOKS & DICTIONARIES

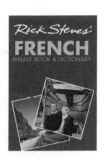

French
French, Italian & German
German
Italian
Portuguese
Spanish

MORE EUROPE FROM RICK STEVES

Easy Access Europe
Europe 101
Europe Through the Back Door
Postcards from Europe

RICK STEVES' EUROPE DVDs

All 43 Shows 2000-2005
Britain
Eastern Europe
France & Benelux
Germany, The Swiss Alps & Travel Skills
Ireland
Italy
Spain & Portugal

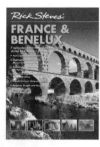

PLANNING MAPS

Britain & Ireland
Europe
France
Germany, Austria & Switzerland
Italy
Spain & Portugal

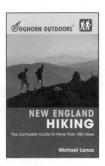
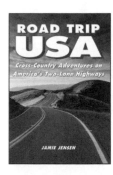

For a complete listing of Rick Steves' books, see page 8.

Honza Vihan would like to dedicate his share of the writing to all of the friends who helped him through a difficult year. Special thanks to Victor Chen, Cimrmanologist par excellence.

Avalon Travel Publishing
1400 65th Street, Suite 250
Emeryville, CA 94608

AVALON
publishing group incorporated

Avalon Travel Publishing
An Imprint of Avalon Publishing Group, Inc.

Printed in the United States of America by Worzalla.
First printing November 2005

Portions of this book were originally published in *Rick Steves' Best of Eastern Europe* © 2004, by Rick Steves and Cameron Hewitt; and in *Rick Steves' Germany, Austria & Switzerland* © 2003, 2002, 2001, 2000, 1999, by Rick Steves.

For the latest on Rick Steves' lectures, guidebooks, tours, and public television series, contact Europe Through the Back Door, Box 2009, Edmonds, WA 98020, tel. 425/771-8303, fax 425/771-0833, www.ricksteves.com, rick@ricksteves.com.

ISBN (10): 1-56691-768-9
ISBN (13): 978-1-56691-768-1
ISSN: 1554-3870

Europe Through the Back Door Managing Editor: Risa Laib
Europe Through the Back Door Editors: Cameron Hewitt, Kevin Yip, Jennifer Hauseman, Gene Openshaw
Avalon Travel Publishing Editor & Series Manager: Patrick Collins
Avalon Travel Publishing Project Editor: Madhu Prasher
Copy Editor: Chris Hayhurst
Indexer: Laura Welcome
Production & Typesetting: Patrick David Barber, Holly McGuire
Cover Design: Kari Gim, Laura Mazer
Interior Design: Laura Mazer, Jane Musser, Amber Pirker
Maps & Graphics: David C. Hoerlein, Laura VanDeventer, Lauren Mills, Mike Morgenfeld
Photography: Cameron Hewitt, Rick Steves, Honza Vihan, Mike Potter
Cover Photos: front image, Church of St Francis Seraphinus dome and Stare Mesto's spires © Jonathan Smith / Lonely Planet Images; back image: Charles Bridge and the old town © Chris Mellor / Lonely Planet Images
Front Matter Color Photo: Prague © Cameron Hewitt

Distributed to the book trade by Publishers Group West, Berkeley, California